A Dream Map to the Sixth Sun

Restoring Harmony and Balance to our Lives

A Dream Map to the Sixth Sun

Restoring Harmony and Balance to our Lives

Eleanor Barron Druckrey, Ph.D.

Copyright © 2017 by Eleanor Barron Druckrey, Ph.D.

Front cover photo by: Elizabeth Gamboa

Library of Congress Control Number:		2017901788
ISBN:	Hardcover	978-1-5245-8076-6
	Softcover	978-1-5245-8075-9
	eBook	978-1-5245-8074-2

All rights reserved. No part of this book may be reproduced or transmitted in any form or by any means, electronic or mechanical, including photocopying, recording, or by any information storage and retrieval system, without permission in writing from the copyright owner.

Any people depicted in stock imagery provided by Thinkstock are models, and such images are being used for illustrative purposes only. Certain stock imagery © Thinkstock.

Print information available on the last page.

Rev. date: 07/12/2017

To order additional copies of this book, contact:
Xlibris
1-888-795-4274
www.Xlibris.com
Orders@Xlibris.com
752689

Contents

Author's Notes xi

Acknowledgments xvii

Introduction xxi

Prologue lv

Chapter 1: Malinalxochitl: Aurora 1

Chapter 2: Gracia: La Llorona 61

Chapter 3: La Curandera: Hearing Coyolxauhqui's Call 137

Epilogue 191

Bibliography 205

Index 209

To Randy,
with love.

A La Diosa

*Help me believe I have the right to remember and
know what at times only my troubled heart
tells me to be true.*

—Cherríe L. Moraga

Author's Notes

I believe the idea for this book was planted when I was in the second grade and I realized I couldn't remember the three steps to solve my mathematical problems. I was a spindly Chicana dreamer kid then—lanky, wiry, energetic, and laughed aloud often. My right eye was turned in. I squinted to read and was seated at the back of the room with the mathematically challenged students. My education all the way to college was fraught with subtle and overt scenarios of being pushed to the back of the room. But as a child, a force beyond my understanding that spoke to me through my dreams and showed me people and places that existed long ago moved me and showed me something greater than my earthly life.

After forty years of meditation, prayer, writing down my dreams, and conducting research on the Toltec, Mayan, and Aztec dream traditions, I felt there was still an understanding I lacked in my waking life; but I couldn't quite name it. The years passed, and my life followed a trajectory of its own. I continued to feel a sense of displacement, of alienation. It wasn't until after this book was written that I was finally able to identify the source of my discontent and malaise: the paradigm of the ancestors and my need to bring my understanding of it into this dimension.

The writing of this book began after a drawing of the Organ Mountains of New Mexico I had absentmindedly drawn. It depicts a people moving away and another returning. Zigzag lines suggest snake and sun energies, and eagles, trees, and four-legged relatives. Small streams of water with abundant energy running throughout provide a hint of a spiritual hand at work. The drawing drew itself; I just provided the paper, color pencils, and pens. I forgot about the drawing and put it away among my journals. A year passed, and I unconsciously began writing a story of a passage of a people from the American Southwest southward. Still unbeknownst to me, the story trickled out ever so subtly, part dream, part research.

Ocelotl is a dream guide who began appearing in my dreams when I was a young woman before the beginning of my journal-keeping. I invited him to speak to me and began seeing images of his walking with a steady sway, eyes cast downward, making me realize I was dreaming while awake. Two years after starting the drawing, I reexamined it and was shocked to discover the story of the migration within it. "We left, with the intention to return someday." I heard Ocelotl's voice ring out to me in a dream.

My books get written backward. This book was no exception. It began with the images in the drawing, and then I filled in the gaps by letting my fingers type without my thinking about content. Then I dreamed the next installment of the story and filled in the gaps with these dreams as the content of the story continued to evolve. At first, I just had a migration story that needed filling out with research, and I began to develop the story with fragments of dreams and the discovery of Ocelotl's role in its unfolding. When I thought the book was completed, my editor suggested that I include an introduction, and then I did further psychological and anthropological research.

The story of Coyolxauhqui, the Dark Goddess of the Aztecs, emerged as I attempted to quench the thirst to find a meaning in stories I was casually coming across in my research. I stopped to examine another thread in the story and realized she would fit into this narrative, but without my realizing it, she had taken center stage and was there as big as life with something significant to say. Internal shifting around and awakening occurred, and consciousness began to say something to me about duality. As I continued to research her, I realized that her absence in Aztec culture had affected my personal development and that it now played quite prominently in my growing awareness of the feminine. Her presence or connection to the sixth sun seamlessly emerged in the last stage of the writing.

After I thought the book was done and had put a neat bow around it a second time, the title came to me. Again, I had to revise the manuscript in order to make sense of the writing that had preceded the emergence of the title. I write without an outline. Some would say this is foolish, but the truth is that I can't put anything down on paper until it has reached its proper time. I write in blind faith. Many years ago I heard a radio program wherein a man discussed compressing time to shorten the gestation of "something that should take nine months to three." I thought, *I'm sure women will think that's a good idea.* His idea was impractical. Now that I recognize the value that the passing of time has for healing wounds or allowing truth to surface, it seems ludicrous that someone would want to shorten a pregnancy to speed things up.

My crowning moment came when a friend asked me if I had communicated with the ancestors about the problems I was having with the computer, and suggested that I ask them for help to wrap up. I giggled and said that I would do just that, thinking that would engender another period of waiting. That night I dreamed:

> *There is a celebration of family members going back generations—women, men, children. I hear the beat of drums, music of a flute, jangle of ayayotes, shells jangling around their ankles, and laughter as they gather around me. I doubt the reality of the dream, but my nephew Christopher who passed on ten years ago comes up to me with a broad smile and says, "Keep working at it. We are waiting for its completion." The music continues until I become aware of the aliveness of my body lying in bed.*

The introduction itself has moved slowly; it has taken three years to write. The lessons it has put me through have shown me how to utilize the power of attraction and how to keep in mind that everything has its own timing and purpose. I'm on schedule if I am patient and allow what needs to unfold slowly.

This story covers nearly forty years of dream journals juxtaposed against Chicana/o culture and writings. This has been a deeply rewarding process for me, and I hope it will serve as a vehicle that brings the reader into greater understanding of traditions that were devalued and all but lost over time. Fortunately, the embers left burning after the collision of cultures were bright and strong enough to withstand the passage of time to resurface as blazing fires within the hearts and souls of the daughters and sons of the survivors from both sides of the battle, some within the first generations of the events five hundred years ago. Although many other writers have written about the destruction, for me it was a vision that necessitated my delving deeply into my personal spiritual and emotional makeup that changed me in the process. The ancestors who traditionally live within our dreams have been vital resources for me personally.

I believe, as traditions hold within oral folklore, that the ancestors are guiding us toward recreating an identity built upon their teachings; they are helping us recognize that the soil under our feet was once theirs and reminding us that we continue to be a part of the stars, wind, air, trees, rivers, oceans, and mountains, along with the four-legged, six-legged, and winged relatives who have always been a part of Mother Earth. Despite new ideologies and paradigms, we Chicana/os can continue to thrive and emerge into our *nepantla* (our center) as multidimensional beings, trusting what beats within. The details are written in the events of our dreams and in the creation stories they left vibrating in ancient songs and poems.

The migration story included in this narrative is an example of a spiritual journey to be attained. It is not an accomplished goal I have attained but rather illustrates (a) the spiritual aspirations of our ancestors and (b) a story of endurance and spiritual attainment for our own evolution. The thoughts and philosophies have come to me by way of my research and study of other religions to understand the expansiveness or immortality of the human spirit. Most importantly, I'd like to think of this edition of the story as an example of the way that our ancestors reveal themselves to us in everyday life, and stories evolve and change.

I have also been influenced by previous writers who refer to the "magical" aspects of Mexican/indigenous cultures. Yes, there is a bleed-through experience between dimensions, but I feel it is important to bring attention to the quality of journeys undertaken with hallucinogenic/ sacred plants. Our young people are hungry for these journeys, perhaps because they have been romanticized by writers, but also because modern times offer drugs in abundance that allow for such experiences to occur in a secular manner. I emphasize that this narrative was written to illustrate that "magical" side of the culture and is a composite of dreams and research without hallucinogenic plants. Usually the stories came together as a result of information that was revealed to me over long periods. However, I must admit that I envied writers who had more spectacular journeys utilizing sacred plants. In hindsight, I can see the effects of my personal challenges, and in this narrative I have edited out misleading stories I've been inclined to include that could confuse the reader with sensational data.

Now that this book is written, I can identify the source of my dismay in looking back on that day in the second grade. With this writing completed, I can see that the need to find the source of my puzzlement was actually an undefined yearning to find the truths that would restore the harmony and balance that my ancestors insisted in my dreams were the home of my true nature.

I invite you to choose your path and join me in finding those places within, where the door opens easily and freedom calls from the other side. Any internal work taken on behalf of dismantling the illusions of this world will facilitate in helping you find your *nepantla* (center). In deciphering your dreams, nothing compares to the beauty found along the way. Exploring beyond the boundaries of common beliefs by decoding the messages of the ancestors in our dreams can be nothing short of miraculous. We have arrived into the thick of the sixth sun as the Mayan and Aztec calendars prophesied. My hope is that you will turn the knob, open the door, and find the harmony and balance your heart longs for. As the Aztec poet Tochihuitzilopochtliin tells,

> It is not true, it is not true
> That we come to this earth to live.
> We come only to sleep, only to dream.

Acknowledgments

Thanks go to many friends and colleagues who have assisted and supported me in the writing of this narrative. I have often seen writers acknowledged for their contributions in the subject fields. This writing also could not have taken shape without the reflections and conclusions of researchers and writers in the Chicana/o movement: thoughts and feelings on the unfolding of our culture, concerns and needs of artists, curanderas/os, writers, historians, and all those who have tirelessly fought for language and cultural freedom of children in schools.

To Cherrie Moraga, for permission to use the quotes from her book *A Xicana Codex of Changing Consciousness: Writings, 2000–2010.* Copyright © 2011; published by Duke University Press in 2011, by permission of Stuart Bernstein Representation for Artists, New York, NY, and protected by the copyright laws of the United States. All rights reserved.

To my friend and spiritual sister Kathleen Baca who has long been a committed supporter of my work and believed in it from the start of our first meeting.

To my friend, colleague, and editor Dra. Yvette Flores, associate professor at the University of California, Davis, who has patiently listened, offered suggestions and insights, and continued to be of immeasurable support for my dream journals from the moment I talked about my visions prior to the formal investigation.

To my friend and mentor Dr. Jill Gover who helped me open the door when my insights seemed like outlandish ideas and fantasies and led me to believe in the possibilities of furthering my education beyond the master's level.

To Kora Schmid, director of chaplaincy and palliative care of Marin General Hospital, for her interest and support in my cross-cultural work with the hospital.

To China Galland from the Graduate Theological Union in Berkeley, CA, and author of *Longing for Darkness: Tara and the Black Madonna*, New York, Penguin Books, 2007, who generously took time to listen in-depth and offer invaluable suggestions.

To John Kriebel and Colleen Moore for their dedication, support, and patience in the editing of this work.

To John DeGaitano of the Santa Rosa Chamber of Commerce for sharing his knowledge of publishing and encouragement to keep writing. Through thick and thin he stood by.

To Ivan Silva, reference librarian at the Tiburon Library, and to other staff who extended themselves to me with technical assistance, finding information and references.

A special thank you to Elizabeth Gamboa for her generous support In offering photographs of Coyolxauhqui for the cover of the book.

To my friends in the Oakland healing community for their enthusiasm, interest, and support—Ancestral Apothecary, Atava Garcia Swiecicki, Marcela Sabin, Veronica Juarez, and Leah Arrellano.

To my friends in the spiritual community in Marin County who cheered me on during the difficult, fallow periods of this writing and offered amazing suggestions and support.

I miss Gary Politzer, my dear friend and webmaster of my website Chicana Dreamer, who for many years was the artist who put my work into the world in creating postcards, adding web pages, flyers, announcements; not only was he a strong supporter of my work, but he was also a committed artist and dreamer who kept a dream journal even longer than I have. Special thanks to Gary's brother, Stephen Politzer, who unselfishly extended himself to provide website assistance after the passing of his brother.

To my nieces for their love, encouragement, and support: Maggie Barron for her avid and enthusiastic interest in the dream traditions and integration of them into her life, Yolanda Barron for her ready assistance with technical support, Melissa Barron James, Julie Chacon, Valerie

Barron Estrella for her valiant exploration of the spiritual and healing traditions, Patricia Barron, and Linda Blaha. My nephews Adam Barron and Joseph Barron for passing on the family tradition of Mexican culture and music to their children.

To My nieces on the Druckrey family side, Gabrielle Hinahara and Natalie Hinahara, for their tremendous creativity and dedication to their art and activism that empowers the next generation to dare being their greatest selves.

Special note of acknowledgment to my nephew Marcos Benjamin Barron, accomplished classical and jazz guitarist, for his focused attention on his art and dedication to culture in his training and musical performances on the guitar; and his wife, Sue Claire Jones Barron, for her art and dedication to music.

To my artist friends and staunch supporters Diana Marto, fine papermaker, and Stu Rabinowitsh, musician.

Acknowledgment and appreciation also go to my brothers John D. Barron and Jose Barron for their kind support of my writing and creativity.

Special thanks to my husband, Randall Druckrey, for his love, support, and encouragement during the writing of this book, but especially for his ability to allow his feminine side to coexist alongside his masculine with complete acceptance and nonjudgment.

Introduction

This story is a dream map revealing some of the truths hidden in the arrival of the sixth sun as promised by the mathematicians of the early cultures of what we now call the land of Mexico. Aurora, Gracia, and La Curandera were born into poor beginnings—migrant workers struggling to make it in Aztlán, El Norte, the American Southwest, the land their ancestors left. They may be confused and troubled in modern times, but they are wickedly steadfast and determined to discover what happened in the past that made their lives seem so puzzling and out of step with the society that surrounds them. The story takes place within modern memory and the range of the sixth sun's light. Their search for identity within Chicana culture takes them into the history of their people, the unwrapping of their sacred gifts, and, ultimately, finding the face of the dark feminine, obscured by the passage of time and the arrival of other religions. In their search for truth, they will stop at nothing short of meeting the ruthless demands of their spiritual paths as they unfold.

The era of the sixth sun is the doorway through which the feminine comes into its power and reclaims its rightful domain of strength. Redefining what the feminine means for us today is the task that is presented to us. This redefinition empowers women and men to enter into the wholeness of Chicana/o culture that has been blurred by the coming together of many cultures in the Americas in the past five hundred years. This introduction also explores modern-day women writers fighting back to regain their standing among society with vitality and purpose.

As a psychologist with a background in history, I write in the tradition of other writers—Cherrie Moraga, Gloria Anzaldúa, Ana Castillo, and others who tell their personal experiences with a backdrop of academic research. This writing too is from my dreams and is a continuation of the ancient dream traditions of the Americas as contrasted against my research of Aztec, Toltec, and Mayan history, as well as emergence of new information.

Legends, gods and goddesses, history, dreams, and life's milestones are integral components for the continuation of a culture and define the identity of a people. In order to understand the spiritual and emotional aspirations and challenges confronting the three women of this narrative, we will examine several social and spiritual facets, values, and narratives of the Chicana/o people at various points in history, including modern times. An in-depth discussion on the indigenous worldview of the Americas can be found in my book *Corn Woman Sings: A Medicine Woman's Dream Map*,[1] and, therefore, I will be commenting only briefly on those details here. However, it is important to keep in mind that the worldview, or paradigm, of the native cultures of North, Central, and South America are distinct and more complex than the worldview commonly held in the dominant anglo culture in America. In some instances throughout this introduction, distinctions between the two paradigms may be difficult to explain since the lived experience of indigenous people includes sound, color, felt sensations, multiple dimensions, and the presence of other beings, not readily accepted as normal, natural, or real in the dominant culture reality. Because of the content of dreams, understanding may become problematic for the more concrete thinker. I apologize in advance for that crossover in paradigms and will attempt to keep the narrative as straightforward as possible.

Arrival of the Sixth Sun

Questions related to identity abound within the Native cultures regarding the promise of the new cycle of time as anticipated by the ancient ones of the Americas—the ending of an age and the beginning of another on December 21, 2012, and lasting until 2021, in accordance with their mathematical calculations. Profesora Yvette Flores, at the University of California, Davis, states in the foreword of *Corn Woman Sings*, "As the fifth sun, the sun of movement according to the Aztecs, reache(d) its final cycle, indigenous nations

---

[1] E. Barron Druckrey (2009).

await(ed) a new age of transformation. During the fifth sun, social movements and demands for justice, upheavals, wars, and manmade disasters prevailed. Mother Earth trembled and wept and reminded us all of the resurgence of *indigenismo* and the (re)awakening of consciousness. Those who had the gift of seeing multiple dimensions and who listened to the messages and music in their dreams began to prepare for the changes to come."[2]

The seed cause of the sixth sun begins with the fact that the mathematicians of the early Mesoamerican cultures, established that repeating cycles of time occur and that this particular cycle called the sixth sun repeats every twenty-six thousand five hundred years. The current age is marked by an alignment in the heavens where the Star of Venus pierces through the center of the Milky Way. Spiritually, the "piercing" signifies a change in consciousness, a commitment to the oneness of all creation and the flow of feminine energies. It means that we can lay aside the ego's self-importance as a seeming driving force, in deference to spirit. Nothing, as will be shown when we discuss legends later in this introduction, overshadows the preeminence of that commitment. In the following section of this introduction, we will examine some examples of what the sixth sun signifies, define masculine and feminine, and discuss Coyolxauhqui, the Dark Feminine, and creativity.

From Tonal (Masculine) to Nagual (Feminine)

Sergio Magaña, author of *The Toltec Secret* and teacher of the Toltec lineage of dreamers, affirms that this new era moves from masculine, action-oriented experience to feminine, intuitive ways of knowing. The early dreamers called the masculine state of mind the *tonal*, common consciousness in the waking state; and the internal, intuitive, attractive, the *nagual*.[3] Coyolxauhqui, the Aztec goddess, was discovered in 1978 at the foot of El Templo Mayor covered over by the Spaniards at the time of invasion in the 1500s in Mexico City.[4] Coyolxauhqui's discovery is not a coincidence, but rather further evidence of moving from the masculine into feminine consciousness. The ancient sages anticipated the uncovering of her symbolic

---

[2] Barron Druckrey (2009).
[3] S. Magaña (2014).
[4] E. Matos Moctezuma (1988).

remains, which represent a spiritual revelation that we have, indeed, entered into intuitive ways of knowing. Coyolxauhqui is the bringer of light into the dark spaces of the night—darkness being representative of the feminine.

Irene Nicholson's[5] work supports the idea of a tradition held within the Nahuatl religion of a consciousness from darkness to light. She states that the Quetzalcoatl had given the people a high task to "beautify the quality of the eagle, the quality of the [jaguar], the holy war, the arrow, and the shield." However, these aspirations, particularly "holy war," were gross misinterpretations, and the violence that was perpetrated against people the Aztecs conquered should have been a "psychological war that in olden times was waged within the consciousness of specially chosen men capable of conquering their own natures." The "holy war" is a spiritual quest into consciousness. The sixth sun is the era during which consciousness moves from masculine into feminine ways of knowing.

Coyolxauhqui, the Dark Feminine

Elena Avila, author of *Woman Who Glows in the Dark*,[6] was the first Chicana writer I found to acknowledge Coyolxauhqui's consciousness in dark spaces. She discusses Coyolxauhqui exactly in this role as bringer of light onto a transformational path. As a registered nurse in a large hospital in Texas, she refers to her personal journey toward transformation, seeking to unearth the healing practices found south of the border related to the early cultures. She shows that Coyolxauhqui bridges the connection of finding one's spirit in the dark spaces of a dream, and states that Coyolxauhqui is the guide in the dark realms of the universe. An Aztec prayer Avila often recites is:

> Mother that glows in the dark, help me
> Ride this weird energy of mine until your
> Luminous, magnetic heart transforms me
> Into love. For I truly want to love. Truly.[7]

---

[5] Nicholson (1967).
[6] E. Avila (1999).
[7] E. Avila (1999) p. 253.

Avila also describes how she brings her patients to the altar in her office to anchor the healing, and points to Coyolxauhqui, saying, "See, she is fragmented, just as we so often feel. She stands for the dualities, the light and the dark, that we all include within us . . . A woman has many names, takes on many roles, and often feels as if there are many different things happening inside her all at once. In Avila's view, we are not simple beings, we are complex. But this goddess can contain all our dualities, no matter how much difficulty we have in reconciling them. She can help us embrace all our paradoxes."[8]

The writer/healer Avila underwent an extensive training in psychiatric nursing in Texas, as well in *curanderismo*, Mexican/Chicana folk medicine. When I read *Woman Who Glows in the Dark*, I registered something different in my feelings about the quality of "dark," but the meaning somehow eluded me until much later. In my journals, I found details of various dreams where "night" had a quality of luring me inward, into feelings yet to come to my attention that seemed to beckon me into deeper levels of knowing. I now realize that feminine energy in dark spaces has power.

In a personal conversation with China Galland, author of *Longing for Darkness: Tara and the Black Madonna*,[9] we talked about the *virgen morenita*, the Dark Virgin, the Virgen de San Juan del Valle in El Rio Grande Valley, Texas, which is a replica of the Madonna at San Juan de los Lagos in Jalisco, Mexico. The two communities focused on the celebration of feast days in conjunction with the church in Jalisco. I remembered a dream I had where I floated in a dark space and was shown a wisdom, powerful but foreign. I overlooked the significance of the night, although the teaching I received pointed toward the sacredness of it. I noticed in my journal-keeping that there was a unique quality to the dreams I had in the dark from those in daylight that had slipped my notice until the title of Galland's book caught my attention and I had that conversation with the author. Perhaps because of my fundamentalist upbringing, at a subconscious level, I viewed night as somewhat sinister, and would take time to integrate this new information.

---

[8] E. Avila (1999) p. 136.
[9] Galland, C. *Longing for Darkness: Tara and the Black Madonna*.

Galland also referred to Coyolxauhqui as the Dark Feminine, a name given to the Black Madonna. Thus, in referring to the goddesses here, Dark Feminine is used interchangeably with the name of the actual goddess. I believe this is an important distinction because of the role that Coyolxauhqui plays in the creation stories and in this narrative, and her impact upon our lives within the sixth sun.

Gloria Anzaldua gives us another example of feminine energy related to the sixth sun in the training of a *curandera* with its range of ecstasies, nightmares, and periods of personal upheaval and uncertainty. She writes of her awakening *conocimiento* and the evolution she underwent while training as a *curandera* and finding snake energy, with its subtle but definite presence in her dreams. Snake energy is ancient, wise, and powerful. Most importantly, snake energy is symbolized through the goddesses and ancient teachings that are now surfacing. These energies are also connected to Coatlicue, the mother of all gods, from Coyolxauhqui, on to Tonantzin, and, ultimately, La Virgen de Guadalupe.[10] Snake energy has always been within indigenous culture, but for us here in El Norte, the sixth sun brings it particularly to our attention.

Creativity

All creative endeavors are an avenue for the innermost workings of a human being's power, and are considered as a feminine consciousness. In the development of creative endeavors, whether music, art, dance, theater, "arts and crafts," or other forms of art, one enters an altered state of consciousness and dialogues with the internal feminine on how it should manifest itself and be expressed. Clarisa Pinkola Estes refers to the story of *La Llorona*, the Weeping Woman, who weeps by the river at night, grieving the loss of the children—the children she killed. Pinkola Estes explains that the river is the flow of the psyche that creates, and the children are the creation of the Wild Woman within who longs for expression. When something goes wrong and she is denied the opportunity for expression, the flow of the river gets backed up and is expressed in distorted forms.

---

[10] G. Anzaldúa (1999).

Other forms of creativity discussed by Pinkola Es sacredness of feminine sexuality. The author notes that beliefs of its opposite, desecrated and maligned sexuality the norm over the centuries in Western thought. Regardless status of feminine sexuality, earlier spiritual beliefs prevalent in European cultures and religions held goddesses protecting the sacredness and beauty of feminine sexuality.[11] It would appear, then, that there is a need for healing of the image of the feminine and that the arrival of the sixth sun is a time for calling for that healing.[12]

In summary of this brief discussion of the sixth sun's inspiring movement from the *tonal* to the *nagual* (masculine to feminine), we can see that the consciousness includes increased awareness or movement from the external toward the internal. Given gifts become more significant in our spiritual development in the coming age of the feminine. The discovery of Coyolxauhqui's remains in the last quarter of the twentieth century reaffirms the significance of the Dark Feminine after five hundred years of being hidden from view.[13] Also, Sergio Magaña's work marks the emergence of an ancient lineage of wisdom keepers who went underground to preserve the teachings that were severely attacked upon the arrival of the conquerors from Spain in the sixteenth century. His work corrects many misconceptions and brings new perspectives about consciousness and the levels of awareness of the *tonal* and *nagual* in the role of the sixth sun. Yet whether we are referring to Coyolxauhqui, the Dark Feminine, snake energy for healing, destiny, and the creative flow, all these aspects of awareness point us toward the energies that the sixth sun brings to aid us in moving from not only the external to the internal and the spiritual, but from masculine to feminine ways of knowing.

---

[11] C. Pinkola Estes.

[12] Many European writers have addressed the ancient goddesses, but for a concise history, Leslene della-Madre's *Midwifing Death: Returning to the Arms of the Ancient Mother* is a good source for restoring feminine sexuality to a balanced view.

[13] Matos Moctezuma (1988).

ıgration Story: Chicana/o Homeland, Chicana/o Identity

For people of Chicana/o culture, clarification of these old practices and ways of seeing our world aid us in understanding our personal spiritual experiences. This background also explains, through our cultural references, who we are and where we come from. We will explore issues of identity and spiritual beliefs from modern religious beliefs, and, as the discussion progresses, how masculine perspectives have impacted Chicana/o culture and have obscured feminine ways. The clearing of this obscuration is vital to experiencing the energies of the sixth sun.

We begin with the Aztec migration story that is a key element of history that impacts this narrative because it answers questions of identity of the three women of this story. The story tells of a migration that took place in the early history of the Aztecs, from an unspecified location in their northern homeland in the Valley of Anahuac, now Mexico City. Irene Nicholson's discussion of the Aztecs' journey to Anahuac tells us that the Aztecs, according to Francisco Xavier Clavijero in the eighteenth century, came from an area "far to the north of the Colorado River." Irene Nicholson describes the myth as a mixture of fact and fiction, guided by a dreamer. Huitzilopochtli, the dreamer who set the migration in motion, set out with seven tribes in AD 1160 to look for a home where they would find a white eagle perched atop a cactus with a snake in its mouth. She also states, "the place of legend in history, and symbolism can and should be larger than life."[14] It is, in reality, a pilgrimage from darkness into light. The legend may be stated that it is a story of spiritual evolution, depicting the immortality of the soul and expansiveness of the human spirit much greater than the human can hold.

Frank Waters in *Book of the Hopi* stresses that many cultures of the early Americas have significant migration stories. The Hopi creation story includes traveling the length of the continents from northernmost of the Americas to the southern tip of South America, and across North America four times before they were to settle in their final homeland.[15] This fact

---

[14] Nicholson, I. (1967), p. 131.
[15] Waters, F. (1977).

is mentioned to illustrate that a journey the Aztecs undertook lasting a fifty-two-year cycle would not be uncommon for early indigenous cultures.

Chicana/o Homeland

In 1969 *El Plan Espiritual de Aztlán* was developed by the First Chicano National Conference in Denver, Colorado. The writings were recorded by essayists in *Aztlán: Essays on the Chicano Homeland*.[16] This anthology explores the abounding myths of the origins of the Aztecs, and examines the necessity of establishing the origins of the Chicana/o people in the land the Aztecs left behind.

Oversimplification does not do justice to the story of the exact location of their origin of the Aztecs. However, it was the group's the consensus at the *congreso* that the Aztecs originated from Aztlán, that Aztlán was in the American Southwest, and that we Chicanas/os are the descendants of the Aztecs. The importance of this section is to recognize that there have been debates and that elements in the culture have accepted the myth of the homeland Aztlán. In the eyes of Chicana/o culture, we are more than hyphenated Americans who arrived recently. We are a considerable group of people that has its roots deep in history and in the land. The Aztecs vowed to return to their homeland. As this narrative will show, these issues of origin bear relevance on the lives of the three women in this story.

The migration story presented in the narrative includes elements of reincarnation, expanded states of consciousness as espoused by religions of the world which are congruent with the Nahuatl religion of the Aztecs as discussed in Barron Druckrey.[17] Other components of the Nahuatl religion as detailed other by writers have also been incorporated.[18] In general in this narrative, states of consciousness are also referred to as the place beyond concepts. For example, *A Course in Miracles* states that the body has no say on how it is used or perceived: "Let this be your agreement with each one; that you be one with him and not apart . . . God keeps his promises; his son keeps his. In his creation did his father say, 'You are

---

[16] Eds. Anaya, R. and Lomeli, F. (1991).
[17] Barron Druckrey (2009).
[18] S. Magaña, 2011; see also C. Castaneda writings.

beloved of me and I of you forever. Be you perfect as myself, for you can never be apart from me.'"[19]

In summary of this discussion on the homeland and identity of the Aztecs, it becomes clear that migration stories were commonly used in the Americas to establish spiritual roots of peoples. The legend tells us that the Aztecs wandered for fifty-two years in search for a new home. They were cognizant of the need to make their legend larger than life. At least one reason for their move from their homeland was caused by, it appears, climate changes. They established their reasons for seeking their home elsewhere in spiritual terms that, in turn, established their identity first and foremost in the spiritual world. As Irene Nicholson stated, they had to make their legend larger than life to spiritually hold the group together. Just as the various groups prior to the departure of the Aztecs from their homeland developed stories bigger than life, the current situation, Chicana/o culture, calls for drastic measures once again. The Aztecs left their land against their will, and promised to return to their beloved country sometime in the future. In the meantime, a holocaust, as anticipated by the dreamers, occurred throughout the land; millions of people died throughout the Americas. Some of the deaths were caused from exhaustion or overwork as a result of being taken into slavery; sometimes through diseases for which the natives had no immunity against; or killed through wars for land and natural resources. A reason bigger than life has to exist today in order to explain why five hundred years later, Chicana/os are viewed as aliens in their homeland. When spirit speaks, faith carries the day and explains the unexplainable. The legend still applies to the people as a cohesive agent to bring them together again.

Legends of the Goddesses and Gods of Mesoamerican Spirituality

We will now examine the spiritual components that comprise the paradigm of the Aztec/Toltec/Mayan cultures, and, particularly, Chicana/o culture, commonly known as Mexican American.[20] The sixth sun reveals

---

[19] Anonymous, *A Course in Miracles*, p. 603.
[20] M. León Portilla (1980), and E. Barron Druckrey (2009).

that for Chicana/os, the legends hold keys to our identity, and requires attention in order to surmount the challenges that come with this age. These legends also touch on the roles that defined the masculine and feminine in early native cultures, and explore how they impact the modern role of the feminine in Chicana/o culture.

God of Duality

There are many faces of the God of Duality. This section discusses the Nahuatl spiritual beliefs in which Spirit has established our natural home and how we can overcome the limitations of the waking world in our search beyond duality. Waking consciousness is riddled with contradictions and opposites that confuse the reality of the individual and make it appear that the waking state is the desired state. Just as in other religions of the world, nothing could be further from the truth. The desired state of attainment lies in the spiritual realms where unity and oneness reign supreme. For example, in the Buddhist practice of dream yoga, one seeks the awareness of both the waking and deeper states of reality to awaken from the dream of life;[21] in the Hindu traditions of India, one seeks serenity and peace of mind to unite with the oneness of the universe, or godhead, in the teachings of Patanjali;[22] in the Christian tradition, one seeks the kingdom of heaven while here on earth through prayer, meditation, and good deeds.

Sergio Magaña[23] discusses "the Twelfth Heaven, the place of complementary duality." He likens Mr. and Mrs. Two with the yin and yang energy of the Chinese tradition and states that their "word" and their "breath" shape creation. Magaña notes that a prayer addressed to the sacred couple in a *temezcal* (sweat lodge) says, "may what is dual unite in order to create . . . may what is created in the subtle world manifest in the physical realm."

In the story of Quetzalcoatl and Huitzilopochtli, where we find the light and dark forces opposing one another, we can also see an example of duality. Huitzilopochtli being the God of War, carries the sword symbolically to fight for truth; Quetzalcoatl, sensuous like the snake, lofty as the eagle,

---

[21] Year-End Retreat (1983), Nyingma Institute, Berkeley, CA.
[22] C. Isherwood (1953).
[23] S. Magaña (2011), p. 56.

is the bringer of music, brotherhood, sisterhood, and love.[24] The point of duality is to go beyond the opposing forces and reach the source of oneness. Willingness to step back from the ego and let it dissolve comes from seeing beyond illusions. Reaching the other side of duality is done by remaining in balance, not pushing, not pulling or forcing our way. Balance is the key.

An important precept central to Aztec religious beliefs is the development of face and heart, which engenders the personal search of the individual toward self-knowledge. Self-knowledge includes discerning our destiny and developing our sacred gifts that are also tools for navigating through life. A vital component of knowing oneself is to return to our *nepantla*, core of our being, which then brings us beyond duality and into the presence of the divine. Lara Medina, a Chicana writer, also describes in detail her process of finding her face and heart and setting about living her life within the ancient healing traditions.[25] Preparation for death was vital to the Aztecs, and their goal was to reach their n*epantla* in anticipation of their journey beyond this life. Gloria Anzaldúa's *Borderlands—La Frontera*—is a tribute to a process she endured in her dreams which she describes in her poem, "Canción a la diosa de la noche" ("Songs to the Goddess of the Night")[26] in which she not only reaches her *nepantla*, but is also called by the Goddess of the Night to serve her through becoming a *curandera*/healer.

This is a shortened discussion on the God of Duality, but vital for recognizing and understanding the concepts of opposites as opportunity for transformation. Going beyond duality and finding our face and heart, and thereby our *nepantla*, also reveals the gifts of creativity within us. The path of understanding what the sixth sun brings necessitates our undergoing a process of transformation. Returning to the prayer mentioned by Magaña, calling on the gods for assistance in surmounting duality and bringing into this realm what has been ordained in other realms is necessary to manifesting the desires of the heart or the gifts destiny has given us. Other examples of duality will be discussed throughout this introduction and narrative to illustrate the magnitude and necessity in attaining our true

---

[24] Nicholson, I. (1967).
[25] Eds. L. Medina in Facio and Lara (2014).
[26] G. Anzaldua, (1999).

spiritual identity. In describing the God of Duality, one can reflect also on tenets of Buddhist dream yogic practices as well as the teachings of Patanjali on the state of mind, or yoga, attained in Hindu traditions, and yet find the spiritual teachings of the Aztecs.

Coatlicue and Coyolxauhqui

Another area of Chicana/o culture related to the sixth sun that impacts identity and ways of seeing masculine and feminine energy emerges from the legends and stories of the past. The legends tell us about the goddesses and gods and define our universe to point the way toward transcendence of the trials of this world. Later in this introduction, a discussion will clarify and illustrate how Chicana/o culture integrates the legends into gender role behavior and customs. In this section, we discuss the legends themselves.

The legend of Huitzilopochtli and Quetzalcoatl's creation begins in the early evening, with Coatlicue sweeping her grand front garden in preparation for the arrival of her four hundred sons, "Heroes" (the stars), as they are oftentimes called. During her task, she finds a tuft of feathers that she casually tucks into her bosom. This being no ordinary tuft of little feathers, Coatlicue becomes pregnant.

Coyolxauhqui, Coatlicue's daughter, has also been known as Earth Monster and has mouths with sharp teeth on her elbows and knees, and wanders through life eating everything in sight. We first learn of her in this legend in the upper worlds when she hears of the coming birth of her brother, Huitzilopochtli. Coyolxauhqui also realizes her father has been too long in the underworld to be the father. Not wanting to ignore this insult to his memory, she calls to her four hundred brothers to avenge their father. Their presence in this legend serves to remind us that at every dawn, the stars are vanquished by the rising sun.[27]

A pair of twins is born, Huitzilopochtli and Quetzalcoatl. Huitzilopochtli, whose role is the sun, is born with sword in hand, dressed and prepared for war. Immediately upon his birth, he takes revenge against Coyolxauhqui to protect the mother from harm by "piercing" Coyolxauhqui's heart, dismembering her and cutting off her head. As she falls through the

---

[27] I. Nicholson (1967). The Heroes are also known as the Centzon Huitzilnahua who were neighbors of the Aztecs who fought a battle with them and lost the war.

heavens, her body becomes the Milky Way, and her head, the moon. The way that Coyolxauhqui is destroyed illustrates a battle within the spirit that creates an avenue of transformation. Symbolically, the light of the morning sun piercing through the darkness is Huitzilopochtli "piercing" Coyolxauhqui's heart.

In another version of the story, twins are born as opposites of one another—one warring and the other caring.[28] Together they kill Coyolxauhqui. Nicholson calls this murder a vanquishing of the stars because the stars are indeed annihilated at dawn with the rise of the sun.[29] The legends tell us that in Coyolxauhqui's destruction by her brothers Huitzilopochtli and Quetzalcoatl, humanity is prompted toward *conocimiento*, or consciousness. Today, we need Coyolxauhqui's breath upon us to go into darkness to make way for transformation. In a world where time and space are imbued with the presence of the divine, one may delve into realms that appear to be hostile and inhospitable to ascertain the messages of transformation that point us in the proper direction.

Though this dismantling may appear as outright murder, in spiritual symbolism she has been transformed into the sacred Dark Feminine that guides the heart and mind out of despair and into balance with the *tonal* and the *nagual*, or masculine and feminine aspects of the self. Just as the Star of Venus "pierces" through the heart of the Milky Way every twenty-six thousand five hundred years, the path is open at this time so that we may also elect to have the faith to leap into the unknown and allow ourselves to be transformed in the spirit by the "piercing" of her heart. When that momentous event took place on December 21, 2012, a tremendous force was unleashed that gave us additional power to remember our true nature and restore us to balance. This is the event awaited for by the ancestors. The event and the new era it sets in motion brings with it a shift in consciousness from the masculine to the feminine.[30]

The plot deepens even further. In a battle in waking life, the *tonal* was also fought where the Aztecs overcame their neighbors to the south, the Huitznahua, and thus, they symbolically vanquished the stars in the

---

[28] K. Taube (1993).
[29] I. Nicholson (1967).
[30] Magaña, S. (2011).

waking realm. In other words, light overcame the night and triumphed over darkness. For five hundred years, the Aztec symbol of Coyolxauhqui has been lying hidden, neglected, and all but forgotten at the bottom of the stairs of the pyramid where the Spaniards buried her symbolic earthly remains.[31] Gregg Braden, author of *Fractal Time, The Secret of 2012 and a New World Age*,[32] reaffirms that the time is upon us now to *remember* or *recover* what we know deeply within ourselves, and bring to the forefront of our consciousness that which has been forgotten by the descendants of the Aztecs—the feminine.

Mayahuel

The story of Mayahuel is used in this narrative to illustrate relations between men and women, or the pursuit of love. Mayahuel, in the legend presented in story, is the goddess that brings to earth an elixir of delight for lovers, *pulque*. She is enticed to come to this world by Quetzalcoatl. The lovers have left the upper realms without Coatlicue's consent. When she discovers the young Mayahuel has left, Coatlicue marches right down to earth, shaking mountains, rivers, rocks, and trees in search of her errant granddaughter. In an effort to evade her, Mayahuel and Quetzalcoatl magically turn themselves into a tree. Coatlicue sees through their ruse and has the tree cut in two and returns to her kingdom. Quetzalcoatl goes on his way, but Mayahuel is left without friend or recourse of any kind.[33] Nicholson discusses the legend and tells that the separation represented by the lovers leaving heaven illustrates that there is a separation from the divine by the mere fact of coming to earth, and there is a necessity to embody love in order to recognize their need of a higher consciousness.[34]

I take poetic license to recount the essence of the myth as told by Karl Taube to point out pitfalls in interpretations evolving over time, and how one might see cultural values of class, race, power, and name, which in this case limit the role of women. There is a difference between examining stories from a spiritual perspective and examining them from a perspective

---

[31] E. Matos Moctezuma.
[32] Braden, G. (2008).
[33] Taube (1993).
[34] I. Nicholson (1967).

of social mores. We recognize the young goddess's predicament in the results of her actions, and the danger in which she finds herself as a woman alone on earth. In a spiritual sense, these could be seen as separation from the divine. In sixteenth century Mexico where the old familiar truths were fading rapidly into the past, a woman alone would face a new order of demands upon her. Mayahuel is left without family, name, man, sister, or friend. She is alone, a stranger in a wild land without the key that will allow her entrance into society, family, or marriage. Her options are quite limited.

In today's translation and reading of the story, how would we judge Mayahuel's actions? Is she separated from heaven or a lone woman adrift, judged by the standards of the day in this realm of reality? The old stories leave Mayahuel, a goddess, vulnerable and abandoned. The cultures of Mexican past saw life as a suffering—unfriendly, mysterious, and unpredictable land where cunning, deceit, and treachery abounded among the shadows of the day. The dream state, however, was the seat of reality and beauty. Separation from the divine would be cause for significant concern. Still, in waking terms, Mayahuel is a disobedient daughter, and the gods shall always have the final say. How will a simple human being judge the essence of the story? Though supposedly she was created for the delight of lovers, she is left without friend or family.[35] In later sections of this introduction, we will discuss in greater detail the problems women face in Mexican society that may be related to this legend.

Music

"How Music Came to Earth" is a poem borrowed from Irene Nicholson[36] to illustrate how the Aztecs believed the gods interacted with our destiny and confronted us with choices to make. Music in indigenous American cultures was held as a sacred gift that must be developed in order to meet with our destiny. The poem is from a sixteenth century Nahua manuscript, and shows us that music is also endowed with spiritual elements connecting mortal with divine. The ethereal feelings the poem stirs within the listener (or reader) are intended to transport us into other realms. Music lifts the

---

[35] See M. León Portilla, *Native Meso-American Spirituality* (1980) for a good source to understand relations between mortals and the Divine.
[36] I. Nicholson (1967), p. 32.

imagination and invites one to be carried by the gods into other realms to feel the golden sound of reverie. This sweet spirituality is the realm of the eagle, the heavens. The soft murmur of the conch trumpet, lofty feelings and reverence to the divine, are used in the poem to invite us to open our spiritual eyes to recognize creation and our reliance on the divine.

If we are called to be musicians, this will be the path to find our destiny. All creative endeavors have a god of their own, but if we truly wish to know and meet our destiny, we develop the sacred gifts that are given us, and joyously give them to the world.[37] Destiny's call is often very subtle, other times quite overt and difficult to ignore. We may find obstacles in our path and wonder if this is, indeed, ours to fulfill. Even a rock gives way to the steady pounding of the waves, and we may find ourselves moving in a direction toward rightful path without knowing how or why it happens. If we have lost our way, finding the right path again is crucial. Music is considered a feminine endeavor.

Not only does the poem illustrate the beauty of Aztec poetry, it also imprints on our consciousness the sacredness of the creative tradition. As the present narrative unfolds, we will see how the struggles of the three women are in conflict with traditions of creativity and how they fight back to resist the limitations set against them through family and culture. The presence of the feminine as it emerges in their dreams is significant and a strength to aid in their quest for identity. How much autonomy do they have, and how can they overcome the inner struggles they encounter, flying in the face of Chicana/o culture that emphasizes masculine superiority over the feminine? Can they survive without family, separated from their culture? These are questions whose answers will be revealed in their lives as the feminine and masculine roles come into balance and harmony with the arrival of the sixth sun.

---

[37] Barron Druckrey (2009). An extended discussion of sacred gifts delves more deeply into the traditions that call us to our destiny, and why we must be at attention to understand and heed the call.

The Collision of Cultures: Chicana/o Culture and the Place of Women

To get a better understanding of what the sixth sun means to the three characters in this narrative and what it might mean to Chicana dreamers of today, we will explore the lived experience of the *tonal* and the *nagual* since the rise of the culture before and after the arrival of the Spaniards. Looking back in time, we can see where legends, history, and cultural values have taken us. The issue of identity continues to be a serious source of concern.

Research reveals that the Catholic Church excluded women from having positions of power at the time of its inception, which then had the net effect of negating the strengths and wisdom upon women to a point that they then became the hated, demonized, and diminished ones. This introduction will show how the diminishment of women happened throughout history in Europe before and subsequent to the arrival of European cultures in the Americas and will also discuss how women have held a secondary status within Chicana/o culture as a result of the Catholic Church's influence upon Aztec culture as the two cultures came together.

Women writers are actively involved in developing a new spirituality reflecting their experience and knowing the answer to their personal needs and the needs of the culture at large. Ana Castillo (1994),[38] Gloria Anzaldúa (1999),[39] Camilla Townsend (2006),[40] and other writers found through their research that indigenous cultures and native religions of the Americas suffered a severe and extreme demonization at the time of the collision between native and Western cultures, leaving large portions of the populace without a clear path to their beliefs. These writers also question the status and treatment of women in early indigenous cultures. In the following section, we will continue our exploration by examining aspects of Chicana/o culture and the origins of social and cultural values that evolved from Aztec and European foundations.

---

[38] A. Castillo (1994).
[39] G. Anzaldúa (1999).
[40] C. Townsend (2006).

As the information mounted in my research, I realized I must make some choices as to the direction and complexity of this introduction. However, there are several important points that must be highlighted in this introduction to illustrate the depth of the challenges present to women in navigating through the *tonal* as their roles became more complex when the European and Native cultures collided. These points are as follows: the Aztecs were a polygamous society, which then became more patriarchal with the arrival of the Spaniards; women were, to a large extent, commodified; the role that was given to Malintzin, Hernan Cortez's translator, became laden with a tremendous weight of guilt and treachery with the passage of time; though the role of goddess had largely receded into the Aztec cultural background, the inclusion of the Virgen de Guadalupe rescued Coyolxauhqui from complete oblivion, and the people continued to revere her. On the Spanish side of history, Old Europe had a long tradition of worship to the Goddess, and gylanic cultures had been known to flourish where the arts and feminine values had been prominent, while war and conquest had been of lesser importance to society; with the Spanish Inquisition, destruction of the remains of paganism dealt the final blow to the values of Old Europe, and women were relegated one step further back from inclusion in European society. These salient points will be discussed in more detail in this section. Despite these complex topics, I have attempted to keep the topic of feminine and masculine as straightforward as possible and still illustrate the extent of tension and severity throughout history. The section on European mores and values will also delve into masculine and feminine roles in Old Europe and the need for resolution of inequality between the sexes that also impacts this narrative.

Aztec Culture

If we look at some of the writings from Miguel León Portilla, we find a noble woman advising her daughter on proper decorum for girls of their position in society; we find that young women were encouraged to be meditative, modest, and to avoid casual contact with boys or anyone who could mar their character. Noble girls were to learn to weave and focus on the fine arts of homemaking.[41]

Camilla Townsend[42] describes the difficulty in finding definite images of women, and chooses instead to look for trends and patterns within Aztec life that best describe the probabilities of choices available to them. The information she finds most abundant comes from the times during which the Spaniards first arrived, but written from memory thirty, forty, or fifty years later. She chooses Malintzin as her model for the role of women in Aztec society. Malintzin was the woman who was chosen to assist Hernan Cortes as an interpreter in the early fifteen hundreds, a role she played for over fifteen years. As Townsend writes about Malintzin, she is able to capture cultural trends and stories from that time frame, but none of the writings come directly from the pen or voice of Malintzin herself. From other events, she is able to piece significant segments of women's role to draw strong conclusions.

The following is a simplified portrait of what Townsend found that reflects on the lives of women in general: at least in the area of the hearth/home, women take their role as spiritual beings as seriously as men do in their role of priests in the temple. The floor plan of the home was identical to the design of the pyramids, and this similarity constituted in making the home a sacred place, where a woman could be goddess of her domain. According to Miguel León Portilla, it was customary for women to awaken before sunrise and take the time to get ready for the day by bathing (perhaps a steam bath), brushing their teeth, combing their hair, and meditating. Weaving and home duties were considered sacred acts that were offered to a god the Aztecs referred to as the "Near and Close."[43]

According to Townsend, the Aztecs were a polygamous society, a fact that had its advantages as well as disadvantages. An advantage could be that at the time of giving birth, the abundance of support allowed a woman the time to rest and recover from delivery before having to return to her duties. Another advantage was that giving birth was a sacred moment

---

[41] M. León Portilla (1980).
[42] C. Townsend (2006).
[43] M. León Portilla (1980).

done in community surrounded by extended family and never a solitary experience.

If a woman was highborn, she could pass on land to her son; no mention was made of being able to pass it on to her daughters. If the woman were second or third in the line of coming into the household, she would have difficulty getting her share of property for her offspring. The further down the chain of marriage, the less power the children had. Infighting was common between half-siblings, where the siblings with a mother with more power and a mother with little or no power could fight over inheritance for years, thus leaving the home divided.

If a woman was a concubine, she often had no rights and no position of any power in the household. Townsend describes the loneliness and isolation that went along with that role, particularly if the woman had been added to the household through purchase as slave. Ana Castillo comments on another aspect of Aztec culture when she reveals that the king of the Aztecs, Moctezuma, had no less than one hundred fifty women in the palace impregnated by him. She goes on further to state that girls were hardly schooled, did not participate in civic life, were chaperoned, and were not permitted to interfere with the business of men.[44]

Slaves were at the bottom rung of the social scale. In lean times or as spoils of war, girls could be sold or given into households as slaves and have no status other than as sexual objects. Townsend describes a world of constant change and social disruption during the years just after the arrival of the Spaniards; she sites many examples of warring for land, which were oftentimes settled with the disposition of women. Townsend mentions that records show that Malintzin was twice-sold into slavery by her family but that she was unable to confirm a definite ancestral lineage for her. The writer concludes that given the circumstances of being passed off to Hernan Cortez, there had to have been a betrayal by a family member since she was in her mid-teens at that time.

Townsend reflects on the loathing and hatred held toward Malintzin during her lifetime and that she is still held with intense disregard to this day. The key here is that there is hatred showered upon the person of Malintzin that is far greater than "one moment in history can hold."

---

[44] A. Castillo, *Massacre of the Dreamers* (1994).

She contends that one woman is being blamed for all the destruction, loss, carnage, enslavement, and theft that took place in Mexico during that period of turmoil five hundred years ago and that the blame and sexualization of women continues into modern times. One of Townsend's conclusions is that there is no definite image that can illustrate precisely why Malintzin received such a negative assessment of her actions, and claims, instead, that the character of Malintzin is sexualized and seen as a traitor.

What one can conclude from the scant information available is that men predominated in public life. Private life was the domain of the women, at least in the upper levels of society. This subject needs more investigation in order to draw more concrete conclusions about the roles of women in early colonial Mexican life that became more complex with the influence of the Catholic Church that arrived with the Spaniards. What can be concluded from Townsend's writing was that although there is no conclusive evidence of the status of women in Aztec society, women's power was limited to the domain of the home and determined by the status of her family. Castillo cautions that one should not ignore how women's roles in Aztec society has impacted social relations between the genders in Mexico and how women have been commodified in Mexican culture and a brotherhood society, which leaves women in a secondary position.[45]

Gylanic and Androcratic Ages in "Old" Europe

Interestingly, history and the coming of a new age have much more in common than one would expect. It is not surprising, the worship of the goddesses in Old Europe and the fact that gylanic and androcratic cultures alternately fluctuated in and out of prominence in Old Europe, prior to the recording of history. These fluctuations can be an indication that periods of *feminine* and *masculine* were common in Old Europe as well. The androcratic ways of society that the Spaniards brought, however, served to strengthen the masculine which now makes the feminine age of the sixth sun all the more significant in its arrival. In this section we will examine attitudes toward women as lived in Europe that were brought to

---

[45] C. Castillo (1994).

the Americas. The spread of a society that had some similarities as well as diverse ways of seeing the role of women, and relations between women and men, must be taken into consideration to understand the development of a new society with its own paradigm and mode of living. Findings of Western psychologists, social scientists, philosophers, anthropologists, and other researchers have been addressing the waxing and waning of feminine and masculine influences upon various societies throughout the ages.

Old Europe—Feminine and Masculine

Researcher and writer Riane Eisler pays particular attention to the pioneering work of Marija Gimbutas,[46] a Lithuanian archeologist who documented eras during which goddesses were prominent throughout Old Europe; Elaine Pagels,[47] who wrote *The Gnostic Gospels*, documents the exclusion of women from the rising Catholic Church shortly after the crucifixion of Jesus Christ. This exclusion has had wide-ranging consequences, and here it is mentioned to emphasize that these attitudes toward exclusion of women in society widened the gap of power between men and women—men having the upper advantage over women.

Riane Eisler wrote *The Chalice and the Blade*[48] in which she discusses in-depth a wide range of fluctuations in power between the feminine and masculine before recorded history. She includes the work of many researchers who write of a time before written history in Old Europe when the Goddess was worshipped, and entire cultures coexisted in relative harmony with one another. In this introduction, we mention her work to highlight that feminine and masculine ages have each taken the forefront and drive of civilizations, just as the wise ones of indigenous cultures had observed through their mathematical calculations. She emphasizes that at the root of these periods there has been acceptance and belief in a feminine god or goddess. Eisler chooses to describe them as gylanic and androcratic eras. She describes gylanic cultures as being nature-based in the goddess, and inclusive of masculine and feminine principles. In these societies, women had greater participation in public life, involvement with

---

[46] M. Gimbutas (1981) in Eisler (1987).
[47] E. Pagels (1979) in Eisler (1987).
[48] E. Eisler (1987).

education, a society more attentive to creativity; more equality between the sexes; greater interest in the welfare of its people; and living a peaceful and loving coexistence. Androcratic societies, on the other hand, were more repressive, less tolerant of feminine values, i.e., creativity and spirituality. The feminine principle was overlooked and excluded from a religion of a universal masculine god; women held a subservient role and were generally considered inferior to the masculine. Androcratic societies also tended to place emphasis on war and overrunning other cultures by might. Eisler comments that the foundations of European cultures were based on the foundation of the androcratic Roman Empire, which are still prevalent today.

Spanish Culture in the Americas

Ramon Gutierrez investigates sixteenth through eighteenth century records in the state of New Mexico before its annexation to the United States and finds that Spanish women were held responsible for the reputation of their families.[49] Any false step on the part of a woman could lead to ruining a family name and causing shame, embarrassment, and a fall from good standing in the community.

The Spanish Inquisition

In *Caliban and the Witch,* Silvia Federicci examines the role and scope of power in the Catholic Church's domain. On November 1, 1478, Pope Sixtus IV responded to Ferdinand and Isabella's desire to expel the non-Spaniards, who appeared to be practicing Catholicism but, in fact, were not, and established the Spanish Inquisition. In 1484–1485, two thousand Jews were executed. This was the beginning of the Inquisition.[50] The church was expanding its power over the choices of individual cultures and demanding loyalty and service from all subjects based on country and government. This power extended particularly to the new "colonies" of the Spanish Crown, and the Catholic Church and Crown worked hand in hand. What is not commonly acknowledged or recognized about the Inquisition is

---

[49] R. Gutierrez, *When Jesus Came, the Corn Mothers Went Away* (1992).
[50] S. Federici (2004).

the hidden hand of discrimination against the ways of knowing that directly affected the building of the Catholic Church in the Americas.

As Ana Castillo discusses in *Massacre of the Dreamers*, the Arab cultures of Spain had influence in the formation of the Catholic Church and subsequently in the colonies. Castillo says the church and the African/Spanish cultures still hold sway over us even today. She points out that the North African followers of Muhammad also subscribe to the Old Testament, and in the version of the creation story of Adam and Eve, woman disobeyed the Father, and thereby became the root of evil. Because there is no reflection of a feminine principle in the god of the Catholic Church, Castillo notes that the dichotomous models open to women are "that of mother as portrayed by the Virgin Mary versus that of whore/traitor portrayed by Eve. These two roles were revisited upon Mexico as the figures of La Virgen de Guadalupe and Malintzin."[51] Thus, the integrity of women was seriously complicated and further undermined with the arrival of the Spaniards in Mexico as the church took power, eliminated the existing religions, and superimposed its doctrine upon the people.

Exclusion from Women's Mysteries

According to Federici, the church, as part of its arsenal of weapons in proclaiming canons and fighting heresy, began a systematic attack on women who held knowledge of the birthing mysteries and the healing arts. The reign of terror created by the Inquisition lasted about two hundred years, and by the eighteenth century, laws were passed as far away as England and France, places that specifically excluded women from obstetrics. The first male midwives took over the role that had previously been the "inviolable mystery" of women, which then became the exclusive domain of men. Federici further notes that obstetrics at that time came almost entirely under state control. With all these events and proceedings, the final blow to the image of woman can be seen and proclaimed: she is inferior, evil, untrustworthy, and her body must be under state control.[52]

---

[51] A. Castillo (1994), p. 116.
[52] S. Federici (2004), p 183.

Effects of the Past on Modern Writers

These past influences had their effect on Chicana writers. In an example from a current Chicana writer, Cherrie Moraga states in *Modern-Day Malinches/2008*:

> It has taken me years to figure out that my resistance to many academic considerations, especially the framing of ethnic studies exclusively within the context of postmodern theories, is that so many people of color, especially women—even here in the United States—have never been full members of modern society; that many of us were born or raised with some other source within us that summoned us to the page, the poem, the politic, and the protest; that we held other ways of knowing that modernity did not reflect; and that we were without the "formal" language to articulate it. [53]

The discomfort that Chicanas experience in academia, and the lack of support and diminished regard they often get from their families, attests to the lack of regard modern writers still carry and the burden of the despised feminine. In *This Bridge Called My Back*, author Gloria Anzaldúa examines her feelings about the role she played in her family, and concludes that families often feed women self-hatred. In the writer's opinion, this is the legacy of the image held in the culture of the life Malintzin (discussed earlier in this introduction) that arises within the writer, in which she feels aligned with the hatred held toward women who defy the mores of the norm. But, as Anzaldúa observes, it is for her "sexual weakness and interchangeability" that Malintzin is most unmercifully criticized. "These types of attitudes and prejudices continue to be seen in that light; we are earmarked to be abusable matter, not just by men of another culture, but all cultures including the one that breeds us."[54]

Carlos Castaneda wrote many books on the teachings of his Yaqui teacher Don Juan, who taught him the protocols for using sacred plants

---

[53] C. Moraga (2011), p.148.
[54] C. Moraga and G. Anzaldúa (1981), p.184.

in exploring other dimensions and bringing back the nuggets of wisdom hidden in other levels of reality. These are complex systems and required years of training and dedication to the teachings. The end result of these journeys is to find the freedom sought with dedication by the old masters, teachers of the past. The first of Castaneda's books was *The Teachings of Don Juan: A Yaqui Way of Knowledge*.[55] There were several other books that followed. These books present an in-depth picture of the Yaqui worldview and ways of knowing.

Sergio Magaña also presents a discussion on dreaming and travel into other dimensions with the end result of awakening and finding one's creativity.[56] He discusses the process of utilizing an obsidian mirror to transform not only our particular past, but also the experiences of our ancestors. He also reviews other techniques for remembering our dreams, and cancelling dreams that reveal danger or frustration for our lives. His methods are the teachings he has received from his teachers connected to the lineage of dreamers who went underground at the time of the arrival of the Catholic Church in Mexico in the mid-sixteenth century.

"Sing the bones alive," as Clarissa Pinkola Estes would say.[57] In the story of *La Llorona*, Weeping Woman, Pinkola Estes illustrates that the creative process has a life of its own that must be nurtured into being. *La Llorona* is the story of the wailing woman who drags her fingers along the bottom of a river looking for the children she has killed. Pinkola Estes says this story reminds us that creativity is a delicate gift, and regret and sorrow are the results of denying the prize. Singing the bones alive would mean gathering the pieces of our creativity bit by bit and reviving them into expression.

Elena Avila, as a psychiatric nurse, also sought training with curandera/os in Mexico learning about dreams, psychological tools, and other practices.[58] Gloria Anzaldúa discussed her process of guidance through her dreams in discovering snake energy.[59] With the arrival of the

---

[55] C. Castaneda (1968).
[56] Magaña, S. (2011) and (2014).
[57] C. Pinkola Estes (1992).
[58] M. Avila (1999).
[59] G. Anzaldúa (1999).

sixth sun, we face the demands upon women to not only utilize their innate way of being, but to welcome and value the challenges of this reawakening. Oftentimes, the heart whispers softly, and "gut feelings" stir within, but we dismiss them as mere hunches, too hazy or blurred to give credibility. Creativity comes like a dazzling spirit so brilliant that one wants to deny its existence. Far easier to ignore the call and feign ignorance.

The birthing process can also serve to illustrate a feminine mode of creativity and "bringing the bones to life." The work of writer Patrisia Gonzales[60] is reviving the tradition of birth ceremony here in El Norte, the United States. She writes of the teachings she received through her dreams while training as a birth worker. In *Red Medicine* she defines the aliveness of all matter, and emphasizes we are that and much more. There is no separation between us and all of nature—the trees, water, earth, the stars. We are one consciousness. Gonzales has trained in an academic setting and is undergoing initiation into *curanderismo*, Mexican cultural medicine ways, wherein she works with ancestors in her dreams who provide guidance, as well as collaborating with established birth workers on both sides of the border who are passing on the tradition. She refers to indigenous intelligence, having encoded knowledge, from which the process of creativity arises. It has a life of its own. Gonzales's personal revival of the birthing tradition is testimony to the farsightedness of the ancestors who continued the old traditions, despite admonitions by the Catholic Church, and at great sacrifices and danger to their lives. As dreamers, they were determined to keep alive the mysteries of their spirituality and healing practices, and dream themselves into other dreamers' dreams as seen traditionally.

Another example of help available when we undertake the process of opening up to our creativity and finding the feminine can be seen in the writings of Eduardo Duran[61] who experienced firsthand going back in time. In ceremony and with the aid of sacred plants, he ventured into the unknown, met with ancestors, and returned with information previously unknown to him that was later confirmed to him through other means. To

---

[60] P. Gonzales, *Red Medicine, Traditional Indigenous Rites of Birthing and Healing* (2000).
[61] E. Duran, *Buddha in Redface* (2000).

the unbeliever, it could never be, but to the dreamer, it is a reality that our ancestors appear in our dreams and lend support in all areas of our lives.

In summary, examples of masculine and feminine in Old Europe can be seen in the Americas as European cultures crossed the Atlantic Ocean and replicated themselves in the colonies as imperialism and colonization expanded. The androcratic values of the Roman Empire were carried and blended in the Americas with an already complex society of masculine domination over the feminine. It can also be noted that self-knowledge is vital to the process of awakening to the sixth sun, the creative feminine; awakening creativity and manifesting our given gifts is a part of the path of self-knowledge, and serving the world; passing on traditions of the past, such as *curanderismo*, ceremony in birthing, and communicating with the ancestors are all valuable in bringing strands of the sixth sun into the waking world. *Corn Woman Sings* also describes the process of being born with a destiny embedded within us. We have the responsibility to uncover our destiny. These examples are merely the tip of the iceberg, but they open the path of discovery, intention, and dedication to live our lives in both worlds—waking and sleeping, thereby ushering in the sixth sun.

This segment on feminine and masculine as reflected in culture and the place of women, loss of Chicana's identity to family, and exclusion from public life, is by no means to be considered the final word on history. But the exclusion of feminine principle itself from the structure of religion further diminishes the link of the feminine in the spiritual realm, thereby affecting the position of women in the new society being developed in the Americas. We can see that both Aztec and Spanish cultures had their prejudices against women, as evidenced by the commodification of women, the prevalence of concubines within the Aztec home, and their absence in public life. The sale of children, though not always a permanent arrangement, but certainly a factor in lean times throughout the Aztec cultures, left large portions of young girls vulnerable to abuse, a situation that persists to this day as discussed by Anzaldúa. Favor and privilege to the first son also continues to this day. Polygamy and the commodification of women in Aztec culture also contributed to the marginalization of women. Though these components of culture may not be the intended outcomes for women, they have played a large part in holding women down in current Chicana/o culture. These long-held beliefs still cut deeply into our experiences. The secondary roles to our brothers that we play within our families and communities, and the restrictions imposed on our individual rights through culture and custom, remain deeply embedded in our psyche.

Despite these disadvantages for women, there is one loophole that existed for the indigenous woman that was not afforded to European women to the same extent. Given that women's mysteries were taken away from women in European cultures, it is quite surprising that *curanderismo* continued to flourish after the Spanish takeover in the Americas. Although Coyolxauhqui's representation was buried for five hundred years, her memory remained in the mind of the culture, and they continued their reverence for the feminine. The work of the *curandera* has survived, and *curanderas* continue to this day to be holders of women's mysteries, and to be trusted by the people to heal illnesses, chant, listen, and to use other ancient medical and psychological technologies to restore and cure. One can always find a practicing *curandera/o* in any Mexican American neighborhood throughout the Southwest, and particularly along the Mexico-US border. A cursory review through the World Wide Web brings forth thousands of websites and communities. It may be possible that one reason for the existence or survival of this component of the culture is that the creation stories naming Coatlicue the Creator played a vital role in maintaining a significantly strong image of woman in the forefront of the people's mind.

Whatever attitudes occurred in the blending of European and Aztec cultures contributed to the new role of women in Mexican culture. We can see that Chicana/o culture mirrors these tendencies to further marginalize women. Attitudes prevalent in family relations reflect a diminished standing for women as seen in the writings of modern Chicana writers. It may be possible that in the fact that the Catholic Church continues to exclude women from priesthood and other positions of power within the church, the status of inferiority continues to prevail.

These remnants of old attitudes, both positive and negative, are extremely important to the relevance of the arrival of the sixth sun. The sages of the old cultures of Central Mexico believed that cycles of feminine-based eras ebb and flow, and theerefore anticipated the return of the age of the feminine as a vital force to be reckoned with. Now, as they anticipated, is the time of the reappearance of the feminine. The sixth sun is the promise in ascendancy of the feminine—values, wisdom, and a return to our authentic, spiritual, and creative self. The era opens the door to identification with our true essence, including identification with all of nature and the land. It's up to us to allow the restoration of harmony and balance. The road is not an open and smooth path, however, given the past obscuration of the native paradigm. The challenges are complex, and the feminine still tucked into the culture at deep levels of memory.

Conclusion

In a world where the gods have been disfigured, maligned, destroyed, and buried for hundreds of years, how do we go about the reconstruction and revitalization of the traditions that can contribute to the restoration of balance and harmony into our lives? How does one usher in the energies of the sixth sun? Evidence of this new era is seen in the knowledge about our Chicana culture that surfaces every year through the writings of contemporary dreamers and *curanderas*/healers. Each generation of writers has its own message, and they all tie together a continuing recovered portrait. I am brought back to why I write this narrative. Both Moraga and Gonzales relate to the need to *remember* and the need to *know*, respectively, and, here I am adding, the need to *tell*. We have seen how writers and other creative people are reawakening to the feminine in their worlds; this introduction has examined facets of history that have held the feminine at bay by traditions and attitudes in both Aztec and European cultures, and then discussed how we might invite the changes within to openly manifest harmony and balance into our lives through the expression of the creative feminine. Most importantly, this introduction has re-opened the door to identity with the Toltecs, Mayans and Aztecs and given some examples of legends that have held us together. Our identity as a people lies in the reclamation of the land and our ancestors' ties to it. We have always been here, and the word "alien" is naturally foreign to a people who have always been a part of the land.

What we do know about the religion and traditions of the Mexican past, we find that, above all, they valued going beyond duality and reaching the levels of the divine which were home of our true existence and domain;

the gods and goddesses of the culture portrayed for us the wisdom and understanding beyond the material world; dreaming was our reality, and the waking state the dream. Humans were meant to seek and decipher the will of the mother and father by developing a face, heart, and identifying with our divinity, i.e., seeking to be our god-self by serving the world with our sacred gifts. With this knowledge, the path to truth lay open. Learning to straddle both spirit and waking worlds is crucial to finding a path to the sixth sun.

However we choose to envision this feminine way of being or finding our creativity, understanding the indigenous paradigm would be helpful. As discussed in *Corn Woman Sings: A Medicine Woman's Dream Map*,[62] navigating the dream world and finding our creativity can be confusing, slow, tedious, painstaking, and it requires time and patience to bring creativity forth. There are cultural traditions, and many ways of allowing ourselves to be used in service to healing the creative feminine.

If we want to manifest the effects of the sixth sun, we take upon ourselves the responsibility to uncover our destiny and live it out in accordance with our Creator's divine plan for us. The quest for our creativity and the feminine is where we find unity and meaning that dissolve the illusions of this world. Traveling in other worlds and understanding our experiences are part and parcel of pursuing the creative feminine, the energy of the sixth sun.

The arrival of the sixth sun is about learning how to utilize power by avoiding to control or manipulate it. The lessons of duality help us recognize that we are much more than what we believe. The opposites we find in daily living are opportunities to find the truth of who we are. Even if we only see it for five seconds, we can never again believe we are victims of fate. The voice of the Coyolxauhqui herself, as presented in this narrative, tells us to risk all and hasten to meet her at the edge of the precipice of duality. That is the intent of the philosophy and beliefs of the ancestors, the belief in a multidimensional world, the efficacy of dreams, and the alternative spirituality of the sixth sun. Going beyond duality and seeing the oneness of all creation means that we have expanded our consciousness and begun to live multidimensionally. This would indicate

---

[62] E Barron Druckrey, 2009

that we recognize illusions for what they really are: distractions from seeing the truth, reasons to separate ourselves from one another, and belief in the tonal—the waking world—as our reality.

Let's see how we can open ourselves to the ancestors' views of time and space to take us through our lives, and lay aside our own plans in order to be guided by our destiny. The bridge between the worlds can be laden with fog and desolation. Enticing one to enter into deeper realms will be an early tasks in our joueney. Awareness has many starts and stops, and dreamers over the centuries have come in and out of this dimension in efforts to find their true selves. The rope holding the connection between the worlds eventually emerges. As consciousness moves toward the anticipated change, training will flow easily. One will intuit and eventually finally remember what the ancient ones prophesied long before this lifetime. History has done its part in confusing cultural memory, the collision of cultures, and other facets of culture that have negated the vitality of the feminine. These now have the opportunity to be corrected.

As I have attempted to illustrate, feminine and masculine patterns of communication are deeply embedded in our collective memory through legend, oral folklore, tradition, and literature. However one may feel about relations between the sexes, there are avenues to pursue to free us from the constraints of habit and custom. Spirituality is a wide door through which to enter. I would say that this narrative has served its function if a man has learned to wield his power by allowing the influences of the sixth sun, in particular, the feminine values of the legends of Coyolxauhqui, to guide him; and that he allows himself the time to wait in the spaces of not knowing with gentleness of spirit, an open heart, patience, and kindness; that he allows tears to flow freely, devotes time to discover his softer, creative self, and incorporates his sacred gifts by reveling in the consciousness of his dreams. It will also have served its purpose if women aligned themselves with Coyolxauhqui, the Dark Feminine, and brought forth their given gifts and continued the practice of expanding their awareness. Communication with nature is vital to the expanded awareness and understanding of consciousness; the awareness that comes from this communication leads to further development of the gifts given, particularly when related to travel into other worlds and dimensions. Identification with and the development of our special gifts, or powers, is dependent on the receiving of such spiritual communications. We are not separate from one another, and this includes union with nature and the aliveness of time and space, but we are not our bodies either. There is tangible wisdom to be learned from all of creation.

We've entered into a beautiful time and space. Now is the time to step forward. Let us explore how Aurora, Gracia, and La Curandera attempt it.

EBD
Tiburon, California
October 27, 2016

Prologue

In Coatlicue's Words

I am the Mother of your mother, providing the spiritual nourishment that will take your last breath and bring you safely into the next stage of awareness. I continue to do my dream work and am aware of your actions in other worlds where you create and cocreate with yourself and sister travelers. Everyone dreams, but most have forgotten that sleep is more than a time to rest. Sleep is for sharpening your spiritual senses, a rich period of creativity. To dream within dreaming is a gift one gives to oneself. The ability to remember increases in time and space.

I am Coatlicue, Mother of the Multiverse, I am the creator of the heavens above and worlds below, Heart of the Earth, Mother of the Southern Stars, the Huitznahua, and Mother of the People of the Corn. I've had many children and guided and nurtured them to their destiny. The Twins are whispered names from the past, but they too continue to play their part in the constellation of space and eternity, the confounding aspects that demand acuity of mind over matter. My daughter Coyolxauhqui, the Milky Way and light in the dark—yes, she succumbed to the hands of her brothers. It was their duty to play their part in destiny, but it was her destiny and her choice to decry the sorry condition of humanity without discernment beyond duality. Her body was strewn hither and yon. Without her consent, there would have been no consciousness in the darkness of this world. It is she who took the stand and gave herself to offer a path out of the emptiness of duality, and hence, to be the call to guide you home.

Coyolxauhqui is the primary guide to the one consciousness. Discover her mysteries beyond duality. Allow the dark, silent spaces of her being to envelop you. Secrets of the multiverse abound in those spaces. Pierce her heart; blast through it and become the light you are meant to be. The gods; the thirteen levels above and nine below; the colors red, white, black, and yellow; time and creation meet there in a glorious array of sound, light, space, and time. Let your spirit be soothed by the ancient symphony that rings throughout time and space. Let her guide you back to me, for I am the consciousness that holds all in eternal oneness, and I long for your return. Release the ego, there is no death. Death is the thought that you are separate from me.

Chapter One

Malinalxochitl: Aurora

Passage*

La Curandera releases my hand, and fades slowly. Gracia fades away. I am left in the kitchen with only Ocelotl and the sound of the rustling leaves of the fig tree outside the open window. The vacuum of their departure feels unbearable. The silence is so profound, thundering in my ears with each breath. After what seems an eternity, he begins.

"Come with me, and I will tell you a story that begins in a sacred place not too far away, a familiar place deep into Mother Earth where our ancestors gathered during the change of seasons to honor the Creator in ceremony to assure our continued existence. There, around a fire, I will tell you the story of how you, Malinalxochitl, as you were called then, and I, Ocelotl, your elder brother, committed with other dreamers to return to earth again and again to assist in carrying forward the consciousness vital to the continuation of life." The sound of his voice is soothing and calming; effortlessly I make myself comfortable near a fire, close my eyes, and begin another dream.

"My relationship with you begins when our people experienced turbulence and radical change—a migration from our northern home, where we were surrounded by seven caves, to the Valley of Anahuac; it was a passage that lasted a full fifty-two-year cycle, one thousand years ago. I was your elder brother then.

"I remember the elders of our clan saying that the beautiful, verdant trees and plants that once abounded throughout the land had withered. Where rivers had flowed, dry beds of cracked, scorched earth lay exposed. Even our food supply of beans, squash, and corn had dwindled. I was told by the elders that many seasons before, there had been rich fields of corn that stretched through large areas of the land; that the corn stocks were tall and heavy with corn; and that the hair protecting the

cob and kernels was thick, long, and abundant. Gradually, the supply dwindled. No longer were the fields thick with harvest, and more often, there was a shortage at the end of the cold season. Families were leaving for greener lands, sometimes traveling toward the morning sun, and other times, the evening sun. Some traveled to the land above the Great Canyon where the winters were longer and colder, but where the fields could grow as they once had in our motherland.

"One night after I began running with the men and warriors on the hunt, when everyone was deep in dreams, I lay still under my deerskin and heard the painful cry of an owl pierce over the rooftops of our dwellings. It was toward the end of the season when the nights were still longer than the days, and the shallow layer of cracked snow was beginning to melt.

"The very next day, very early on a crisp and cold morning, the mothers of our clan called for a meeting that marks the beginning of this story. They gathered all the people, young and old alike, weavers, potters, artisans, and warriors. Down the ladders that protected our dwellings and across the valley floor we went, until we came to the mouth of a cave where a large boulder defined the sacred space.

This dream recall is actually part-cultural legend on the identity of the Aztecs; the narrator of the migration story is a dream figure that came to the writer as a sprit attempting to communicate with her over the forty years of her journal-keeping, and finally broke through the barriers of the waking plane because he became so commonplace in the dreams of the author that she finally accepted him as a dream guide and resource for the unfolding of the beginning of the book. Therefore, it is a composite of actual legends of the identity of the Aztecs, actual parts of the climate history of the American Southwest as found in the Internet, and part-dream as it was experienced by the author.

(See Corn Woman Sings: A Medicine Woman's Dream Map, *Barron Druckrey [2009].)*

"'It has become apparent that we must leave the land we love, and move into new lands. Children have been starving, and the elders are suffering from disease.' I heard our mother begin with a resignation that spoke volumes of sorrow in having to leave behind the world our people had always known. This was our home, where our protectors stood guard for us in the mountains, surrounding us with their watchful and tender eyes. Her words fell upon the people with a deadly resonance. We sat in a large cluster wrapped in deerskins, covering ourselves from the cold, stunned and unable to respond.

"The mountains that surrounded our valley, with their beautiful movement in shades of dark blue jagged rock and ever-changing fiery moods, were our markers of assured continuation and safety. To think that we would leave the dwellings of the sacred beings and the places containing the history of our ancestors was truly unimaginable. Sitting at my place among the warriors, I listened as waves of fear rolled down my body, a chill penetrating my heart and leaving me shivering. Even my bones had no answer for the words wildly slamming against the ancient stone. No, this could not be. We could never leave her—the Mother, protector, soother of sorrow, giver of life and wisdom. She who sustained the gods who protected and guided us. She who surrounded us with compassion and goodness, and drew us closer to her in times of strife. She who bared her soul to sustain us. This could not be.

"An elder who traded shells with neighboring tribes for countless seasons spoke after the long pause, 'I've heard that several other tribes, relatives of many of us, are preparing to migrate in the direction where the rains come from.' His comment increased the weight of the discussion since it was apparent that others of the region were further along the path of coming to grips with this decision. 'They believe they will manage well with the children. Of course, they plan to leave most of their belongings behind, and *have debated long and hard. We must think of our children and future generations,' he concluded.*

"*Our mother went on, 'A dreamer who lives many a days' walk, where Grandfather Sun begins his movement across the sky, tells that he had a vision guided by our God Huitzilopochtli. He saw what our people must do. He divines that an eagle with a snake in its mouth perched atop a cactus will signify where the people will have found their new home, to roam no further. He describes a rich green valley with gardens of hanging bright red and blue flowers, bountiful herds of deer, a beautiful blue green lake sheltered by high surrounding mountains, and many rivers running through the valley.'*

"*Silence fell upon us again, and another mother added, 'Our God Huitzilopochtli would never mislead us. We cannot deny that he too protected our ancestors.' Talk continued until the sun was high above us, but the consensus was unanimous—we needed to leave in search of a new homeland.*

"*Shivers and restlessness disturbed me throughout that night, and before Grandfather Sun brought the new day's light, I decided to seek out the holy man for counsel. He pointed me in the direction of the Mother. I set out with no food and water across the valley floor again with a saddened heart in search of answers. I needed to lean my face against her body, to tell her of the incomprehensible misfortune about to befall us. I desperately needed the assurance that she and our destinies were bound together forever, that we would never wander far from her warmth.*

"*The ground was frozen, though for this time of year in past times, it would have been buried under heavy layers of snow. Now there were only meager patches spread throughout the area. Stubbles of plants were evident. Life was barely visible. When Grandfather Sun cast long shadows from the mountain the following evening, I found the trail of boulders drawing me toward my destination.*

Dormant stems of wild sage lay wherever I stepped through, and reminded me that the world was still at rest under the protection of long, cold nights. The markings, having been arranged by the ancient ones many, many cycles behind, announced that I had reached the sacred grounds.

"*I descended through the spaces and openings I knew so well until I came to the circle of the stones deep in the Mother's womb. Thirsty, breathless, and trembling with weary bones, I lay my head down. The fatigue enshrouded me, and I began to dream. Very subtly, I opened to communion with our ancestors. They nudged my back gently but steadily, and confirmed the worst of my fears. Tears welled in my eyes and flowed silently onto the ground. I began to convulse and writhe with intense anguish in my heart.*

"*The splendor of her stillness further conveyed to me that our time together was shorter than the arrival of the hot, scorching weather, and maybe even on the heels of the all-too-short rainy season before that. I felt certain that she was turning her back on our people, but in the silence, I knew in the depths of my soul the truth that could not be denied. She would have to hold her pain in order to comfort and soothe ours. She was the strong one. I remained there for a day before making the trek back to our community. I walked with stick in hand to support myself, weakened by the lack of water and food, through dense fog, over boulders and hardened ground. Unsteady and barely able to walk, I arrived home with a conviction that she would, indeed, provide for us and guide our way to our new homeland.*

"*During the new moon, when the snows had completely melted and the days had grown longer, preparations for joining our neighbors began. Breaking up our community and deciding who and what would stay behind were decisions labored on long and seriously. Our tribe had its final meal on the land we so loved. The holy man raised the lit sacred plant with its dreamy white smoke, while he whispered incantations that carried the message of our plight across the valley, bouncing back to us in shrill sobs of Mother Mountain's grief. This was our farewell to her and to our relatives staying behind.*

"Before the sun rose the next day, with a vast chasm of the unknown in front of us, we set afoot in search of our new home. Heavy-hearted, eyes averted from one another, especially Mother Mountain and the loved ones remaining, we moved in a haze of uncertainty away from her. Many of the elders stayed behind with rations to sustain them through to the coming warm season. Many families remained behind for various reasons—some to join us at another time, some to go north to be with their relatives in the sacred grounds of the deep valley, others, to move north into the mountains and forests.

"Our close circle included our mother and her family, our grandmother, our aunts and their families, and our father. We quietly embraced the elders and the others remaining. We waved farewell and set out to join the trail of pilgrims in the direction of the rising sun, inching our way forward to the rhythmic sound of beating drums."

Passage Begins

"With Huitzilopochtli ensconced as our guide at the front of the caravan, dogged determination carried us through scorching weather toward cooler green lands. Movement was hardly noticeable, but after many weeks of travel, we left the familiar and entered upon green terrains that rolled and undulated. The rugged spine of another aspect of the Mother, the holy mountains, was continually at our right side. Gladly, we saw that she continued her watch over us. Children were most susceptible to heat or cold, and we buried many. The few elders who agreed to travel soon set themselves in places protected from the

weather, or joined relatives in other communities, and waved us farewell with their blessings. Water was often scarce and hard to find. Only the very strong could survive such harsh conditions.

"Once arriving in more hospitable surroundings with shade and water, we took to resting and replenishing our supplies. The tight formal boundaries that identified us with our traditions began to melt and blend with others in the long procession. Without perceiving it at first, the constant movement and change of view rattled loose personal aspects of our lives. The daily patterns of habit that we left in the abandoned abodes carved into the cliffs above the valley dissolved. I often wonder how our smaller groups would have navigated crossing those unseen borders without Huitzilopochtli's profound wisdom and strong medicine.

"We carried within our secret dreams and expectations. No longer tied to the land, they spilled onto the ground like living waters on those days that seemed most unbearable. The swaying of our bodies as we tread the uneven path was conducive toward bringing out those images. One could float aloud partially formed visions since everything else was in flux, and tradition no longer restricted our thinking. Malinalxochitl, it was during these periods that your thoughts and feelings revealed the power of the medicine shaping your inner life. Even for your nine winters, you had a depth of perception and insight that seemed particularly remarkable, a wisdom that could be culled for the common good and survival of our newly forming extended tribe.

Dreamers' Agreement

"Early one fresh summer morning after a light rain, our dream group gathered. The summer leaves were budding. We sat under the sparse shade of a cedar tree when the sun was not yet hot. Long blades of grass covering the ground

lent cushion for our bodies. A full creek nearby sang its melody loudly. Sitting quietly on the trunk of a fallen tree, Huitzilopochtli reported his impressions of the future to us: 'In my travels to the real world, I have met with dreamers who dream together in bringing our people into the ages ahead of us. We all agree that a cycle of great growth is coming but that it will also be followed by a long period of darkness. As dreamers, we are planning to assist our nation across the eventual abyss before us. The time is coming when humanity will join into one great tribe, when we help one another transcend the travails of this world and stand united in the consciousness that dreamers have always known.

"'We as a people will grow into a powerful nation where our warriors will conquer boundless lands and tribes to make us one great people. We will till the soil, grow abundant crops of corn, squash, and beans, and our children's children will know great wealth and live in harmony with one another.

"'But some will lose their humanity. We are a reflection of all creation. Just as it moves from its center, in this world, we move from our center, pulling further away from our beginning. When the Great Star passes through the center of Coyolxauhqui, the Milky Way, which happens only once in the longest of cycles of time, there will be an alignment of the all levels above and all those below, and the consciousness of humanity will be changed forever. This is the time the gods await, when duality is in perfect balance and humanity can seize this most uncommon opportunity to transcend the travails of this world and be catapulted into the divine essence of consciousness.'"

Ocelotl continued with Huitzilopochtli's prophecy, "'I want you to keep in mind this very important message I have for you from the dreamers: your spirits are continuous, and you come to this world to live more than once. The Great Mystery organizes your lives for when you are in *this realm, but it is up to each of you to listen, and follow through with sacred gifts which are lent to you for the protection and wisdom of the people. Each one of you has a destiny, which will unfold with the help of these sacred gifts. Ask yourselves: Did you come to serve life with music and calming whispers of the wind? Did you come to reveal the Invisible One through color and light, dance or poetry? Perhaps you come to teach harmony, valor, and wisdom. Remember your soul's purpose and blossom into that which makes your heart sing. We dream our lives! The Great Mystery sends messengers and guides (dreamers) to assist you in remembering the immensity of truth. Fulfill that destiny and calling. Remaining conscious is a difficult road, but is always a path of great value that leads toward transcendence of the soul.*

"'*In my encounters with other dreamers,*' Huitzilopochtli continued, '*I have seen that your lives will be fruitful, abundant, and anchored under the protection of the Invisible One, the Creator of all worlds. You will live in a world filled with radiant colors of bright pink, red, and blue flowers, and fragrances enlivened with magic and wonder. You will make music, and work with white, yellow, red, green, and other metals. You will have ornaments of these precious metals to wear woven with the quetzal's blue feathers. The pageantry will dazzle your eyes and send you in unison into other worlds where you will meet the gods and the creators of the universe—worlds beyond your dreams.*

"'*But a time will come, long, long after many lifetimes, when a foreign consciousness will predominate. During that period, our lands will be taken from us. Our temples will be destroyed, and the drums will fall silent. There will be no dancers, musicians, or poets to sing praises to the gods for cycles of seasons upon seasons. Our people will suffer enslavement—the young, the old, everyone will suffer a great loss of life and freedom. But, regardless of the suffering, the dreamers, the great messengers, will show you lasting truths to help you travel through this dim, dismal period.*

"'Fear not, your descendants will see the time when reality as we know it to include worlds within worlds, the aliveness of the land, the sun, the stars, our four-legged relatives, the rivers, and the mountains will remain forever alert and aware, and we will be the richer and stronger for our efforts in the dream time, when we become awake and embrace the gods in their magnificence. The cycles of the past will bring forth their wisdom, and we will join them in the brightness of their light and the vividness of their knowledge.'"

"Ocelotl, this is a beautiful story," I said to him, "but how is it possible for us to avail ourselves of the wisdom that you say we acquired at that time? I can't just snap my fingers and make it so. How will I ever be able to remember everything, when I have serious doubts about remembering even this dream? How will I be able to remember something that happened at another time and place so long ago? It's not like there's a telephone and I can call dreamers and say, 'Hello, you have some teachings you must impart to others. Come on over!'" I said, trying to grasp the immensity of the task with humor.

"There's another part of the story that will answer that question," he responded. "Let me continue. It's easier than you think. Just think of me. I will be there. My task in this part of your journey has been simply to remind you of all the aspects of the agreement we made centuries ago. We agreed to directly and specifically find the edges of duality, and plunge into the depths of the vastness and become awake. We agreed to remind people that we abide in eternal wisdom and malleable borderless realms. The wind has consciousness, light, awareness, and nature is vibrant and alive. Direction, time, and space have awareness and *can guide you in remembering and taking up your part in what you agreed to do.*

"Most importantly, we committed at that time to hold the consciousness. The passage of time, the travails of this world, famines, warring among ourselves, expedient moves such as the migrations south and eventual return, large-scale destruction of our peoples, enslavement, and other catastrophic events during collisions of cultures—all around the world. These all conspire to close the curtain and bring upon humanity a dreamless sleep that hides the truth. People have accepted the belief in a one-dimensional reality where they see themselves as miniscule beings subject to the tides of change, and victims of their thoughts of lack and suffering, alone and without the benefit of a long memory. But there's another way, a way of living beyond this duality, of finding the oneness that belongs to us. By finding the joy, uncovering the sacred gifts we are born with, we are able to find the time and space within ourselves to experience the essence of our true being, and experience the boundlessness of the multiverse. You must—you will wake up and remember!"

Ocelotl continued with Huitzilopochtli's prophecy: "Our original group under Huitzilopochtli's guidance continued to become a cohesive band of strong dreamers. In our dream voyages, he led us to the group of dreamers who dream and incarnate to help the human race awaken to truth while in the human body. By practicing a form of dream meditation (and sometimes with the help of a green button and other sacred plants), we grew adept at meeting in other realms. At a place at the top of the multiverse where our ancestors conduct their teachings to us, we saw our vital role many cycles into the future, bringing back the teachings of the vastness of our existence.

"We also learned to be focused in our waking state so that we could have an impact from other realms into this one. Awareness is not only within the dream state,

but is used especially for our meetings with destiny and helping others remember their true identity. We must keep our spiritual eyes focused to remember.

"The gods were generous with their teachings and blessed us with visions and communications. Since everything occurs simultaneously, in that lifetime we went into realms where we could see our lives as they were destined. Huitzilopochtli would wait for all of us to arrive in the dream state before beginning his instruction. The lessons were as clear and straightforward as though we were sitting on holy ground under the shade of a cedar tree in the waking world. We arrived one at a time or in clusters of spirit—students charged with excitement and expectation to meet with the master.

"Ask yourself: did you come to serve life with music and calming whispers of the wind? Did you come to reveal the Invisible One through color and light, dance or poetry? Perhaps you come to teach harmony, valor, and wisdom. Remember your soul's purpose, and blossom into that which makes your heart sing. Draw from your experiences prior to this lifetime to help you evolve spiritually. Drink from the feelings in dreams that enliven you with joy and song. Waking life pales compared to the array of treasures the soul offers. Use those prized memories to set you afire with intention. Endless possibilities await you. Life is in the spirit realms. We dream our lives!

"Dreamers know the truth. Multidimensional travel is second nature to us. When our creators made us, they included aspects of themselves to be reflected in our actions. But, more importantly, the universe is ultimately a multiverse with aliveness and sacred geometry woven into all matter. The absence of light is not emptiness, but a space of power like strong gravity. We understand that our divine right is to expand our awareness that encompasses our consciousness in all worlds. We are constantly weaving throughout many realms. But awareness in this world

requires the support of dreamers from many realms. My role in this life—in this third-dimensional, seemingly solitary path—is to support and remind you, Malinalxochitl, to reawaken to all reality. Each lifetime requires focused intention, the wisdom from the Four Tezcatlipocas (the four directions), the interaction of the sun and moon, and the cycles of the sun, moon, and stars interacting with one another.

"*Influenced by Huitzilopochtli's teachings, we laid our plans to become awake within the dream of life. The course of history has repeating cycles and repeating shorter cycles exist within these larger ones. We became seekers of awareness—to remember we also exist in other worlds, and to bring the essence of the sacred for the benefit of our people. It was then that we too committed to devote ourselves to planting the spiritual seeds of consciousness for the proper harvest time as seen in our travels to the great dreamers.*

Temporary Home

"*Seasons passed after Huitzilopochtli's prophecy. After many winters of pushing steadily southward, fatigue set in, and the strength of rank and file travelers began to sag. Political disputes arose about the efficacy of our intentions. The elders made a decision soon after the rains came one season. A great crackle and lightning over the hills was seen that split the tree around which we gathered daily, bringing it down in two equal sides. Huitzilopochtli and many others saw this as a sign from our god. The decision was long overdue. A group splintered off and moved over the mountain range toward the shores of deep waters. But mostly, followers of the original vision remained faithful, even to the ends of their lives.*

"*We traveled on and shortly found a beautiful lagoon surrounded by gentle hills with pine trees and a generous supply of deer, pheasants, and other small animals. The scouts that explored the area reported that they had found many caves, about seven in all, in the surrounding hills and distant mountains. Naturally, we saw this as an auspicious sign that this was holy ground. The weather was temperate and mild. Leaders of the group and heads of family mutually agreed that we would stay in this tranquil, pleasant world longer than usual to replenish our animals, plant corn, squash, and beans, and redirect our plan for the future. Still, no sight of the eagle on the cactus was spotted. The mothers and fathers knew the people had reached their limits.*

"We set about building dwellings from a mixture of mud and grass. After a period of settling down, potters and jewelers began to spring forth with the riches of the land. Potters found clay and produced new designs for cooking and carrying water. Silversmiths made fine jewelry with precious blue stones, and weavers perfected new and brilliant garments. Even the rivers were cultivated, trenches built so that the flow of water was distributed throughout the area for growing our crops. We called our new home Chicomostoc.

Toward the Final Destination

"By the time we regrouped to assess our wealth in preparation to resume the search from our temporary home to our final destination, twenty winters had passed, and we faced a considerable number of changes in the leadership. The generation of dreamers Huitzilopochtli developed during the pilgrimage had moved on to other tribes to pass on the teachings. They too were unable to make the next leg of the journey. The younger dreamers he had fortified and prepared through the wisdom and foresight of his vision in the interim renewed the fervor and ignited the ambitions of the adventurous and the strong.

Hundreds from our original travelers had died from old age and various causes, but a formidable group of the new generation that had grown up on the land was yet willing to embark upon the hardships ahead with guidance from experienced travelers. Huitzilopochtli, an elder then, was still willing but unable to travel. From among our priests, educators, warriors, and artisans, a sizeable committed group set out once again. They were fully prepared. Some were not ignoring the possibility of glory and power that lay ahead for the benefit of all. Naturally, they wanted to please Huitzilopochtli, the God, and, in the final analysis, it was the strength of the dreamer's vision that carried the weight of the decision. Once again, the white plant was lit, and blessings were invoked for the final leg of the journey.

Challenges and Signs

"You as Aurora came into the world prepared to undergo the isolation and loneliness you experienced as a child. But in this endeavor, don't expect avalanches of gratitude and love. I am warning you of this. You will uncover a level of unimaginable loneliness. You will uncover a new meaning of rejection, betrayal, and abandonment. You will think yourself a second Malinche. Let this be permanently written in your mind. Put this in front of your dresser mirror where you will be reminded upon awakening, in front of your kitchen sink where you will see it many times throughout the day, on the dashboard of your car, and in front of your books. Write it on the back of your hand to be indelibly written for all time. This is the danger of putting the mirror of consciousness in front of people's faces. Just remember, as always happens in this plane, the outer will crumble, and you will feel a profound chill of loss and sense of isolation down to the marrow of your bones. There will be many other challenges, but each one will draw you closer to truth."

> *With Ocelotl's story completed, he and I leave the sacred underground area and I gradually become aware of the kitchen where he bids me farewell. Putting his forehead against mine, he smiles and affirms, "You'll be just fine. Remember, Malinalxochitl is also the name of the goddess who guided the people to their new homeland, so you travel in good company. Whatever happens has already happened to you and others on this quest dozens of times. You'll recall the lesson."*

Slowly, my body becomes acclimated to the feel of the bed beneath me and the sheet's smoothness on the backs of my legs. I begin to hear the soft sounds of the street—motors of occasional cars passing by, the neighbor's sprinklers. I hear the early summer morning breeze rustling the leaves of the fig tree. It's time to move into the day. I wonder how long I've been dreaming. It must be three days, I exaggerate. I savor the sweetness of seeing Grandmother, La Curandera, Gracia, and Ocelotl; it's just too soon, and the memory too vibrant to come back to this world. Yet I know it's time. It's time to rise, but not quite yet. I replay the experience with my eyes shut, remembering the smell of being underground, remembering Ocelotl's voice, Grandmother's sweetness and love.

Time to return; my eyes still closed. I feel the weight of the sheet on the tips of my toes, with the memory crystal clear, and the longing beating in my heart. However, I know they now reside in my heart. I breathe in. I open my eyes.

Before: La Biografía de Mi Mamá

"Mamá, cuéntame de tus tiempos," I ask my mother one afternoon when she is making a blue gingham dress for me. I have nothing to do but keep her company. The shades in the dining room are drawn to keep the cool air of the air conditioner in. It is summer, and temperatures are hitting the high nineties. Mamá pauses for a moment and looks up from the fabric on which she has just laid the pattern. There is a window that looks into a utility room at the back of the house. The faraway look in her eyes tells me she is traveling over the years—thirty, maybe forty?

"Teníamos casa en el pueblo," she begins her story, "había dos puertas grandes para los caballos . . ." From the carriage entrance to their home in Rayón, San Luís Potosí, Mexico, she invites me to join with her.

"Life was so hard," she began. "La Revolución del mil novecientos diez (the Mexican Revolution of 1910), turned the ranchitos into unsettled little hamlets. When the Carransistas came through Rayón, we would flee into the surrounding *monte* for safety. We would stay out there for days, sometimes weeks. There was no protection for us. I had a little brother who died of *susto*, fright, in one of the times that we fled out of town. The feet of a body hanging from a tree struck his forehead, and he fell ill and died within two days. My sister was kidnapped—*se la robaron.*"

"Did you ever see her again?" I inquired.

"No. later we heard that she was taken to Pachuca, a town quite some distance."

"Did anybody try to find her?"

"These are peaceful times here. It's hard to explain how people felt. I'm not sure how we found out that she was living in Pachuca. When I left Mexico, I couldn't afford to look back, and I didn't for many, many years. Also, my father went on drinking binges. Sometimes, for a week or two at a time, my mother would gather us up when he was on a rampage, and take us to her family's home. We had a *rancho*, but he lost it all through his drinking. We were lucky your grandmother's family could take all of us in, and there were six of us kids."

My mother says she was sixteen when she boarded the ocean liner as a governess to an American family. They were bound for Los Angeles, via South America. She carried all her possessions in a brown leather suitcase.

They had lived through the worst of the Mexican Revolution. Ten years after arriving in Los Angeles, she met my father and they married, barely escaping the Depression of the 1930s.

Mother, my brother Chepe, and I visited Mexico City, and I remember the first time she saw La Virgen at La Basílica. I'd read my mother's facial expressions and knew them well, and I could tell this was a precious moment for her. She stood silently in front of La Virgen, and sighed a deep breath when she stepped away from her reverie.

"Oye, Cata, y no extrañas a México, o a la Virgen?" asked her cousin Josefina. This was a double question because one referred to whether she missed the mountains and rivers and relatives in Mexico, and the other to the spiritual, her new religion without saints and La Virgen.

"Sí, Pepa," she answered, looking down and holding back her pain. She missed all of it. "Sometimes I think I'm doing fine, and then I receive a letter from you telling me about the family, and I feel very sad for days. I get over it, but it comes back with the next letter."

Looking back on that day that we "worked" together on my blue gingham dress, and the stories she related, I see that my mother's silences were loaded with her longing for La Virgen, her family and its network of aunts, uncles, and cousins, and the feminine warmth that we basked in when we visited Mexico. So when I recall the events that led up to my mother's death, I know she died of a broken heart—the border between the two countries was like a canyon that kept her heart divided, and I don't think she ever did come to terms with her life up here. In a way, I think that's how I learned that sadness is an accumulation of events that one can't change, which are etched in one's heart and family forever—the losses, the distance, the absence, the longing, the missing. Perhaps that's one of the reasons why music had to come to earth; why I feel I must do my part to make earth a beautiful home, make it welcoming and joyful. My mother didn't have the opportunity, but maybe I do.

My First Blue Dress

I always loved the dresses my mother made for me, but my very favorite was a simple little blue sleeveless dress with black piping around the collar and down the front alongside three big black buttons. Tiers ever widened the skirt that flared when I twirled round and round. My mother bought it at the Mercado de La Villa de Santa María in Mexico City. It was our first trip to Mexico. I was twelve years old that summer. My jet-black hair was still in long silky braids. It was morning, about ten o'clock; the day had a slight humid haze. The warm, balmy air brushed lightly against my face and my arms, but, most amazingly, the laughter, loud music, and language I was hearing was mine—familiar and caressing. I walked arm in arm with my cousin Marysela. My mother and Aunt Josefina walked behind us down La Villa, as it was called, a wide, busy, six-lane boulevard.

Tortillas de maíz cooked in makeshift stands at street corners—the aroma of the cooking corn seeping into my pores, transporting me to my ancient past. *Antojitos*, short-order dishes of *frijoles, carnitas, aguacate*, and *salsa* rolled into hot, fresh *tortillas*. Trumpets, violins, guitars, and voices blared the passion of a new love from jukeboxes in open-air stalls. Rapture and tenderness and tears of joy, all rolled into one.

I was bathed in Spanish, with sensations of delight tingling over my skin. The roll of the Spanish double "rr" thundered proudly. Everything on the radio was in Spanish. Everyone in the street spoke Spanish. My ears rang with sweet words. Further yet, new words, famous landmarks—Popocatepetl, El Bosque de Chapultepéc, Alameda de Las Américas; Spanish names of presidents, Porfirio Días, mythical figures, famous leaders, now streets and parks—all reflecting my soul; poetry, lyrics, jokes, songs; and the brown faces—ah, the brown skin, where brown was the norm. I was the norm. This was everyday life, not just Sunday afternoon at the Jamaica in Stockton. I felt as though I'd put a great seashell to my ear and could hear the distant voices of my grandmothers. In Mexico City, there was no one who would dare point the finger as if to say, "Behold, an intruder," where a tightening of someone's lips or slight stiffening of their backs betrayed their thoughts. Gone was the fear of whispering something in my mother tongue and the reprimand that could follow. Not at all—this was home, and I belonged.

"En la Capital." I even loved the noisy diesel trucks and the old rickety buses spewing their fumes, packed to the brim with passengers; buses barely stopping for boarding passengers braving to jump onto the moving vehicle; assistant conductors shouting "Listo!" with a quick bang on the back of the bus signaling "All clear."

Exploring through the huge *mercado*. I don't know how big it was—it could have been as large as a city block or two. It was a maze of sections featuring all range of household goods—radios in large maple and mahogany cabinets, RCA and Motorola phonographs, kitchen supplies, from heavy ornate silver to flimsy stainless steel knives and forks to large wooden spoons for stirring *mole*, the spicy chocolate sauces for special occasion *enchiladas* or *guajolote*, foods that resonated in my heart and said, "Honey, this is yours." No need for translations, no explanations in English—it was all here, a feast to the stomach, the eye, and the heart.

We walked past the huge meat section with the smell of beef, lamb, and other types of meat and fish on display. Then came the vegetables, another huge section—squash, beans, corn, and more *tortillitas* cooking on grills; *orégano, chiles,* and bell peppers cooking together. My mother's face radiated with joy, as though she had just walked into her mother's kitchen. She and Josefina checked prices and compared the quality of produce that was brought in from surrounding *ranchitos*, touching and smelling *las tunas, los tomates, elote* she had not felt and smelled in decades. Impatient, I tugged at her to get to the more interesting stuff—*rebozos*, sweaters, shoes and dresses. Across several aisles, I could see guitars and the huge *guitarrones*, guitars with big round bellies that ring out happy Mexican *mariachi* songs. Further down, I could see what it was I wanted. Some shops were still opening, raising the corrugated aluminum doors that went from floor to ceiling in their fronts.

Finally, we walked in the direction I wanted and came to a woman who had dresses hanging outside her shop. They were simple, sleeveless dresses in pastel blues, bright pinks, and yellows. I loved all of them and finally picked the blue dress. My mother measured it against my body and asked how much it was. "Treinta y cinco pesos, marchantita." It was thirty-five pesos, slightly over three American dollars. My mother handed her the money without bargaining. The woman took it, making the sign of the cross before turning her back and putting it in the cash drawer—her bra.

Today I still feel champagne bubbles up and down my spine whenever I think of that blue dress. But that's not all—the shopkeeper's blessing went even further, these feelings rippling into the past and future. It felt as though her prayer appealed to the gods to surround everyone with mercy and protection. The small action of crossing herself with the exchange she made for the dress still invokes dreams that inspire in me a longing unimaginable in earthly terms. In the place where dreams are reality, the dress wraps me in the knowledge of the soul's beautiful Beloved, where I dance to the music of heavenly spheres; where he twirls me tightly in his arms and imbues me with sweet emotions from his heart, the flare of the skirt intoxicating me in rhythm to the movement of the stars. But, even more remarkably, the little blue dress we bought at El Mercado en La Villa de Santa Maria brought me into the presence of the divine in a hundred different ways. Wearing the dress, I sang a song that lifted me above the Milky Way and brought me face to face with them, the Gods of Love and Music. Their resplendent lights enshrouded me in blessings of ecstasy that promised to last a thousand lifetimes. That dress still exists in my dreams, and still reminds me of my resplendent existence.

My Passion

At four years old, I developed a passion. Sacred gifts are exactly that—sacred and gifts—to be handled delicately and reverently. I was given one that I haven't treated with respect, and yet, when life pushes me away from it, I manage to find my way back. The end result has created a disappointed muse within that aches and longs to have his love requited. The instrument beckons me; the muse stalks me in attempts to revive the fire. I hear the music; I wonder what could have been; I wander and stumble unfulfilled until I return. Call me hopeless or dimwitted, but three times I have walked away from my love of the piano only to come back and begin anew with the intention of reviving the original flame. However, I believe that destiny plays a large part in what we do, and it can offer us more than one gift. There must be a reason why I leave and return to it over and over.

In my family, everyone had an instrument—except me. John had a brand new shiny brass trumpet, Gilbert had a sparkling new guitar with not a scratch on it, and Chepe had a new trumpet that he blasted for all the world to hear. I loved watching them open up the cases. The light in the room magically sparkled off the trumpets as they lay in the soft, velvet-lined, dark-green cases. My father's rule was "Carry your instrument wherever you go," and that's exactly what they did, when going to church or to someone's house for the evening. Instruments into the case and into the car.

Instead of playing on Olvera Street as he did in the 1930s and 1940s in Los Angeles, now my father's joy was to play for God. The family belonged to a church where we lived in Stockton, California. Once a month, the Pentecostal churches in the San Joaquin Valley would gather for all-day conferences. It was during one of these conferences at the church in Sacramento when I became conscious of the piano. They were simple two- or three-room buildings with metal folding chairs arranged in rows in the sanctuary. The pulpit area was covered with embroidered and crocheted white cotton napkins, thickly starched and pressed. But this one had something different. Pointing to a wooden structure that looked like a dresser to me, I asked my father, knowing full well what the answer was, "What is that?" I had seen and heard one before, but this one felt alive to me, as though seeing one for the first time.

"That's a piano. Sylvia is going to play it," he answered matter-of-factly. Sylvia was the minister's beautiful sixteen-year-old daughter, petite with light skin, pretty pink lips, deep brown eyes, and the richest jet-black hair I had ever seen. I waited patiently for her to strike the first chord. She came in wearing the traditional uniform for young adults, white blouse and black skirt, her hair flowing down her back like a graceful river, and sat down, opening the cover carefully. She looked at my father who sat at her left with mandolin ready, nodded, and struck the keys with a clarity that instantly brought the congregation to their feet.

A feeling of virtue and the heavenly music combined within my heart, and I was marked for life. Throughout the singing of "Onward Christian Soldiers" in Spanish, I heard nothing else but the piano, and felt the pounding of the beat in my chest. Sylvia's agile fingers flying over the keys mesmerized me, and I vowed to someday play just like her.

That Christmas, my parents gave me a baby grand toy piano. For me, it was the real thing I could touch and play. I would play for hours. I'm not sure if my mother had the patience to put up with the racket because she wanted to foster my interests, or if I could really play, as she appeared to enjoy it. My impressions were that I was actually making music, and she delighted in it.

As I recall, my first time to sit at a real piano was in Pico Rivera, where we were visiting some friends. We walked into the living room, or maybe it was just an entry room, but this room was big enough to fit a narrow couch, a chair, and a huge upright piano. I saw the piano and immediately made a beeline toward it. I began piecing together "Rock of Ages." I was about six or seven years old by then.

Time passed, and I began playing the piano for our church. My father gave me the introductory lessons, and I learned the scales and arpeggios for all the keys. Whenever I heard music, I listened for the piano. Often, I would imagine a piano in front of me and pretend to play as I heard the music in my head. Little by little I stopped listening or caring. For years our home life was disrupted by leaving our home to work seasonally on ranches throughout the California Central Valley, and I was sent to live with different families in the Mexican community.

But these disruptions did have a purpose. Finally, my parents made the big decision. After school one day, I walked into the house, and my mother had a peculiar look on her face, trying to hold back a smile as she stood in the middle of the hallway near the front door. My father and Chepe, my youngest brother, were full of anticipation. I walked into the dining room, where we dumped everything we were carrying onto the table, and I saw something unusual out of the corner of my eye. Slowly, I came over to the piano and ran my fingers over it; the tone was deep and luxurious. They were silent, waiting for my next reaction. I looked at my father in disbelief. I don't know where the tears came from or even how I had such an emotional response, but I said, "Everyone else has gotten a new instrument. How come I get an old beat-up piano?"

"Hija, this cost thirty-five dollars. That's all we could afford right now," my father tried to reason. I hated the subject of money coming up since it was the cause of my being sent away for those dreaded work seasons. I ran out of the house crying. Time passed. Occasionally I would sit at the piano, but the agony was too great for me; I was too heartbroken to understand. Soon, I hardly even looked at it. It saddens me to think that I snubbed the piano and jeopardized my relationship to it on that day.

As I reflect on the years between ages six and twelve, I can see the family pain taking its course. But who could explain to me the importance of developing a relationship to something as significant as my love for the piano? It was as though the loneliness and isolation I experienced while I was away from home could not be adequately explained away. If I happened by chance to be in the neighborhood during the times my mother was away, and I walked into the house, the loneliness and emptiness was unbearable. The house was cold and lifeless. Little did I grasp that the same process was working within my creativity.

For my twelfth birthday, my mother said, again as I came home from school, "We found a piano we think you will like."

"A piano?" I asked, not wanting to believe her words. "A new piano?" Somehow "new" and "old" was mixed up with my personhood—I wasn't worthy.

"Well, it's not new, but we think you'll like it. Do you want to go see it?"

We drove across town and spoke to the music director of the Catholic school that was selling it. I ran my fingers over the keys, and the notes danced off the walls of the auditorium. I loved it, but thought it wiser to hide my joy. It was a dark mahogany Wurlitzer spinet. Within a few weeks, I was taking lessons from Don Wilson, a tall, slim Caucasian man with a classical piano background. He had studied in England and learned to speak with a British accent as well. His enthusiasm was infectious, and I quickly responded to the challenge of learning to read music and embracing the classics.

When I prepared for my first piano recital, Don remarked to my parents that "Aurora could have gone to Carnegie Hall if we had started her earlier." That remark has haunted me over the years when life presses me in other directions and I turn my back again on my first love. Deep within, the glorious sound of the piano is entwined with the grandeur of music I hear in my dreams that sweetly and patiently calls for my return to it. I've been careless and thoughtless in handling this God-given gift. I suffer, hold my breath, worry, and cry. Beneath the noise and distractions I manage to create, however, there is a lovely melody that brings my attention back to the piano. It invites me to be still and listen; to dance to its rhythm and enjoy the light of day; it softens life's twists that carry me into uncharted waters in difficult times and spaces. If I could only take back time!

After: My Life Laid Out

I don't remember much of the summer Mamá died. I was eighteen years old, and time stopped, the wind ceased its path, and even the birds declared a moratorium from singing. What I do recall vividly is that I began having conversations with her in her crypt where she allowed me to visit and see how she was adjusting to her new life. In all, I had seven unusual experiences. As it actually happened, she had seven medical emergencies in her last year of life, was rushed to the hospital, and then returned home to recuperate from all of them except the seventh. In these encounters with Mamá after she died, the pattern repeated itself identically, and on my seventh visit, she seemed resolved to stop trying to beat destiny. The passage of time showed itself in her gnarled gray fingernails, her eyes worn through and eaten by death, her yellow teeth with signs of decay. "Ya es tiempo que no vengas"—It's time you stopped visiting—she said in a stern but sad voice to dissuade me from returning. I awake from the dream, my heart beating wildly, in a sweat yet happy to be relieved of this gruesome task of witnessing her body decaying. But, as I look back, I can't really blame her. She allowed me to observe her grief, or at least didn't try to mask it in my presence, but I knew that it was time for her to move on to her next life.

In my culture, we believe in dreams as reality. My grief takes me to her, since I cannot bring her back. Grief for me has been a profound need to reverse time; to bring her back to life and hold her once again in my arms; to feel her warm breath on my cheek. In these visits, I am consciously aware of traveling to another dimension and seeing her face-to-face, as clearly and easily as boarding a shuttle bus across town.

Summer turned to fall. My father worked nights, I worked days, and the emptiness of the house without Mamá exaggerated the pain of loss. Only the Great Mystery knew what lay ahead for me. But for the time being, my assignment was to adjust to life at the telephone company where I worked as a long distance operator.

There was an indefinable gap or space in Mamá's passing. When I was alone in the house, I clearly heard inexplicable sounds that teased me to look around corners or darkened places; that lead my steps into the subterranean world I used to see when in her company. For now, I am the translator of these mysterious occurrences, whereas before, she explained them to me.

The Romano girls, in my sister-in-law's family who lived in San Francisco, invited me to come and join them at a residence for young women run by nuns at Waller and Steiner Streets. I applied for a transfer through my job at the telephone company. With time standing still, I seemed to be navigating through a world without gravity. The shadows of the tree outside my bedroom window crept across the wall with the setting sun and came alive under the moonlight.

The day finally arrived when the chief operator approached me and said, "Your request for transfer to San Francisco has gone through." I felt a twitch in my stomach with the thought of moving to the big city. It was as though we were underwater; I could see her lips moving, but the words sounded garbled, missing every other sound. "Thank you," I managed to mutter.

I packed my bags, and within two weeks, my father and I were driving through the rolling hills between the Central Valley and the San Francisco Bay Area. They moved slowly by, as if in frames I could photograph with my camera. My father hardly spoke, and there was mostly silence in the car, but that's how things were with him. He didn't reveal his thoughts, nor I mine. There was nothing to say. I was leaving town, and he was left behind with his partner of thirty years gone. One by one, through marriages and attrition, the family had shrunk, and he remained behind, alone in the house we had known for the past twenty-five years.

Two Years Later

I sat at the kitchen table for two while the sun slipped between the high-rises and, for a moment, shed its direct light on the Sunday want ads. One looked promising: "Stenographer for insurance company. Shorthand 100 wpm, typing 60 wpm, good grammar, dependable, fast pace. Call 433-2000, Mr. Simmons." It was my first day back in San Francisco after a year's absence to attend secretarial school in Stockton. It was only one year, but now I had solid marketable skills as a secretary. It was my mother's dream that I would someday be a secretary, working for the president of a bank. Secretarial school was the fastest training I could think of that would also get me out of my brother's house, where I lived with his growing family.

Things didn't go well the first time I came to San Francisco, and I returned to Stockton. Now, with my new skills, I could say good-bye to Ma Bell. For a roommate, I had a friend I met while living with the nuns. She had a studio, but we planned on looking for a bigger apartment. My first Monday back in San Francisco, I got the job with the insurance company. The clerical staff was all women. I began working as a stenographer for the insurance agents, men of all ages and ethnicities. I quickly became part of the lunchroom group, which gathered at noon every day. I had my trials with the job itself, but I felt comfortable, despite my seeming displacement, being among white businessmen. I missed Stockton and hearing Spanish. I missed the clatter of kids at the corner where the Mendozas lived—all thirteen of them—and where I played as a kid.

I'd been at the job for six months now. We'd fallen into a routine during lunch time. I liked it because we ate together. Something unusual happened one during lunchtime, and I am not sure why it felt so disconcerting to me. At noon we sat at the round white lunchroom table, and we began talking of old customs. I told about the time a "hobo" came to the front door at home to offer to sharpen knives and scissors. That was commonplace when we were kids. My mother gave him her sewing scissors, and he promised to come back in five minutes. He never returned. I'm not even sure this had anything to do with the subject at hand, but they commented on my story. One of the women, Jasmine Bayshore, who was the eldest and the psychic one among us, remarked, "It's from a bygone era, and machines do the work now, but we don't see knife sharpeners anymore."

Georgina, one of my coworkers, and I decided to take a walk alongside the cable cars that come down Russian Hill on California Street. It was a lovely sunny day, and foot traffic was heavy. As we passed the Tadich Grill, we noticed a jalopy flatbed truck with wooden panels on the sides that said "Jack the Knife" painted in faded red bubble letters. It was parked in front of the restaurant. Two men stood beside the truck talking. They wore faded old denim overalls. They had the look of another time and place as men in gray and navy blue gabardine suits walked by. As we passed them, we heard them discussing a new knife and scissors sharpening machine on the flatbed. Curiosity grabbed me, and I suggested to Georgina that we stop to admire the machine. We giggled as we examined the machine from the sidewalk. I leaned close to her and whispered, "This is weird. We were just talking about it, but who sharpens knives downtown?" She shrugged, and we both laughed at the coincidence. "This is weird," she agreed.

That night, a visitor woke me out of my sleep. "Do you want to know?" he asked. He was right up against my face. I could almost feel his mustache brushing against my nose. He looked like the man on the street with the knife sharpener, but this was too much of a stretch for me. I'd seen spirits in the past—heard nails pounded into wooden boxes and then dragged across the floor, which terrified me and even made me pray to Jesus as anyone would do in a moment of naked fear. This face was just as terrifying at such close range—not because he appeared menacing. I said, "No." I was not interested, or would a better word be "ready"?

The next morning, still bothered by the dream (or whatever it was), I stopped at Jasmine's office and told her about the tradesman's visit. "What do you think? Do you suppose this was a coincidence?" I asked her.

"No," she answered. "It's too extraordinary to be a coincidence. Some things just can't be explained."

I didn't draw any conclusions, but something about the man's face resonated. I knew him from somewhere . . . I had a sense I would be seeing him again.

La Virgen Calls

There had to be something more to life than dancing to the jig of an insurance company. I made a short run to New York to see a little more of the world, but I came back practically as soon as I landed because something didn't fit right. Nothing seemed to be falling into place, and I couldn't quite fit into my surroundings. I came back in short time, six months, and made the conscious decision to wait and see what to do next, as though I was tapping my foot and waiting for the music to start. I began to have a series of dreams that inspired the next stage of my life.

The images came slowly, and the changes within even more subtly, yet they became more insistent. They began with the Virgen de Guadalupe, appearing to me as in the following dream. Her appearance called forth something foreign in me that I had never experienced before, and it gave me pause to listen for what was opening in my heart. The feelings were akin to hearing a familiar soft voice, nurturing and gentle tenderness unknown to me in my human form.

The Tree of Life Dream

> A huge sprawling oak has sprouted suddenly in a cathedral where I await services to begin. A soft glow emanates from it and fills my being with peace and tranquility as I gaze upon it. It's in the deep of winter, and the only lights we have come from this tree of life. Next to it, a tall evergreen hung with beautiful green, red, and blue lights touches the magnificent ceiling. A tiny green light reflects off a shiny ornament of a figurine of La Virgen de Guadalupe that catches my eye. As I concentrate on La Virgen, I notice that there are hundreds of ornaments, all exquisite and fine in detail and design. A shooting star suspended in space glistens and sparkles, amplifying the array of lights and beauty. The congregation basks in the magnificent atmosphere and acknowledges its connection with the spirit that binds us all together. We are bound together in the silence.

> *I become aware that this is no ordinary cathedral, but rather my living room converted into an artist's studio. I have two children—girls, twins, dark ebony. It is lunchtime, and I am putting food on a miniature table for them. I study the setting and admire that this is my home, my children are here, and something extraordinary is happening. Just as I think this, one of the girls takes the plate and dumps it on the floor. Looking at the mess, I try to come up with the most effective comment to get her under control. I'm confused as to how this madness can exist side by side with this beauty. Just then, the other twin takes the table and turns it on its side. Pandemonium breaks out as they tip their heads back in uproarious laughter.*
>
> *Amid this confusion, I refocus on the star, the lights, and the beautiful trees. Ever so softly, I begin to hear the magnificent sounds of a celestial orchestra playing a glorious symphony that resonates throughout the universe and envelopes everything within it, including my home. Even the hilly forest and the creek that runs along the south side of my cottage hold still in awe and amazement.*
>
> *Gradually, I become aware of my body on the bed and my senses gently returning to waking time.*

In the weeks, months, and years that followed this dream, the memory of La Virgen stayed with me and inspired me to seek communion with the divine. I hadn't paid much attention to the religion of my parents, but this new reverie awakening within bonded me to the eternal and made me feel worthy of pursuing a way of life that I had never before considered. I also thought of that epic dream that connected me to my culture. More importantly, I began to focus more intently on my spiritual life in a way that was not related to any known religion, but rather a feeling silencing my restlessness and seeking peace.

Growing up when my brothers had bright, shiny new instruments, and my father held them together as a group of musicians, I somehow did not fit in with the scheme of the family. Perhaps if I had been more amenable, more outgoing, and more willing to show my talent, I would have been included. But this dream and the dreams that followed enabled me to begin thinking of myself as a musician.

I knew it was time to sit up straight, discipline myself, and allow myself to be carried into the wonderland I discovered in that dream, where sweetness surrounded me, and the gentle breeze guided me toward the surrender to the Beloved—the music I heard as a child.

There are so many ways in which my attention has been divided, but for today, I interpret this dream as a call to hasten to my first love when I was a girl. I wonder if it's possible to be a musician while other musicians, men, seem more accomplished, advanced, and, above all, talented. I need to do this.

My dreams continue to help me. These are some that are supporting me to reawaken my love of music and the piano. I feel they are beckoning me and preparing the way for me to imagine a new life, filled with love and appreciation for true essence.

The Alvenu Malkenu Dream

It is night: lying on my bed, I can see sparkling dots reaching to infinity, and then I hear the Alvenu Malkenu chanted as a haunting melody by a chorus of a thousand voices.

Dreaming of Drummers

A long line of drummers plays in a most exquisite synchronized fashion. The first drummer plays gracefully, lifting his arm, and the next one follows, and then the next, onto infinity.

Unable to control my awareness from meandering in space, I next find myself taking a train ride with my mother, brothers, and cousins from Mexico City. I step into one of the Pullman compartments and tip my head back to see upward. A magnificent tree of life with pink and white blossoms stretches from this tiny room high into the dark sky. The place is new, but I know I've visited this realm many times before.

When I awake, the expansiveness of the drummers and the tree of life still vibrate within me. They are reminding me that it is another magical/blissful feeling I can only experience in other realities that are meant to be used as fuel for my burgeoning new life. The feelings left tingling in my memory are the glue that will help me imagine myself a musician and hold my own in a man's world.

I continue in this expansiveness of widening vistas and new images of becoming.

Out of Sync Dream

A worship team with two singers, two guitarists, a bass, and drummer stand on the platform of a church of my childhood, sounding very good. Suddenly, one of the guitarists begins improvising and going off on his own without regard to the singing. This guy is such a renegade that he has his own amp turned up so high, drowning out the others; and, to make matters worse, the amplifier has a loud and annoying buzz, bringing the congregation to protest with riotous voices and fists.

He is good, but out of sync with the others. After the service, I walk up to the front of the church and take the leader to the side. "You guys sound good, but you need more practice so that you play the proper chord changes and stay synchronized," I advise.

Feeling smug with the "invaluable" advice I have just imparted to this beleaguered group, I walk outside into the sweltering afternoon. The oven-hot air inside the car hits me full force on the face when I open the door. Damn—that guy's like me: he makes up his own rules, keeps himself out of sync, and wonders why people don't keep up with him. He's imitating me! We are marching to the beat of our own drumming and not watching where the parade behind us is turning.

I insert the key into the ignition and drive off, still thinking of this revelation.

Yes, I do feel like the outsider, unable to catch the rhythm. The thought that I don't fit in torments me. I must not listen to this voice that misdirects me toward failure. I must and can overcome my fears and become the musician that I am.

Mamá's Assignment

The sun is bright the morning that my mother stands in front of her students, assigning their tasks for the day. I stand back from the crowd, not feeling included, and waiting for my turn. I am the last one to step forward and speak with her. My task, of all improbable things, is to wait on a crotchety, mildly senile, detached, and uninvolved old man whom I had met some time in the past, and now he is incapacitated and unable to care for himself.

Before going to see him, I go swimming in one of the pools in a huge glass structure with a myriad of skylights, pools, and gigantic thick ferns. There are pools like hot tubs and others that look like tide pools. Enjoying myself at first, floating on my back and soaking in the warmth of the water, I begin to notice that I am further out in the ocean than I realized and that I've even traveled beyond the marked pools and outside the overhead shelter. The currents are carrying me toward the open sea.

With the elements changing, I am less protected and more exposed and vulnerable as the acceleration of the currents increases. At first I continue to act as though I am in the safety of the first contained bathing pool, but it is becoming more and more apparent that I've entered irreversible danger. To guard against this, I expand my consciousness to handle the magnitude of the situation. I calculate the depth of my breath and inhale long and calmly to stay ahead of the increasing pull of the tide. My consciousness takes me to the top of a ledge, where I can see the waters raging and crashing against the jagged rocks below.

Fearing that I cannot manage these changes, I decide to look away from the rocks and take in my surroundings from another perspective. My eyes are riveted to the water that is beckoning me to take the plunge. With all my will, I manage to extricate my eyes and lift them toward the horizon. As far as I can see, there is nothing but beautiful sun, bright blue skies, and still waters. As calm as the waters appear, I am keenly aware of the danger below the surface, yet the dazzling light bathes me in its embrace and releases me from the pull of the undercurrent.

I turn to look inland and realize I am on a small tropical island in the Pacific. I feel my heartbeat slowing down. A calm has enshrouded me, and I begin to think of the people in the village and how I must be returning to them. Something continues to hold me spellbound. The quiet natural wonders touch the depths of my soul as though massaging my feelings back to life and safety.

On my way back to the location where Mamá gave out the assignments, I walk past a music store out in the open and see that dozens of grand pianos have been left in nature, open to the weather—new ones, small ones, old pianos that need restoration, and long elegant pianos. One stands alone—that's the one I want, grand, simple, and timeless. I walk up to it and run my fingers over the keys. The notes that vibrate from its strings are exquisite. My heart melts with love, and I realize that this is the kind of music that will restore me.

Returning to the group, I can't forget the beauty of the sun, the blues of the skies, and serenity of the deep waters. With the knowledge of the rich tones of music that I am being called to create, I have the certainty that we are truly immortal. As I continue my trek back to the group, I look down at what I am wearing—a black bathing suit with only thin spaghetti straps in the front and in the back. My breasts are exposed! I have been to the edges of eternity, and now I am more vulnerable than ever before. Will I manage this assignment?

My friend fear is haunting me again. Yet, as seen with the following of my breath and expansion of my consciousness, I can stand up to it; I know I can do it. With all the travails in this dream, the fear of being overtaken by rough waters, I can see how deep the fear runs. But to be seen in public naked, my breasts exposed, I am vulnerable, and again, a woman in a man's world. I have no choice. My father is the old man. Strange though it seems to me, I didn't think I had a troubled relationship with him, but when he passed away, I began to see that he was self-contained, that he took the slightest rejection to heart without saying anything, and turned his back on me at the slightest rejection from me when I was a girl. He became the symbol of music to me. I turned my back on him when I retreated from the piano. In these dreams, my mother provides an element of surprise. She has spoken, and I must nurture the love of music she instilled in me through her encouragement and support by giving me the opportunity to revive what I lost with my father. By rebuilding my relationship with him, I will be guided back to music.

My Soul on a Maybeck Estate

An old estate stands on a small island at the bottom of the hill from where I live. The mansion was designed by the Berkeley architect Bernard Maybeck, and has aristocratic arched wooden window frames. I imagine large ballrooms with smooth hardwood floors covered with thick oriental rugs; windows with soft, dark green velvet draperies; and rooms filled with rich antique tables with elaborate gold-leaf painted vases. I ask my sister-in-law Victoria if she wants to come down the hill with me to have a look inside.

It is rumored that the old landlords have died, and the heirs have decided to remove the house from the island so that they may rebuild to their own specifications. I notice that a barge is attached to the land. Instead of raising the house and taking it away in pieces, the ground underneath will be loosened in order to carry the house and whatever they can of the grounds by barge.

We walk down the hill and come to the garden with tangled overgrown bougainvillea vines that create the sense of a bygone era where gardeners once worked full-time. Weeds and faded flowers give memory to the days when the house was in its glory and full of children's dreams. A lavender wisteria tree droops over the front stairs. We stop for a moment before knocking at the front door. I notice that thick burgundy velvet curtains cover the windows, but a gap reveals a single naked light bulb hanging from the ceiling that illuminates the entire room. I have a vague recollection about the family—nothing I can remember clearly now, but it brings the family to life for me in my memory, and I begin to recall their lives, hopes, and dreams.

I check the doorknob. It's loose and it opens easily with no key. We enter through a dining room. The table and every little nook and cranny around the room are covered with dolls and other toys the elder woman who last lived there kept, some of the toys still in their original packaging. She didn't have children of her own, but she collected toys to have them available when children visited, which happened frequently.

I half whisper to Victoria, "I'm disappointed. They lived ordinary lives. I expected to see grand ballrooms, harps, and grand pianos as evidence of the elegant parties they hosted. Look at this clutter—toys for kids! Is that all they spent their money on?" Victoria just turns her head toward me and smiles at my ignorance, but otherwise pays no attention.

On the opposite side of the room, there is another bay of windows, which looks into what used to be another private garden. I see nothing but weeds and dry hydrangea bushes. Off to the side there's a small, dark, and musty parlor with the curtains in tatters that were once lush green velvet. I notice sales tags on some of the furniture, evidence that there's been an estate sale and most of the nice furniture has been sold.

I spot a grand piano under a plain gray quilted covering and walk directly to it. No one is observing me, and I feel free to let my curiosity explore at will. I hear a car pull up and walk toward the window to look outside. A policeman has arrived. He is doing a usual inspection, but I panic because, in truth, I have no explanation as to why we are here, and he could think we have broken in. Just then, a woman in charge of the estate sale comes into the room and assures me that everything is fine and that I may continue my exploration.

My first thought is to uncover the piano. As I walk around it, studying its underbelly, I marvel at the ebony finish, smooth as silk. "It's a grand piano, not a baby grand, but a grand piano." I murmur to Victoria, carefully opening the lid over the keys. To my amazement, the individual ivories have been hand-painted and etched in red roses and pink and blue chrysanthemums. In amazement, I call Victoria to come and examine the indescribable of beauty of this piano.

I strike a chord, and the sound and strength of it takes me by surprise. I laugh when I discover that an attachment inside the harp adjusts to my playing so that even though I am not proficient in my technique, the piano fills in the notes to create the effect of an accomplished musician.

"How much is it?" I ask, knowing I don't have the money for any amount she might ask.

"It's a very good piano, but we've been waiting for you to come for it. How would $1600 be?"

"Sixteen hundred for this great big beautiful piano? I can't pass this up." I get the brilliant idea that I could ask my father for the money, and he would be more than delighted to pay for it. "I'll take it." I announce, knowing that this is an act of faith because getting it out of the house and off the island will be another challenge in itself.

The beauty of the feelings in this dream encouraged me to revel in the possibility of returning to my first love, my love of music, and allow myself to imagine what it would be like to think of myself as a musician.

The following is a nother dream of encouragement. I look at the symbols of the pianos calling my attention. I must gather them and bring them in from the weather, no matter what stands in my way. I must develop the pianist within myself.

Songs from a Dream of Other Worlds

My niece Julie, an accomplished composer and pianist, needs my opinion concerning the outfit she is making for her piano début. The dress must be "just right." As she pushes the blue satin fabric under the needle of the sewing machine, her spirit or consciousness expands with each stitch sewn. When she comes to the end of the seam, she holds up the dress to show me her work.

"How does it look?" she asks, smiling radiantly.

"You're doing just fine," I remark, inspecting the seam. Light reflects off the dress and pierces through me like a laser beam. The thrilling sensations of the beam grow in me like champagne bubbles, and my perception becomes sharpened and acute.

A large crowd gathers in the adjoining room of this large Victorian house we're in, and for some reason, I decide to sit down to meditate. My friend Frank, an accomplished guitarist, comes in to ask if I want to shoot some baskets with him. The bubbly sensations are transformed into beams of light that echo songs and poems from other worlds. I revel in the feelings as though soaring like a bird in the tides and currents of the sky. I sit motionlessly, savoring the moment until the joyous feelings bring me back to waking awareness.

Dreaming of My Father as Master of Ceremonies

I'm performing a piano concert and putting the order of the program together. My brothers and their families have arrived at the concert hall that, with its wide marble stairways and tall hallways, looks and feels like the old San Francisco Opera House. I come into the audience area that's laid out with tables instead of rows of seats to greet everyone. I am pleased to see old friends of the family, and stop at a few tables to express my appreciation for their presence at my debut.

The windows and doors are open; there's a bit of a draft, and my wild, curly, black hair is blowing across my face. I must get dressed, and I check my watch to make sure I have enough time. My father steps up to let me know that he will be master of ceremonies. I smile joyously. Even in my dream, I recognize that this is a departure from the usual tension between us, but he is jovial and happy to be supporting me, and I am ecstatic at his participation. It's getting late, but I am enjoying myself talking with people, and I feel the sweet tingle of anticipation up and down my spine.

I make my way to the dressing room. I find the folder with the order of the program that my father will need in order to announce the pieces, and give it to the stage manager who stops by to see if I am on schedule. I am aglow with a broad smile, and hand him the notes.

I hear people walking down the hallway on the way to their tables, and I can't help but revel in the newness of these developments—me, at long last, playing the piano as I've always dreamed and, even more miraculous, my father's holding his talented daughter as a prenda *(a treasure or trophy) with* orgullo *(pride) to the greater community. The sensations of joy and ecstasy bring my consciousness to my resting body in the living room of my house.*

I rest for a moment, lying on my side on the sofa, looking into the patio where I've just planted red geraniums and purple petunias. I had forgotten that I once had a tender relationship with my father, where I knew he was proud of his daughter as a musician. All has not been lost, but reopening my connection with the piano has opened the door to other feelings long ago forgotten, however short they existed. My life has changed—our house on Hunter Street in Stockton was sold, my father moved away, and life as I knew it back then no longer exists. But it's nice to imagine and wonder what could have been, what could be, with the piano. Encouragement and support from my father is the magic I need to push me onward.

La Pianista

A large audience has already assembled. She is lovely in her simplicity. The stage: the backdrop, a thick, luxurious, black velvet curtain; a Steinway grand piano; the pianist wearing a long, sleeveless black velvet dress.

Sitting in our comfortable chairs, the audience is moved by the exquisite music as though transported to other worlds of refined beauty and sensitivity. When the concert is over, we leave in quiet procession, and she continues playing softly. Coming out in the open, the procession moves slowly down the hill toward the ocean. I listen to every note and feel the music growing stronger. I look around me for speakers, which may be bringing the music closer to us. No speakers, just the quality of her music. She is getting stronger, I say to myself. I listen with my body, and feel the rhythm with my heart. The surrounding cypress trees stand majestically still as though enraptured by the music.

All is calm.

Mother Earth whirls in rhythm.

The tree relatives raise their arms higher.

Our water relatives in the sea undulate silently through Mother Ocean.

Even the birds stop their song.

We listen reverently, and continue our way toward the water.

Whether or not it's possible for me to become a musician in my mid twenties, I feel that so much time has been wasted and that I will never recover the abilities I had in my childhood. I feel sad about it, yet these dreams reassure me about having a glimmer of connection to the past. I can do it because music runs in the cells of my blood.

I still have my Wurlitzer to this day. I've begun the tedious task of practicing scales and limbering up my fingers. I've started with Bach's "Well-Tempered Clavier, Book I," and go on to two-part inventions. Encouragement comes from dreams to keep up the practice, despite the seeming frozen stance and monotonous dirge of waking up the musical memory. The music I hear in my dreams raises me out of the mundane and shows me another aspect of the Mother and reality, a boundless space where I can lean back and observe the changing reds and purples of the sunset, and Mother Ocean's hypnotic voice transports me into a world of angelic musicians.

I finally contact my music teacher.

Meeting the Tarot Reader

Power Dream

River water is ice-cold in the springtime after the snow melts. This first day of warm sun after the blistery winter days, when the sun is hidden behind a gray sky, is when we've come to bathe and wash our hair. My sisters, entering the water timidly, scream with glee when they take that first plunge. They taunt me, their eldest, to come in, and threaten to pull me in if I take much longer. I submerge myself in the freezing temperature, and they laughingly splash at me when I emerge. My younger sister sneaks up behind me and adds mayhem to the spring ritual of our first dip. I chase her and keep splashing her as she tries to get away. Soon, all of us are shouting and playing in the water. The fog has evaporated, and the sun has come out and miraculously heated the water.

I hear my brother's voice calling my name. I know he wouldn't be there unless there was good reason because this part of the river is off-limits to the men. Besides, he is a warrior and hunter and should be away on a hunt. Hearing his voice so far from the village adds to the urgency. Others look up and look at me to see if I've heard his call.

"Something is happening in the village," one says to me. "Should I come with you?"

"No, no. I'll be back soon," I respond.

Sorry to miss the frolicking, I quickly dry myself off with a thin deerskin and wrap myself in a brown garment of buffalo with openings for my arms. The ground is still frozen, and I can feel its sharpness as I run up the path, jumping over patches of snow and mud.

I've been called to the meeting room underground, where the elders are gathered. I began my menses during the past winter. The kiva is for men only. I have a queasy feeling in my stomach as I step down the ladder quietly, trembling to be called by the elders. The light from a small fire reflects on their faces, and I sense a tension in the air.

When I reach bottom, I hear the crack of a drum as though announcing my arrival. It's a loud, crisp whack from the spirit world, for I realize there are no drums or drummers present.

"And there's more power where that comes from," one of the men mentions to the others. Looking directly at me, he adds, "Remember." That's all he says, "Remember," as though I've consented to a covert agreement. The elders nod in unison. Something stirs in the pit of my stomach that I am overlooking something important. I know these elders. I know them from somewhere.

The slam of a door caused by a breeze in the hallway of my flat wakes me. The light shines blaringly through the windows that run across the west side of my sunroom. It must be late in the morning. I should have been up hours ago. I'm too groggy and left with questions and incoherent feelings of having overlooked something of great magnitude. It's not exactly as though I've actually forgotten, though, but definitely the essence of a vital matter is missing—something I should know. Who are these elders? I know them, but they're certainly not part of my waking community today. What am I supposed to "remember"?

As I lie in bed under my blue green striped cotton blanket, I remember the early dawn that a man with a thick mustache and floated above my face. With the light streaming through the loosely woven burlap curtains, I could see his face clearly. I could trust his dark kind eyes, but it was quite rankling and terrifying at the time to find a disembodied being this close to me. Remembering the distinctive quality of his voice again rattled something in my brain. "Do you want to know?" he had asked with insistence in a husky voice. Now I wish I hadn't been so naive. Thinking again more clearly, I realize it must be from that migration dream I had in Stockton. That was years ago. What was his name?

In my psychic class, we've been discussing the tarot. I decide to get up and spend time looking for books on the topic at the used bookstore down the hill at Ninth Avenue. Maybe I'll go for a walk in Golden Gate

Park and find a good place to read. It's Tuesday, there shouldn't be many people. I shower, get ready, and heat up some potatoes and fry two eggs for breakfast. I head out the door, still wondering how the elders and my music go together.

Two hours later, with *The Flight of Feathered Serpent* under my arm, I direct my feet toward the arboretum. I always enjoy its stillness, but for some reason, I pass it and turn toward the Steinhardt Hall of Science. I buy a hotdog at the vendor, find a comfortable bench near the bandstand, and sit down to enjoy the hotdog and my new book. I notice a sign several rows down that says, "Tarot Readings, $2." It's draped over the back of a green park bench. The benches have been moved to face each other, a sense of space the reader has created for conversation.

The tarot reader is a Chicana, petite, with a pixie haircut and jet-black eyes, probably in her late thirties. I've seen her many times in the neighborhood on Ninth Avenue. The sign itself makes her approachable, and she speaks openly to passersby who stop to ask questions. Her ready smile frequently induces the truly curious to stay for a reading. I've also seen her in the arboretum, talking with a young man—I'm a people watcher, and I notice those things. Another time, I saw her at a restaurant with a nice looking, hazel-eyed, curly-haired white man, both looking like they were in a world of their own, seeing things no one else saw. She's in her element now, laughing and engaging her customers to reveal of themselves to round out the secret of the tarot.

A group of boys stop for a drink of water at a nearby fountain, and one of them leaves the group to speak to her. He seems unusually self-confident, a boy of about fifteen or sixteen years with a quality of grounded wisdom that is unusual for his age. In any case, he reads the sign and asks her for a reading. He tells his friends to wait for him. I pretend to be engrossed in my book. The gentle autumn breeze carries away most of the words, but I get a gist of the reading. She tells him he will have pressure to follow a career that his parents wish for him, but to be strong and listen to the musings of the heart. He seems to grasp her warning.

A man comes up shortly after the boys leave. He's a small thin man of Nordic background with short sandy blond hair. He's wearing a dark red and black Pendleton shirt and has an aura of seriousness, as though he carries a heavy burden from the past. His eyes are averted, and he moves in tense, jerky movements—not someone I would take for wanting a reading. He seems happy with the cards' message. By the time he leaves, he seems more relaxed.

The sun is high above, and I didn't bring enough to keep warm. I should head home before the fog rolls in. I look toward Fulton Street and notice that the street looks different, almost like from another time, like the 1930s or '40s. I have the sensation that something is off, but I quite can't define it.

She gets up and comes over to me. "I noticed you were listening. Are you a tßarot reader?" she asks.

Rather embarrassed, I answer under my breath, covering my book, "No. I'm just curious."

"It's funny how the stories unfold through the cards, and things I've never thought about come out of my mouth. I get strong impressions, and I just tell my questioners what the cards are telling me," she says in a friendly voice, reading my thoughts. That's exactly what I was wondering—how could she have so much to say to total strangers off just three cards? I like the sound of her voice and the way she talks—sort of a singsong that Chicanas from the Central Valley have. I feel comfortable with her.

"My name is Gracia de la Cruz," she says. She asks if I want to stop for lunch at a Mexican restaurant near Ninth and Irving. As it turns out, we both live near there on the south side of the park. We're both from the Central Valley, she from Modesto, a town about twenty-five miles south of Stockton.

We arrive at a small joint and find a table. Her conversation is nonstop, especially about the dream journals she's kept for almost fifteen years.

"Something unusual happens in my dreams," she comments.

"Like what?" I ask.

"I can't say what, but I get pissed off when I bring an exciting dream to therapy, and my therapist interprets it from a Freudian perspective. Turning the spotlight on me rather than the content itself."

"Well, isn't that what therapy is about?" I nudge timidly, trying to get her to be more specific.

"You know," she says, controlling her tone. "That's exactly what I mean. Instead of pursuing what's different, my therapist goes over my head as though to argue I'm wrong—that's what it feels like, anyway. She could say, 'Oh yeah, Gracia? Tell me what's different,' and really mean it. I think there's something cultural I'm seeing, but she cuts me off at the pass by relying on what she knows, instead of venturing into the unknown with me and exploring it together. I hate it—she keeps the upper hand, no matter f—g what."

"I have a hunch of what you're saying. As a girl, I visited Mexico during the summers with my family, and I used to hear stories of the past. Whatever it was, it felt real to me because I have experiences like what they talked about. It's a different reality, another world. Time is different," I said.

"There's a lot of folklore and stories, but region to region there's no consistency in what we hear," she continues. "What's worse, most aspects of our culture are dismissed as superstitious. What we do know isn't positive. Racism blots out a sense of pride. 'The music is pretty,' they say, and it ends there. I have a sense of what 'it' is, but I want to make a connection with our culture. Sometimes I wake up in the night because I feel something, and someone is standing near me. In my braver moments, I try to communicate with them, but it hasn't worked so far. I get scared, and lose control of my dialogue with them. There's an elder I'm starting to make some headway with."

"What do you mean?" I ask, leaning forward. Now we were getting close to something I've never discussed with anybody, too personal like this morning's dream, so I let her keep talking.

"One time, I felt a hand on my back, and I turned around and there was a dark-skinned man standing next to my bed. I could only see his legs, but I was afraid I would see his balls, so I tried to scream instead. It was just a guttural noise, I'm sure. But I jumped out of the bed to get a better view of him. The poor guy disappeared. I'll see if he ever comes back," she said.

We both break into a fit of laughter.

"It's not only these oddities of the culture. There's the racial issue," she says. "But it's the stories that fascinate me. In my opinion, the dreams and these experiences in this world are connected. We don't learn about culture in our schools. I had to go out of my way to find a positive picture of our ancestors. I did my BA in history at Cal. I was horrified at the repetition of enslavement, slaughter, and theft—country after country—as I read the histories of the Americas. It was uniform. Oftentimes, the way it was written was as offensive and demeaning, referring to Natives and Mexicans as 'lazy' and 'filthy.' I'm concerned for future generations. We're cut off from our real culture here in El Norte. Mexico has beautiful traditions of the heart that our young people never get to see or fully appreciate."

"Yes," I chime in, "when I visited, I'd see guys on motorcycles, and instead of leather fringes on the handlebars, they'd tie flowers. For La Virgen's birthday in December, people set up altars next to their *puestos*, booths, with colorful floral arrangements around her image. I'd see people arriving at La Basílica on their knees, coming from their homes miles away. It was very moving."

"We're too much in our heads up here," she continues. "Mexican wisdom got fuzzy or lost once the border was redefined. Poetry, flowers, and music are such a vital part of the culture. It's a shame how we learn to be linear up here. We're missing a vibration that can't be translated. I'm puzzled by what I see and experience in my dreams. I need to, and must, figure out what this other reality is. Sometimes it feels that the lines of reality are blurring. I meet these guys that know me well, advise me on different things, and I'm even recognizing one of them that appears from time to time. I call him Ocelotl. I'm not sure where the name came from. I'd really like to know more about that, but who has relationships with dream people? I don't know anyone else who does, do you?" she asks.

"Not really," I comment, rolling over in my mind spirits I have seen and felt in my own dreams. Ocelotl—that has a familiar feel or ring to me. Impossible, and I brush the thought away. "No, I don't think so," I confirm.

"I practice lying-down meditation and dream yoga, where I try to maintain awareness throughout the night," she goes on. "I always drop below consciousness, but I try anyway. Occasionally, I am aware of my body in bed as I dream. I work with people with life-threatening illness, and sometimes I join them at their time of transition. If I talked about that in my therapy sessions, they wouldn't know what to do with me. They'd find a way to pathologize the experience.

"Harold and I practice tantric meditation. I should say occasionally, and rather modified tantric meditation. We just sit with our backs together, feeling our energies, or face-to-face, with our knees and hands touching while looking into each other's eyes. It's very powerful to do. Sometimes we don't realize how this impacts our consciousness after sitting for forty-five minutes. When I come out of the mediation, without noticing it at first, I find there's a delay in recognizing familiar objects. Or I'll see a friend, and the face just doesn't register."

That would explain the time I saw her looking dazed with a white man with curly brown hair and hazel eyes, almost as though they were seeing something in a long daydream. Her topics fascinate and draw me in. I've never known anyone quite like her. Her interests and the way she sees the world captivate me.

It must be around five o'clock when we finally leave the restaurant. We walk down Irving Street; I make a left at Seventh Avenue, where I live in a studio in a grand old house. She keeps going to Third Avenue, where she lives with her boyfriend. As I think about her, I find that there is something so familiar about her, an inkling feeling that we've known each other before. Ocelotl's name finally echoes in my head.

Other Connections

I mention my meeting Gracia to a friend's mother, and she says, "I know her! She's Gracia de la Cruz. I know her from Stockton. We attended Stockton Delta College together. I knew her brothers from when they played with the Pete Martinez Band. This was back in the fifties, when they used to play around the Central Valley and other parts of California. I loved their dances. My girlfriends and I would drive miles to go hear them play. Man, did we kick up our heels!"

"You know her?" I ask, astounded.

"Yes, occasionally she and I see each other on Irving for a cup of coffee. She's a dreamer. She's been keeping a journal for many years now. And she communicates with her dream spirits," she said. "She's always been quirky, always into the Grand Mystery in some way. I never know what she's going to do next. I've never known anyone like her. She can change directions on a dime."

Over the following couple of years, I see Gracia periodically; we discuss dreams and meditation. She tells me that she has escorted people to their next life, and other things about her work with people in medical crisis.

"You escort people to their next life?" I ask incredulously over a cup of coffee at Just Desserts one foggy Saturday morning. She tells me about it.

"*Curanderas* do that all the time. We live in a multidimensional world, you know. This space/life isn't the only realm of reality. In fact, I don't think it's a reality at all! Why wouldn't I be able to escort people to their next life?"

"How do you do that?"

"Well, first of all, I don't plan it, nor do I make up my mind about it—it just happens. The first time I remember it happening, I had a friend who had cancer who I was visiting at the hospital. I had known her for a couple of years. I understood her fear of dying, and in my dream at her time of death, I assisted her in rejoining with her ancestors. In my dream, I visit her at the hospital, and later that same night, I begin choking and gasping for air. I sail down a long, dark chute and realize that she is following me. We land on a moist mound of soil in the middle of a river, and I see that her ancestors are waiting for her across the river. I've been watching her process, and it is her time to cross. My mother, who has already transitioned, motions me by the wave of her hand that it is not my time yet. When I open my eyes, I know this has been real and that she has just transitioned.

"On another occasion, I worked with a friend who had a condition of her heart hardening. Her parents had been survivors of the concentration camps in Germany. She told me about a dream she had about water coming into her basement. I interpreted that dream as death nearing. She didn't seem weak, but she was having trouble with her lungs, and was on dialysis as well, so I concluded that she was ready to transition. Less than a week later, she was rushed to the hospital. In that instance, I merely gave her the opportunity to process her thoughts and feelings without telling her what I saw. When her time came, she was at peace with leaving. Her children and family gathered around her to say good-bye. She died peacefully, very quickly."

I notice that there's a parallel in my life that steers the direction of my interests, though I can't say how—Gracia's life experiences inform mine before they happen. It's fascinating how she has information on what I'm thinking and following in my thoughts or feelings, and she's already lived what I'm about to enter into. I've never talked to anyone about my dreams, but we seem to have a quality of experiences that feels familiar.

Her meditation of several hours daily sets a good example to get me to meditate, and it helps me create a container for my life. Her passion for examining and probing is quite rare. Her curiosity about consciousness makes me want to pursue awareness and take my music more seriously. I too go back to school at City College of San Francisco to begin studying music.

After not seeing or speaking with Gracia for several months, I give her a call. Her boyfriend answers, and I ask for her.

"Gracia is not here. She got married and moved to Hawaii," he says, recognizing my voice.

"Married?" I ask in shock. "How could she be married? I didn't know you guys had broken up." It was too soon to break up, meet someone, get married, and move two thousand miles away.

"We changed our relationship, and she began dating some guy she knew at the center where she did her internship."

"How can I get in touch with her?"

"Are you kidding? She didn't tell me where she was going. I'm sure people at the center know."

The years have gone by quickly since I've last seen Gracia, and I had another strange dream of her, a feeling of connection to her that is quite odd.

Meeting Myself Dream

I arrive early and set up my cushion at the meditation center I attend. I'm ready to begin the retreat, but the atmosphere in the room is not conducive toward quieting the mind. There is a basketball game with all the excitement. A flexible partition divides the room. The dribbling of the ball, the squeaking of the rubber soles on the floor, and the crowd distract me as I attempt to sit on my cushion. Suddenly, I feel a pair of eyes settle upon the back of my head. I spontaneously turn around and open my eyes. We are almost face-to-face, Gracia and I. She wears a black pair of pants and a blue sweater, an identical outfit to mine. Instantly, I panic. I am seeing myself at another stage of my life. She at age forty, I at twenty-three. I am she, she is I! I feel a push on my forehead and resist the pressure to fall back; I have the urge to flee out of the room, but I remain in my place, shaken. At the break, I look for her but can't find her. I ask the instructor about her, but he says he doesn't know the name. I ask to see the attendance roster. Her name is not on it.

This dream is confusing. I am seeing myself in the future. This is terrifying in the dream, but with eyes open, I wonder how much of the dream is true. It feels so real. In cultural terms, I can exist now/then. But where does Gracia fit into in all this? Very puzzling.

The Dance of Love Dream

I open the closet to bring out the dress I am wearing for the party this evening. We're celebrating twenty-five years of marriage for a couple who lives in Manteca. I vaguely know them, but I am going with the Romano girls, who are coming to pick me up. I walk into the closet and thumb through my dresses to find the new see-through silk blue scarf with silver dots that look like stars in the randomness of their spacing.

I stretch out my hand and touch the fabric. My sense of time and space begin to shift rapidly. The transforming world of the stars envelops me with sensations of wavy light flowing through me that can only be attributed to the divine; gracious emotions wash through me as though I am flying on the wing of an eagle, teasing, caressing, and enlivening.

Nearing the entrance to the hall where the party is held, I hear the smooth, sweet stirrings of a flute. Elena and I walk in. The shades are drawn to keep the hot sun out, and we find a round dinner table covered by a white tablecloth, where we sit down. The husband of the celebrant couple is the flautist. His music is sweet and as though calling from another world. It begins to vibrate within me. I stand up and go to the dance floor, and sway in rhythm to the melody. I let myself move slowly, as though leaning into the arms of a beloved—smiling, eyes closed, ecstatic, and sublime. My dress is not really a dress, but a long, flowing scarf wrapped around me that I can hold and wave about between my fingertips, my arms extended and waving about in time to the soft tones of the lovely sound. I become like a belly dancer—the undulations of my body and the rhythm in my movement follow the music like a low, quiet wind blowing around the bend of a desert monument, a teaching of the essence of love. The music ripples through me, through the group, and we are stirred by the magic of the moment.

The door blows open, and sunlight shines brightly behind the shadow of a petite woman carrying a large basket. The shadow is dense and long, like the obelisk in Washington, DC. She is the wife of the flautist, the guest of honor. After the passage of so many years, I recognize her! It's Gracia, though now her hair is salt-and-pepper in one long, thick braid down her back, and she is an elder. The basket seems from an ancient source, relief and sustenance effusing from its contents. She appears to be a messenger from another realm.

From the distance of the dance floor, I surmise that Gracia is emotionally agitated, judging from her quick, shallow breath. She sets the basket down at our table, murmurs something to Elena, and leaves quickly. When the music stops, I reorient myself, still feeling the caresses of the soft breeze on my face, and join Elena again at the table.

It's mystifying seeing Gracia in a dream. I had that funny sensation again, of having a connection to her that I feel when I see her, like a strange, puzzling certainty of knowing her more deeply than I actually do. I wonder how she is doing. I haven't seen her for at least twenty-five years.

Resolution

Time resolved my quandary of choosing between dreams and music. Dreams are the staple of life that pushes me onward, yet, studying music, I was able to integrate my life so that there was not such a drastic split between the two. I get up in the morning and write, examine my dreams. The rest of the day is basically focused on music and teaching. It balances the quality of my life, and it allows me to engage with young students and give them the emotional and cultural support I feel is important to help them develop and mature in a meaningful, spiritual way. Who knows how my dreams will be used? For now, leaving the door open is a good way to not manipulate how the spirit wants to use me. I do not feel complete with one only, they must both be interlaced throughout my experience.

The following dream put the question to rest, and I have been able to be at peace with myself.

Night into Day

At midnight, I stand on a platform with Grandmother at my side. She is giving me a directive that I don't quite grasp when I first hear it. "Turn night into day," she whispers in my ear.

"Night into day?" I ask.

"Night into day," she affirms for the second time.

I have no sense of what she asks of me, but I meekly get on my knees, stretch my hands out on the floor in front of me, put my forehead to the floor, and softly say, "Night into Day." The words vibrate within, and I get the gist of what Grandmother is commanding me to do. I see the picture in my mind's eye of a line between night and day—not a stark demarcation, but a line somewhere between light and dark. The second time, my words are a command, clear and direct, "Night into day." I hear a clap of thunder, and the sky that was previously dark becomes a pale blue bowl over our heads that gets lighter as I gaze upon it.

It seems to me that there is more a process to turning night into day than making day appear at midnight. I have to examine how I live my life and serve the greater purpose of my culture. There is something within that needs my attention. I can take care of my music, and yet I must first follow as the ancestors have ordained. They are quite persistent, but I like it that way.

With the passage of time, the demarcations between living my dreams and being a musician are not really distinct anymore. They both require my attention, but the trick is not to believe that I am one exclusive from the other. It is clear that Ocelotl is a companion that did not scare away easily, and came to settle upon my consciousness like a soft butterfly that heralds from the ancestors with his calm words.

Elders' Help Dream

I come into an auditorium like in a school or university. I hear Father William talking about my arrival, and he is directing people to step back a little and open the circle to make room for me. Waving his hand, he motions me to come stand with him in the big circle he has made to commence the convocation.

Three elders arrive at the front door. It occurs to me that I know one of them from other dreams. We can see their silhouettes against the morning sun behind them, and I get the sense that they are here to help me in this endeavor. Instantly, I realize that I have left the circle and am flying through dimensions. I am leading, rather than just tagging along. Again, I feel as though we are traveling through underground caverns. We change speeds, moving at high speeds, and then slowing down to almost a standstill. We fly through thin lines of demarcation between dimensions. I'm doing the exercises easily and effortlessly, and I begin to think that perhaps I am being given the opportunity to be enlightened. The space opens up, and I sail through the air on a swing, my hair blowing in the breeze freely.

When we return to the auditorium, we come back to a small dark room with a large two-way plate glass mirror, and I am reminded of the time that I focused and projected through a thick glass obstacle at a learning center many years before. Something about flying through dimensions reminds me of Ocelotl, of the dream of many moons ago, many years, when I was a young woman.

I run out of dreamtime and find myself back in my bed, with the cells in my body vibrating from the experience.

Here's Ocelotl again, from that dreamers' agreement dream I had when I still lived in Stockton. We've really been travelers together. Then too, Gracia came into my life and turned my head around. Is it possible that the ancestors, from their spiritual domain, can orchestrate something so that we may feel the essence of the heavens? Lights so sublime that they can be described in terms of the gods? I do know now that I have been here before. Ocelotl is my brother from that lifetime.

Yes, we agreed to do something in this lifetime. Yes, I am a dreamer, and yes, I am a musician. It's taken me more than the second half of my life to acknowledge the validity of that dream. I have an agreement to keep.

Snakes at the Top of the Pyramid

I stand atop a pyramid; my head is tilted back, my spine is straight, and my hands are relaxed at my side, facing forward with two vibrant snakes wrapped around each of my wrists. I am ready to keep my word.

Chapter Two

Gracia: La Llorona

The Story of Mayahuel: How Love Came to Earth*

Grandmother was highly displeased when she learned I had run off with Quetzalcoatl. Actually, I had never seen her in the fury I witnessed that day. I was just a wisp of a girl at the time, when he came to me one night as I slept in the girl's sleeping quarters and invited me to go with him to bring love to the newly forming Mother Earth. With his lips feathering my ear as he whispered his invitation, I jumped at the chance to spend eternity with him. Unfortunately, Grandmother had other plans for me, and when she discovered my folly, she flew, looking to fix my star.

There was no mistaking when I heard the thunder of her footsteps as she landed on Mother Earth with a thump, shaking mountains and causing avalanches. In an attempt to foil her intention, Quetzalcoatl and I used magic and disguised ourselves as a tree, but she was no fool. She was as wily as I was stupid, and immediately marched in our direction. When she found us, the henchmen who accompanied her went about the job of splitting the tree in half. And thus, our plans came to a halt. Grandmother returned to her kingdom, and I became the medicine for joy and celebration, the beautiful plant of the maguey. And Quetzalcoatl? *He abandoned me*! Who deserts their lover like this? He disappeared to save his ass. He left me here with no one! This is a world of conflict: good and bad, obedience and loyalty, devotion and betrayal.

We shall see what Quetzalcoatl does next. He is a man now, and men in this world can display opposite traits or choose one side—to be forceful or kind and gentle, just or unreasonable, considerate or capricious. A man's word is his worth, and honor is his name—he must have one to save the other. Men have privilege and priority; they can cast us aside with the wave of the hand. If he is a man of valor, one whose spirit remembers the Mother and knows the true substance of woman, then he can be relied on to be selfless and expansive; to be loyal, devoted, and chaste, just as women are expected to be.

But there is a portion of men that spoil the reputation of others. These men are the ruthless. "Come with me," they'll say to an unsuspecting young girl. "I love you. I want to marry you." They will ply their prey with flowers, candy, and song; show respect to her family. But one must be careful, as they are hailed by their friends, admired for their sophistication, and regaled for their conquests.

For a woman, it's a different story. A woman is a mere pawn here. Through deceit or lies, one slip, and her name is ruined and mocked, her family doomed. This is a treacherous world! I begin with a disadvantage. I've betrayed my family name. I've become a disobedient daughter without mother, father, family, or name; a faceless woman; loose, without *dueño, sin verguenza*; a woman whose virtue has been smirched. We shall see how I fare in this world of opposites, in this world of class, race, power, and name. I should have known. I didn't believe it could happen to me. I dread the outcome that lies ahead.

Perchance we shall meet again, Quetzalcoatl and me. But shall I pin my hopes on him? Shall I dream of motherhood? Or shall I choose to pull the strings behind the curtain; to be in dreams, change, reshape, recreate, and roam free? Let me dream and weave my story.

*This is a rewritten version of the old legend of how love came to earth. The author takes poetic license in rewriting the story with contemporary references alluding to the state or condition of the role women play within Chicana/o culture as perceived by the protagonist Gracia, the second of the three characters of this narrative. For references of research, please see Corn Woman Sings: A Medicine Woman's Dream Map *(Barron Druckrey, 2009).*

Introspection

I Do x Four Dream

Backstage in an elegant old theater, I walk along rows of costumes and multicolored satin ribbons which hang from the ceiling. The room with flat black walls is dimly lit by floor lamps. I can see masks—African and Mexican, twenty or thirty—hung around the room that create the effect of spirits observing me.

I stop at one of the racks. A light rose wedding dress is on display, as if in a bridal boutique. I push the dresses aside one by one—one beige, one a deep blue floor-length velvet, and the last one, white lace. I take the blue and white dresses and hang them on separate hooks along the dark walls.

Before going through the thick emerald velvet curtains to leave, I turn to see the effect of the dresses hanging on the wall. I can tell I am stirring in my sleep from the anxiety this dream is causing in me.

I lie in bed for a few moments and stare at the aging white ceiling. When I had this dream ten years ago, I ended up leaving my second marriage. I thought I wasn't the kind of woman to leave a man so easily, but I did. Though I didn't think I would survive the ordeal, I did, and lived to get into a third marriage. Here I am.

This might sound insane, but I think this dream is telling me that I'm going to have four or five marriages. I had this dream ten years ago. I'm not sure why I woke up thinking about it. I hate it when I start seeing something ahead of me before I'm prepared to see it.

What is this place? The walls, the sheets, my nightgown are a dingy white; the old plain cotton curtains have a worn quality and a tinge of antiquity. Everything is white, except me—brown skin, black hair, black eyes—and the dark mahogany armoire next to the window. I open it to find something to wear for this early spring day. I see a man's blue shirt with a button-down collar, a black paisley full skirt, a white blouse with lace trim around the collar. I look out the window. My husband, dressed in blue jeans and a colorless shirt, is pulling weeds in the garden. The sky is a beautiful blue. About a mile down the hill, the stunning blue Pacific Ocean glistens and dances, its calm, steady waves breaking on the shore.

I turn back to the closet. I need new clothes. These belong to someone who has been on the island too long—soft, flowing fabrics, blues, whites, and pale pinks.

Later, I remember being fully asleep with the bright silver moon high above. I remember that much, for sure. Let me recall—was I here? Did my husband drive me home from—? My mind stretches to remember something. My head is spinning, and I lose perspective on the room again. I wish I could attribute the loss of memory to having one too many drinks, but it isn't that simple. Something else is going on, and I've yet to figure it out.

Laying my head back on the pillow, a memory cracks through the chipped wall. Ah, a plane flight, arriving on a beautiful island with sky and water blending, the horizon broken only by a jagged rock jutting out of the water. A ceremony.

I feel a grip in my stomach. I can't remember my name! A void opens before me as though the earth has swallowed itself. I stare blankly at the ceiling, shaken by this strange sensation of being nameless. The spinning slows down. Gradually, the void closes, the familiar begins to return through the top of my head, neck, shoulders, chest, and down to the tips of my toes. I awaken into the present moment, grateful for having a body. My arms move close to my sides. Yes—it's Chela.

Is it? No, that can't be it. There must be a real name: A name making me worthy of standing straight, head-to-head and toe-to-toe with the world.

Come on! Come on! You have a name, girl. You do have a name—Gracia? No, no. That's my sister-in-law's. Is it Gracia?

The dizziness returns to me. I sit down at the foot of the bed. The armoire door is still open. The clothes are there, yet no recognition.

Yes, it is Gracia.

Did I take her name, or did she steal it from me? I'm flooded with memories as an eleven-year-old girl. The warm summer day my brother brought her home to introduce us, I stood in my bedroom with the wallpaper of pink roses. The front window was open to the porch; and another, the other on the side of the house, because it was adjacent to a grove of olive trees, making the room feel cool. They came in. "Chela, I'd like you to meet Gracia."

She was sixteen, and I eleven. "We have the same name." she said, and added that her birthday was a day before mine, October 26. We laughed at the coincidences. I liked her immediately.

She's the one! She's the one! As though the fog is lifting from my mind, the clothes in the closet become familiar. Then, I begin to see reality—my name was stolen! Little by little, she became my mother's friend; day by day, my mother's confidante. I stepped back and remained silent. I let them. I didn't take a stand. She gradually took the place of my sister who died before I was born. She was also Gracia. I chose to remain Chelita—it's coming back to me now.

Well, maybe it wasn't that severe, but something caused me to question events as I see them today.

The memory of the eleven-year-old haunts me with her jet-black eyes. She knows. Slowly, seamlessly, I lost my place in the family. They forgot they had a daughter. I retreated and remained silent.

You are—I am Gracia

Say it—yes, I am Gracia.

Shout it!

I AM GRACIA! I AM GRACIA—

A rap-tap-tap at the door brings me out of my reverie, giving me hope that there are other people besides Holden. I open the door. Holden's deep blue eyes look directly into mine, startling me. Taken aback, I lower my gaze momentarily. He greets me with a barely audible "Good morning" and leaves a hand-carved wooden Hawaiian tray with a small pale blue plate of soft scrambled eggs and a slice of lightly toasted wheat bread. He is quickly gone. Have I been out for a couple of days? Too restless to eat, I have a small bite of the toast and then a little of the eggs. I change quickly into jeans and a blue t-shirt, and venture into the unknown of my surroundings. I hear birds and the sound of rustling leaves; a cardinal in its brilliant red and black tuxedo lands on the veranda railing and picks at a piece of mango undoubtedly dropped by another little animal. The breeze has blown blossoms from the jacaranda shading the eastern side of the yard. I hear no sound of human voices at work or play.

Walking along the terrace, I admire the elegance of the hotel where we live that's in a state of dilapidation—grayish chipped paint on the ceilings and walls, shabby sofas and armchairs, and cracked tiled floors. Other telltale signs of the 1950s décor lead me to believe that more than a generation has passed since its days of glory. Except for Holden and me, it seems no one else is here. I decide to go down the hill to explore the terrain. I hope the trees hide any houses or other buildings because I see nothing for miles around. We've been here a short time, and I haven't explored the area yet.

I must be on a foliage farm because I see huge schefflera plants, various species of ferns, varieties of palm trees, large monstera leaves in clusters, and many, many other tropical plants that seem to spread out for acres. The shrubbery is thick in some places. There's an order to the layout of the gardens. I start running toward the water, thinking that if I'm fast enough, I'll catch a glimpse of people before they have a chance to hide.

I cross a road and come to an open space, a park with barbecue pits. The area looks deserted, but I hear a man's voice speaking Spanish. Then, there's laughter and Hawaiian music. I follow the voices and see a large extended family—grandmother, husbands, wives, brothers, sisters, and children of all ages on the picnic grounds. From afar, I can't see the details, but they're obviously enjoying a wonderful spread of meats and tropical fruits. The aroma of chicken on the grill reminds me that it's been hours since I last ate. They're speaking Hawaiian actually, but I run up to them anyway, hoping they're familiar somehow. I don't recognize them. I am not one of their kin. They're friendly, gentle people with dark eyes and beautiful, expressive round faces.

Through my confusion, the absurdity of my plan occurs to me. Even still, I overlook my trepidation and step into the inner sanctum of the family. I trespass the carefully woven bond, admitting I'm the stranger, the intruder in the midst of a private affair. Instantly, I slink my way out backward like a cautious cat. They've seen the desperation in my eyes, but the grandmother steps forward with an extended hand. I gather my composure, straighten my spine, and pretending everything's fine with me, I thank her for her invitation. I must find my people, though I know I am far from the familiar. I am out of breath, tired, thirsty, and my chest is aching—the dull pain stabs at me again. Her softness and tenderness bring forth the sadness and memories I've been suppressing, and they gush down my cheeks.

With Grandmother's attention on me, buried images come into focus. I know I've met her, but that seems impossible. She tells me that the hotel where I now live is an old resort used mostly for small groups or retreats. It's on the road to Hana, not too far from Paia. The road to Hana is famous for its beauty, and narrow, winding turns. "You'll be okay now. I will visit you. I have much to tell you. We're family. Visit me when you want," she encourages. "I know where you live. I worked there as a maid when I was young. I know your quarters. But, for now, join us for lunch. My daughter Kalea will take you home later." Reluctantly, I join them at the long green picnic table, but wait anxiously for Kalea to be available.

It's 3:30 p.m. when I get back home again, and I feel more oriented in the surroundings. I feel as though I am running away from something—a pressure against my back that relentlessly pushes me onward, but disappears when I turn to face it. Or am I reaching toward something that is pinned to my heart that pulls to fly me like a kite? Perhaps now is a good time to answer these questions and figure out how I came to be so far from home. I miss hearing Spanish spoken. I miss hearing the racket of Mexican radio and commercials. I've become a wanderer, peeking through windows, looking for my people. Where *is* home?

House in Renovation Dream

I'm living in a house owned by the Sierra family, and I am going to be living in a back bedroom. I'm not happy with the prospect. I'll be there only temporarily. It feels lonely, and the room is quite dirty and in need of lots of fixing. The paint is old and thick. I'll need to take it off and repaint it. There are many windows, and I have no privacy. I recall that in other dreams I would have been terrified of anyone being able to look into my house, but this time it feels manageable. If I really want to, I can put some sheer curtains up that will not block out light, yet will give me the privacy I need. I am concerned that winter will soon be here, and the room will be cold and damp. I could

> *move into the living room for warmth from the fireplace. I walk into the living room with beautiful oak panels all around. The window frames, floor, and walls are nicely polished, and the light gives a cheerful, lovely feel to the room. The thought of remodeling troubles me; it will be a considerable project, and the backroom will need to be closed off.*

We've been married three years now, and when I had the dream, it was the very day after the wedding. I thought, *Oh no, major overhauling.* Why didn't I have this dream *before* we got married? Not that I would have yielded to wisdom. This dream told me all I really need to know—that the marriage would be hard work and that I would feel a terrible loneliness, vulnerability. In short, I really don't want to know what's up ahead. Don't tell me, I *knew* it—in the deep underground, there was going to be serious renovation. How did I miss the cues? I was oblivious to what was before me. I had zero recognition.

Hawaii is magical. If there is any place to do the soul-searching that lies ahead, I can think of no other place on earth to be. This time of introspection is for finding what lies within, and facing the necessary renovation. It feels strange to be so far from the familiar, alone and disconnected from what is important to the heart and spirit. These are just words, but maybe if I look back, I'll find some clues, the reasons for being here and what I can do to salvage this time and use it wisely.

It's been a year since I met Grandmother. I'm still processing my feelings, but psychotherapy has been reduced to just once a week. My memory has returned. And I've been making adjustments to living in Hawaii.

Holden and I knew each other for several years before we got married. He was part of the community in Tiburon, California, where we both facilitated in support groups for family members of people with life-threatening illness. Our groups met every Tuesday evening. My car dropped the transmission, so he started giving me a ride home to San Francisco, and we became friends.

Over a period of several weeks, repairs were done to the Golden Gate Bridge, and we'd have an extra fifteen to twenty minutes of waiting to cross the bridge. I was living with an attorney connected to my meditation center in Berkeley, and was a graduate student at San Francisco State University.

My relationship was fraught with small and great disparities, so we agreed to end it. Holden offered to help me move, and shortly afterward, we started dating.

I liked his steadiness, his reliability, and his solid foundation. Casually, I suggested that we have a day out in nature. I lived close to the ocean. The following day, Saturday, we went for a walk along the beach and stopped at the Cliff House to watch the sunset. We were both surprised at how relaxed and comfortable we felt together.

We got together a month before a woman was to visit him from Spain. Within a couple of weeks, we were involved more intimately, so together we made the decision that he would tell her not to come. Maybe I was the one to push for that.

A week later, I asked, "Was the trip called off?"

"She felt bad, and said it was such short a notice. She still wanted to come out."

Somehow, I got the idea that if he gave me a transitional gift, I could survive the ordeal. So I said to him, "I'd like a gift of something that will let me know you're thinking of me and that you will be back. How about a gold or silver heart for a necklace?" What I was really saying was that since I didn't have his heart, we could pretend he cared, and I could pretend I trusted our relationship.

Friends who knew him were supportive. No one dared to say, "Hey, put your foot down. They don't have to sleep together," or, "You can always bail out if you don't like it." On my own, the thought never crossed my mind, but I still dreaded the ordeal. I was afraid we would not survive it. This was before the AIDS epidemic, when relationships were built in one day and just as nonchalantly terminated. But because of our long-standing friendship, I thought we had something more substantial than a casual dating relationship. Having come out of the sixties, when I rebelled against all convention, I thought I was big enough to agree to let him "do his thing." As blatantly absurd as the situation was, I overlooked the deeper feelings and rearranged my thoughts to make it look like a day at the beach.

The three weeks crept by slowly. I would get a call from him in the afternoon at work, and he would say, "I miss you." I wasn't calling him in

the evening or calling him at home, and as the days went by, I ha~~
of being "the other woman." It's painful to look back and remember
I waited for his phone calls in the afternoon, and obliterated my thoughts
about him in the evening. One weekend, I went for a walk in Golden Gate
Park and saw a blue Mercedes like his parked near the De Young Museum.
Something inside me shut down in that moment. This was more than I could
bear. If I saw them together, I wasn't sure how I would react: pretend I
didn't know him? Cry? Throw a tantrum? The thought was overwhelming,
and yet I continued forward, hoping to run into them. I can only say that
a longing for union with another human being at any cost kept me in the
denial of what was happening to me.

Once she left for Spain and clean linens replaced the old ones, we resumed our relationship that very evening. I felt an emptiness that hadn't existed before. Our first date after her departure, I thought I would breathe a sigh of relief. Instead, I kept looking behind me, wondering where our relationship had gone. At the restaurant, I heard myself laughing a hollow laugh. I no longer saw him behind the twinkle of his eyes.

The innocence of our relationship was crushed. I had essentially been cast aside temporarily and hurled back in. That was a familiar feeling for me, living in foster homes and coming home after months of being away. I relegated the feelings to the deep freeze and went on with my frozen feelings as though nothing had ever happened, unaware of the emptiness I felt. It wasn't too many months later that I moved in with him, and we became engaged.

After our wedding, the feelings continued to bother me, and I continued to ignore the discomfort. One of my favorite songs at the time had lyrics that went something like this: "I don't believe, I don't believe, I don't believe you." I loved hearing the song; I loved the chord changes, but I never wondered why I was fascinated by it until Holden commented that he felt like I was telling him that I didn't believe him. It was true. I didn't trust him anymore, and I didn't believe in "us." I didn't believe he loved me. But I didn't leave, and he didn't leave. Instead, we got married and moved to Hawaii. And here we are, living in this converted hotel under renovation, away from loved ones and alone with each other. Something feels amiss. I didn't expect my life to look like this, but the mature thing to do is to stay with the feelings. "Stay with the feelings," I tell myself. My "house" is under renovation.

My dreams always tell the truth about my feelings, about what's happened or what's up ahead, on some level, if I could only decipher and accept them. I've accumulated several dreams that tell me that I am looking for a home. I can't say for sure if I am longing to return to the mainland, or that I miss my family, or that I am actually excavating to find something that feels ancient. The following dream tells me that I am looking for a home. I have a home here, why would I be looking elsewhere? I'm not desperately unhappy. We light the candles, turn on the music, and have romantic evenings. We're connected to a church community. We have friends. Yet, it does appear to me that I am no longer "here." I've lost myself. I am looking for me.

Looking for a Home Dream

I'm walking through a shady neighborhood looking at beautiful Victorian houses.
One two-story white house in particular looks inviting—sitting up on a hill, a wisteria tree at the front entrance, beveled glass windows, a wraparound porch, looking cozy and inviting. I have a yearning to have a place of my own, home sweet home, where I am safe and secure.

This looks foreboding, combined with the dream of a house in renovation being temporary: I am looking for a new home. Let me stop the clock. I don't want to move forward. No, I can't be thinking that it's time to move on. I can't be thinking that I want to leave. I can't be thinking of going back to California by myself. No. Say it isn't so.

Traveling by Train Dream

Throughout the night I am riding through the Sierra Nevada by train. I can feel myself thrashing between the sheets. Long slow curves, the shifting movement of a gently

> *swaying train taking me to the next phase of my life. Through valleys, rugged boulders, and desolate, thickly carpeted green, I hear the sound of rustling in the night. Animal calls and roars, high sierras covered with snow, bridges, long narrow tunnels. Nights and days I travel the countryside moving slowly.*
>
> *I stir and moan in my sleep; throw blankets back one minute, cover myself the next; thrash about the bed in reaction to the unfamiliar terrain—the strange, uninviting places. Weeks and months seem to pass.*
>
> *"Remember! Remember! Remember!" keeps repeating all night long.*

Once more, the writing is on the wall. But it feels like I'm making it up, and I'm trying to break free of the prison I feel closing in on me. There is something I have forgotten. What is it? There's a mixture of current issues: needing to move on, yes, but what am I overlooking? It feels ancient—something I've promised to do or committed to. What is this feeling? I take the tape recorder and whisper into it, "Become aware of your breath, *sloooowly*, breathe in deeply and hold your breath. Let it go, all the way, all the way. Breathe out. Remember. You know what it is . . ."

The feelings of displacement continue in pursuit.

Wilderness Dream

> *I feel the cold, slimy spit of rejection land on my heart. My friends are turning their backs on me and are heading toward the wetlands. Like old movies of cowboys running from Indians in hot pursuit, they look over their shoulders to see if I am gaining on them. The faster I go, the more they elude me. My breath slows me down as they climb toward the ridge of the rolling hills. I keep chasing.*
>
> *The outcast, the untouchable. I hunger for contact with them, wanting desperately to belong. I stop at a theater and see a man and woman, friends of the others. There also, I am blemished. They see me coming and turn their backs to avoid my glance. The man hands the woman a*

> *tape cassette, and she inserts it into a pinball machine. The sweet, soft notes of "In the Garden" begins to play.*
>
> *"Ah, that's my favorite song. My favorite song," I tell them. They ignore me. "And he walks with me and he talks with me, and he tells me I am his own . . ."*

I wake up and can't get beyond the rejection and the pain of loneliness. These are such old feelings that have lived with me. I've gone through life with the devil on my shoulder, and here it is whispering to me again, "You're the outsider, go home." I can't do it. I don't want to. At the same time, in the lyrics of the song, there is a call from the eternal Mother/Father. "The world may do as it pleases, but to her/him, I am lovable." The rejection is part of being in the "wilderness" or "the Valley of the Shadow of Death," which is another name for "life." Which will I choose? What would anyone in her right mind choose? These words, these thoughts of being so far from home—living outside the mother, outside of Spirit—do not make sense to me. I feel so alone. Let me choose to be comforted by love.

My quest for truth continued.

My Family Name Dream

> *Tears rolling down my cheeks, fists clenched on the keys, I sit at the black grand Steinway, cursing and raging as my mother watches, fighting back her tears. Crying and pounding the keys, I lean my head against the piano. "I'm going to bring our family name down. I'll bring our family name down," I repeat, whispering. The sobs grow out of control, choking me, throwing me on the floor and making me writhe there until finally leaving me spent and nothing is left—not even a whimper.*

As I enter the door that takes me through the caverns of the underground of my mind, I uncover memories related to the feelings I am dealing with in therapy. These seem to be fairly intense memories of my younger years, without my family. Maybe I am feeling the effects of being in the middle of the ocean, far from familiar sounds and family. It is one thing to be on this beautiful island, but being so far away from my brothers is another matter. It makes sense that these dreams are feeding the feelings of loneliness and isolation, feelings I had never allowed or admitted in the past. They are unrelenting. I'll ride the tide and see where they take me.

Dream Interrupted

It's taken me forty years to figure out what happened the Sunday morning I got kicked out of church. I felt different that warm summer day of 1955 in Modesto, California. I had just come back from a four-month stay with the Mendietas in Hayward. I remember the day clearly, as though I am writing in my high school diary at my mother's kitchen table. Since then, my brothers have gotten married and had children, and their children have had children of their own. My mother has died. My father sold the house and moved to Tijuana. I moved to San Francisco. My father died twenty-five years ago. But that day in Modesto is somehow etched in the grooves of my mind, with the precision of an old maze neatly tended and trimmed by a constant, meticulous gardener.

The church my family attended was across town, away from our working class neighborhood, where sidewalks marked the edge of the street and lawns were mowed regularly and trimmed with an edger. Templo Getsemani was a plain white reconverted mess hall in the heart of El Barrio. Weeds stuck out or around the concrete blocks that held up the wooden frame. Narrow concrete stairs with a metal pipe railing led to the plain double front doors. An unpaved parking lot with potholes and hard-packed earth stretched along the property that accommodated about eight to ten cars. Adjacent to that was an empty lot overgrown with tall yellow grass.

Some of the houses in the surrounding neighborhood were nicely kept with relatively new white paint. Occasional rose bushes and maple trees in their gardens were seen, but most houses were bare essentials with dull, chipping paint and either overgrown wild gardens, or old rusty cans filled with flowers in front on dry, parched earth.

I was accustomed to change. I was six when my mother started working in the *bracero* camps in the Stockton Delta as a cook, and my life began to march to the calendar of seasonal workers. Every February to June, and every September to November for years I was shifted from home to the homes of various people of our church community around the Central Valley as far away as the San Francisco Bay Area. I was no stranger to change. But this Sunday was different. We had a new pastor, Hermano Martinez, who spoke English, which was unheard of for a pastor to be at home in English. He lacked in the hallmarks of an experienced trusted elder. He was young, tall, and thin, with olive light skin, sharp Spanish features, and straight dark hair. His wife was attractive and slim, also fair with brown hair and eyes, and was the choir director. They had two active small children, a boy still a toddler and a girl ready to start kindergarten. His election had occurred while I was away, and I knew nothing else about him except that even from a distance, I sensed discomfort, something I couldn't quite name.

This was the first week of summer vacation. I had been away since February. The months away from home had been fraught with unsuccessful attempts at fitting in with the family long after the welcome had worn out. The girls and I started out as friends, and as the months passed, a silence had developed between us. On top of this, I tended to be inconsistent with my studies. I managed to squeak by and get B and C grades in a crowd of kids talking about attending Cal Berkeley after graduation. By June, I was anxious to get back home to my own room, back with my family and Napoleon, our black-and-white collie. A mother at the church in Hayward tattled to my foster mother that I had phoned her son. It was shameful—girls with any dignity did not call boys. Anabela wasn't cruel when she spoke to me about it. "You shouldn't call boys." It was in the monotone voice and stern face in which she said it. I wanted so badly to have allies or friends to stand up for me. I was alone. The feeling was becoming familiar, that gnawing in my stomach that screamed "outsider."

Privately, I expected to come back to church and find the elders, at least, glad to see me, throwing their arms around me, kissing me, and saying, "Como has cresido" or "How you've grown." I was hoping they would see positive things about me—my long hair, that I'd matured, my *quinceañera*. I was fifteen years old, a time for celebration into community. I would have welcomed any crumb of recognition. These were private thoughts, unacknowledged in my own head, and more akin to an irritating mosquito flying close to my ear. When I came in from the glare of the sun and into the dark of the shaded room, people didn't even glance up from their songbooks.

Through furtive looks and side glances during the service, I realized that some kids had formed boy-girl relationships while I was away. Going steady was forbidden by the church elders, another sign of how much things had changed. I felt a pang, realizing that I had missed out on the picking and choosing. When it came time for class, the kids filed out of the sanctuary and walked around the back of the church to the three rooms where the pastor lived with his family. Walking through the parking lot alone, I saw the girls' clique I once belonged to walking arm-in-arm ahead of me. I noticed their new pastel and floral print cotton dresses flared out by starched petticoats, dresses I hadn't seen before. All these observations were the subtle changes that happened during my absence.

Without realizing it, I was having flashes of running away from this place that was supposedly home. I had seen mothers in the church cry deeply over the loss of their daughters or sons to the "world," a passage when a young member of a family left the community in search of answers in the outside world. Perhaps it was the outgrowing of small ideas of the select few who would attain a place in heaven, or perhaps it was this foreign intruder that was whispering in my ear. I had never heard a name for what was happening to me. In the church, this flight was seen as a rebellious act and a turning away from God, family, and community. The sorrow rippled down to the children in all the families. Drawing closer to God and the community in prayer was our only recourse to relieve the families' suffering. No one wanted to cause heartache. I certainly didn't, but for the first time in the years of leaving and returning, I felt self-conscious being home again. I was wearing lipstick, another taboo in the church. My return home was riddled with the evidence I felt as an outsider.

In class, ten of us were squeezed into two short wooden benches in the pastor's small kitchen. He stood in front of the seated group in his navy blazer, white shirt, plain navy tie, and gray pants. I don't remember the lesson. I just remember there were twenty verses for ten of us to read. I was sitting in the front row between my best friend Celia and her cousin Tito. We were the last to read. After the other seven have each read two verses, the assault came quietly. "Tito, read three verses," he said in a typical Mexican accent. Then, skipping over me, he had Celia read the last three. I looked around to see if anyone had noticed. They were intently paying attention to the reading. If I could have expressed my dismay, I merely hunched my shoulders, certain they could see stains of blood on my back, seeping through my yellow cotton dress.

The next night, Monday choir practice, sitting at the piano, the pastor's wife Eva handpicked members for the choir, selecting them on both sides of me. I realized I had not been selected when she left me standing alone and turned to the choir, saying, "Open the green songbook." I watched as they took their places on the platform. "What page?" echoed around the platform. I walked outside to wait for my brother to pick me up.

I sat at the top of the front steps, and a boy I had liked before going away was late. I said, "Hi, Bobby."

Without skipping a beat, he said to me, "Are you going to accept Christ as your Savior?"

This was my first time to see him in months. There was harshness in his voice, as though he had joined the others in passing judgment on me. After a short pause, I answered, "No." Without looking at me, he nodded, opened the door, and walked in.

In the autumn of that year, my parents sat at our kitchen table when I came home from school, and my mother asked, "Would you like to go to church with Mary?" Mamá was referring to the Anglo-Episcopal church downtown, where my school friend Mary Bailey went. I felt a twinge in my stomach at the thought of being among strangers in such a personal realm. I promised to give it a try.

The decision seemed to make sense at the time, but there was no connection between the people and me. They seemed to try to pretend that I wasn't there. I was introduced to the priest, and he said hello, but no one articulated the question, "Why are you here? Why aren't you with your own?" I had been relegated to a foster home situation where I was silent, invisible, and alone.

Emptiness Dream

My footsteps clang on the metal stairway leading toward the classroom. I'm early and the area is disserted—not even voices filtering out of classrooms, just the sound of my footsteps winding up the stairwell. It is ten flights up. The last step at the top is like a thud to my ears. My heart is beating fast, and I am out of breath. The first to arrive, I sit down to wait, dreading their arrival. I pull out a book to distract myself for a few minutes.

In groups of twos and threes they start trickling in. Aware of my reading, and the low murmur of conversations, I pause to listen. Nothing stands out. There are animated conversations, but the sounds blur and clash against each other. I look up from my book, and people are gathered around me now.

I turn to say hello, but vacant eyes stare back at me, or they avert their eyes from the piercing of my onyx eyes. I return to my book and try to eavesdrop. Still nothing I can grasp. Chatter, but nothing that stays with me—no words or ideas. Sounds flow through me, wafting past like feathery clouds. The room is full. I'm not seen. If I just put my book down, perhaps, maybe, they will see me. Perhaps a word will come out, or come in—"Hello." Not even that.

Classes begin, and I move into a smaller area in a circular wall with four other students. As though in an insulated plastic cylinder, I can see them but hear nothing. Their glances bounce off my shield. No acknowledgment. Invisible. Silent.

The day passes. Classes are over. The instructor puts her books away and I, mine. By chance I hear her say, "These ideas are for people of your generation." Is a response required of me? I look behind me. A man in his early thirties is standing there. No, not for me, another generation.

Outside, I pull up my collar. Air. Breathe in air. The sky is gray, silent.

I finally arrive home. Safe, quiet. My father's been there and gone again. The house is empty. I live there alone, the house that once belonged to my family, vacant for years. No one visits, no one calls. Just me, alone. Tears dry from the years of silence.

It's early dawn. I chance to go outside. Afraid neighbors will see me in my white flannel nightgown, I quickly gather my father's file and telephone and bring them in.

If a writer were recording the scene, perhaps she would mention "the shadowy figure" outside the door. But there is no recorder. The space between the door and the doorjamb—oh, God, a peephole for the world to see inside and watch all my activities. I'm locking a lock that won't click, fumbling, locking out the potential intruder. I hear noises behind me when no one's there.

There is just the dullness of the gray walls, echoes of voices long dead, footsteps from years past.

I, in the house of my childhood.
Silence.
Alone.

I recall clearly how the house felt empty and deserted when my mother was away. I didn't like being there. If I had reason to stop by, I would get what I needed and head right out. The feelings became unbearable after she died. The house was sold years later. The silence has remained after all the years. Being there is as though stepping into a mausoleum and feeling the spirits of those already gone. The significance of the silence reminds me of the interrupted dream—the idyllic dream that I should never be separated from my family and that my mother should always be there at the end of the day. Without noticing it at first, Mamá's absence initiated the final stage of the dismantling of our family. When we each went our separate ways, there was nothing to hold us together. The silence in the dream was a punctuation mark that emphasized the death of an era, a time and place in the community, and the death of a dream.

Dime La Verdad, Mamá
Tell Me the Truth, Mother

Dime la verdad, Mamá. Tell me that you have always loved me. Tell me that your dreams for me extended beyond the river, the mountains, the horizon, the sun and the stars; that you handed your dreams on to me for guidance by flames of altar candles, prayers, and gentle words; that open arms awaited you from your first breath and were then your legacy to me.

Tell me that your passage from the beginning was filled with music, incantations for joy and love; that the sweet sound of melodic voices singing your name in celebration awoke you at your birth; that you danced in brightly colored costumes with silver and gold chimes, and your dresses flowed gracefully in rhythm to horns, guitars, gourds, rattles, and drums.

Tell me that your great-grandmother had a place set for her at the dinner table; that she was surrounded by lovely flowers; that she was given the spiritual truths from her grandmothers; and that the heartstrings continued forever forward.

My dreams tell me that I am a stranger at dinner tables, where I am hungry and invisible; where I take small morsels and say little; where I am a shadow that slips through doors unseen; where only at night do I dare to speak my thoughts and dance alone under the dark moon.

Tell me that I was never sent to places beyond the warmth of our family, where voices cracked through stunned silence as muffled noises that awakened *los espiritus malos*, malevolent spirits.

Tell me that I was never scorned, never seen as the wretched forgotten child of a family, *la rechazada*, who hid behind tattered curtains, denying lies she heard about a bewildered little stranger, her soul longing for comfort and respite.

Tell me that this is someone else's nightmare; that my life began filled with music, incantations for joy and love; that the sweet sound of melodic voices singing in celebration awoke me at my birth; and that I danced in brightly colored skirts with silver and gold chimes that flowed gracefully in rhythm to horns, guitars, gourds, rattles, and drums.

As I write this poem, I feel the sadness of not having personal experience with cultural traditions that were available generations past, before Mamá set sail for North America, via South America. It's more than sadness—the feeling is irreversible, irretrievable. There is a sense that something's gone awry, missing for generations.

I look at Holden; he seems to be content with our situation. If he is bothered by the "emptiness," he doesn't show it. I don't tell him what's going on in therapy for me. It's too difficult to talk about it.

To my mind, something in my mother's heart shut down when she altered family ties beyond her lifetime. When I think of my mother's life, I imagine her feelings as she encountered her personal interrupted dream. I imagine her packing her suitcase and not looking back for many years until she could begin to fathom all she'd lost in leaving her pueblo of Rayon, in Southeastern Mexico. Yes, she lost the chaos and repeated disruptions during *La Revolución and her father's drinking,* but also the faces and voices of loved ones that assured her a place in the family, the warmth and aromas from the kitchen, *la tortillería, la panadería en el pueblo.* She lost everything that secured the underground of her dreams together and drew pictures of safety and familiarity. Her letters from home caused her days of longing for the nearness of her family. I'd observe her sitting quietly at the top of our back door steps overlooking a vacant lot overgrown with dry weeds. Sighing pensively, she'd return to her chores with an air of resignation. Maybe in some way, I carry her unspoken sadness, and long to recreate at least a fragment of the spiritual truths she left behind. Even today, I often feel that I am living out a part of her appointment with destiny.

Papá was born in northern Mexico, the state of Sonora, after the Arizona border split his Yaqui community, making the northern half of it part of the United States. As the Tigres del Norte song says, "We didn't cross the border, the border crossed us." I recall his accounts as a young man, but I don't believe he felt any angst about the border, or any sense of nostalgia for what may have been lost. He was born in 1900, fifty years after the drastic change in maps occurred. It seems to me that in the hearts of the people, El Rio Bravo still roared its song and remained a channel carrying the old way of life. But I didn't hear any complaints about how things changed, nor that his mother had any comments to make about the change. He was a man of the moment. When he took the giant step in 1918, to Los Angeles, he arrived with his guitar and mandolin. His musical instruments were all he needed; they were his love and his passion. It's as though he carried his destiny firmly in hand, and whatever twists fate had in store for him, one might say he arrived prepared to face them.

El destino, I am learning, is something far greater than we think it is in the West, or the European-based cultures. Yes, it is thought of something that is unmovable or unshakeable, but the truth about destiny is that it isn't handed out neatly on a golden platter. Rather, one has to kick, bite, and scratch to discern its essence and then have the wisdom to follow its commands. Mamá, Papá, and our entire church community for that matter, read the hand of destiny in the simplest of actions. A successful drive across town to visit a friend could be seen as a completed act of God's will. "Si Dios me da lisencia"—if God permits it, if it is God's will, we will see each other. Nothing is taken for granted. In a world as unpredictable as that, one learns to do her/his part and to let go of results. So when I think of the drastic changes on one side of a river that separates El Norte from El Sur del Rio Bravo, I am speaking of the difference between corn and wheat, Spanish and English, Spain and England, and La Virgen and the Virgin Mary.

I wonder if it was my destiny to have this bittersweet, indefinable ache that relentlessly pushes me to scrape together what was "lost" in my parents' move north. It could have been many other seeds planted along the way. Even though this poem, "Dime La Verdad, Mamá," barely masks the dismay I feel in being sent away from home six months of the year to live with other families while my mother worked as a cook in the *bracero* camps, I can't help but feel that at a deeper level, this poem is more about the discontinuity in not only my mother's life, but of our entire culture. I can't help but marvel at my mother's courage to come by herself. She came with a suitcase full of dreams, I am sure, though I cannot confirm that now.

There is an underground parallel that runs in Mayahuel's story of loss and abandonment that speaks to the years of my mother's vacating her home base for six months out of the year, leaving each member of the family to his/her own resources. It shook her sense of womanhood or motherhood, I am almost certain of that.

Before poverty turned our family upside down, Mamá's role in life was like any other woman's role—homemaker, wife, mother, friend. This was a contract she signed when she packed her brown leather suitcase. She had dreams of being the lady of the house. But leaving the house empty for that length of time shattered her sense of self in unspeakable ways. That same disjointedness binds me to her because I also paid a high price for being sent away, and together, she and I are bound to Mayahuel in our interrupted dreams. We charted unexplored terrain; we each had to find our way through a maze of unmapped territory. One might say that anyone that crosses that river between the United States of America and Mexico does so at great sacrifice to the spirit and the dream of life.

My mother's dream for me was that people could say, "Que bonito Gracia toca el piano"—how beautifully Gracia plays the piano. As I came into my teens, knowing what she wanted for me was enough to make me fly in the opposite direction. And that was how I missed out on the best of my childhood. I rejected everything I loved. I do wonder if life would have been sweeter and more accommodating had I bowed to the call of the piano that I loved so much. But destiny played its part. I mustn't forget that my church community complicated for me the layers of encrustation of self-protection.

Still, I can't deny that Mamá and Papá uprooted themselves to create a better life for themselves, and then took as many steps forward to set up the family so that we could have a better chance in life than they did. I can't sit idly by and let the tides just spin me around and spit me out after they sacrificed so much. As I sit here at my desk looking into the garden with petunias and impatiens in bloom, I wonder about these things and whether there's a softer way of following through with destiny's dictates. There must be another way.

A Man's World

My mother often said, "Amarren sus gallinas porqué mis gallos andan sueltos"—tie up your chickens because my roosters are on the loose. She thought that was very clever. Without realizing it, she was admonishing me about the ways of life—that men have the upper hand, and women must be wary, just as, I am sure, the myth about Mayahuel's status teaches. Perhaps the myth has nothing to say about women's station in life, but something that I have fabricated to contextualize in today's terms. These following dreams describe my travels in attempting to fathom the cause of my current dissatisfaction, dismay, and restlessness.

Fallen Woman at Sixteen Dream

Time is drawing near to my marriage with Raul, Roberto's elder brother. Through the grapevine, I hear he is in love with a white woman and is leaving me. My heart is heavy with the knowledge that I've been rejected yet again. The shame digs into me, and the pain grips me from the inside. Their house at the other end of the block leaves no escape for me. I am bound to see him sooner or later.

Weeks pass by. I do see him in a casual encounter on the street.

"How come you didn't show up?" I ask point blank.

"I was afraid," he replies.

"Afraid of intimacy?"

"Yes," he admits and adds, "There was no other woman. I made that up to get out of the commitment." I feel a relief that I still have a chance to save face. I could deal with his fear, but not with being shunned and rejected by him.

I continue up the block by myself and reach his house. I go around the back door, the way I used to when I was a girl, and open it. I need to urinate and so head straight to the bathroom. Afraid to be seen in the house, I walk up one of the back stairways. His sister Marina is getting married; and the wedding gown, a rich brown velvet, is hanging over the washbasin. I hold my breath as I wash my hands. There is no room for error here. I don't want people to have one more criticism to add to the long list of faults about me. How dare she! How could she? To soil the brown wedding gown with her own hands. The house has as many bedrooms as there are children, thirteen. A grand estate where the mother is queen of the house and has many servants to help.

I am a shameful and fallen woman—at sixteen. I've become sister of the dark moon, neither wife, mother, nor daughter; despised, destined to travel the alleys and back ways of despair and isolation, of disgrace and dishonor. These are deep feelings within my psyche. Perhaps if I could go back, if I could just relive the time differently and be relieved of these dreadful vines that immobilize my steps, maybe then they would recognize me as one of them.

These feelings can't hide the deep despair I feel. The shame of being the "other." A girl without rights, without belonging—poor Mayahuel, she and I have a similar fate! Or is it our culture that says be attached to a man or be damned! Whatever cleansing I am experiencing, I am being purged of the shame of being a woman, and I am afraid to be without a man. The renovation is underway in the basement of my life. Would that I could end it and be spared being dragged through the underground caverns. There must be a reason. Did I actually sign my name to this suffering? Set me free of it, and let me be restored.

Two Lovers—Dream

When the scandal first breaks out, people in the community gossip and add their own version to the story. As the weeks pass, it becomes apparent that I've become a traitor of sorts, kept outside the circle of important discussions in the community. What I've gained for the thrill of cheap escapades holds no value compared to being included in this small group of souls. In the long run, the losses far outweigh my small gains in freedom.

I can't very well flaunt my exploits in the elders' faces, and the two lovers I have taken have become weary of my unavailability—even if they have agreed to share me. The rejection and being the outcast is so severe that I have no choice but to look beyond the borders of the families. I want inclusion. I am one of them, but my behavior is too akin to that of the queen of affronts and insults. I live in a cottage at the edge of town by myself, and people are making a wide berth around me, never stopping to chat, and even stepping off the curb to avoid speaking. All that has been familiar to me and all that I could ever want is beyond my fingertips. They've agreed in unison to turn their backs against me. I can hide the pain. I do my shopping, carry my groceries home, hold my head up, but the pain has a texture and a color inside, and it is quickly becoming my own undoing.

Instead of a red letter on my breast, a red purse becomes the symbol of the shame I have brought upon the community. When people see it, they walk past me, their eyes steady and straight forward, their faces blank, ignoring a lifetime of friendship and kinship. I don't wear the badge proudly like Hester Prynn; I cower in shame and loathe who I've become. I've become La Malinche, homeless and without country.

I decide to leave the area and start with a clean slate. I dread the fallow period that lies ahead—packing the dishes, the pots and pans, especially being in that groundless period where one's foot is in mid-air, and time stands still before it finds the next rung on the ladder. Homeless, until I've become familiar with the arrangement of the dishes in the new cupboards and can automatically find the spices, the knives and forks. And friends? When—six months, a year, two years? All those rainy evenings ahead when it's too cold to go to a movie and I've gotten bored with my books, and the black phone sits alone on the table, mute and still. Whatever, it is obvious I have nothing to lose in leaving. Even my lovers point the finger at me. Even they have had enough and are siding with my enemies.

The feelings of shame and marginalization singe everything in sight and leave me naked and alone. Give me comfort, warmth and company; give me reason for this suffering. Don't turn your back on me. I am alone, pitiful and friendless, rejected by those I thought loved me. Extend your hand to me and offer me solace until I find my grounding. I am a woman alone, like Mayahuel, without lover, family, or name.

Wait a minute—two lovers? A split in loyalty, uncharted waters, a break with the past, a new way of life? It doesn't seem possible. This spiritual isolation is unbearable. I have a husband, but I feel so empty and alone.

Por Ser Morena

I give a lecture on spirituality, and the audience stands applauding and shouting, "Bravo! Bravo!" I stand at the center of the platform, drinking in the appreciation. In the midst of the applause, Eduardo Peña shows up. He comes up to me and whispers in my ear, "It's too bad you have a tainted past. The Nominating Committee has decided against your ordination."

We step outside the cathedral, and I can see the pulpit, the large gathering and the sun shining through the huge plate glass window. He speaks softly and gently to me, but I see through the thin veneer of his gestures. I am being ostracized for something they know nothing about. Digging my finger into his chest, I lean forward, saying to him, "Now, listen here . . ."

Just then, out of the corner of my eye I see that the congregation is watching this interaction and that I am causing him embarrassment by chastising him in public. Besides, my defensiveness is too intense. But deep down, deep down, I know the darkness that lurks in his intention. I remember. I remember. In another lifetime, I've vowed to bring down our family name, if need be, to vindicate my own. There is something else I am overlooking, something that has a deeper meaning and calls for me to stand tall and be recognized, but for now, I can only sink into the shame and rejection the committee has planned out for me.

Rebellion. This is the price to pay for rebellion. I wear it like a scarlet letter on my chest. The world can point the finger at me and shout, "It's she. She's the guilty one. The dark one. Kill her! Kill her!" They can kill me, but I won't go down silently!

Relieve me of this suffering, this embarrassment and marginalization. The heat is unbearable. Bring me to safety. Show me I am worthy and loved. Show me what it feels like to belong, to be cherished. Hold me, bring me warmth, and tell me I am cherished. Show me the way home. It is a strange feeling, that I don't have the right to speak out, that I must remain silent, or suffer the consequences of being a renegade for speaking out.

Y Sin Dueño Dream

I stand at the art deco dresser with the huge round mirror and hold up my silver hand mirror with the engraved "G" and turn to see how obvious the hook is. It is broad as daylight, a hook like any hook one could find in a closet. But this one is made of old wrinkled skin, and shriveled tissue is growing out the right side of my shoulder.

There is no way to hide it because my bathing suit has thin spaghetti straps with no front to it. I either expose my breasts or expose the hook. I keep turning around in disbelief and dread. I am damned—a red sign that labels me la puta del rancho—*like a washing machine agitator, back and forth, back and forth.*

The breasts or the hook?
The breasts?
The hook?
Either way, damned.
Damned, forever.
Exposed and naked.

Something in me is shifting, and whatever it is, I feel a deep shame for being different, my body causing me reason to feel shame. A girl among boys, a wife deciding to get out of her marriage—but don't let me think that yet. Lift me up. Bring me to safety. Cleanse me of this shame. Give me reason to accept. Which bothers me more, rejection or isolation? My family turned me out as a child without a compass. They went on their ways, and I got stuck in time and space alone. Now I am afraid to turn my back; I am afraid to face the truth. Am I "abusable"? These feelings are surfacing now, but they have been festering for generations. Spare me!

Héchenla de Cabeza Dream

> *We drive up Mt. Tamalpaias in my blue Mercedes, two Caucasian women, myself, and two children. I seem to be attending to the needs of a beautiful blonde curly-haired girl of about six years. Her infectious cheerfulness draws me to her, and I fawn over her, straightening out her pretty floral pink cotton dress, touching her soft long blonde curls. I consciously ignore the other child—the one who is crippled, aloof, and very dark-skinned.*
>
> *We arrive at our destination, and the driver and mother of the fair child and I begin walking up a hill toward the start of the trail. I become concerned for the crippled child. We are on a steep incline, and she is having difficulty walking with her crippled foot.*
>
> *Retracing my steps to assess her situation, I find her moving slowly with effortful movements. Her demeanor reminds me of an adult in grief. I try to pick her up but almost trip over her because she is too heavy. Her thoughts literally weigh her down. But in this short interaction, something happens between us: my heart toward her softens, and I love her as though she were my own. She is accustomed to being ignored. My concern is an intrusion into her loneliness. She gives me a look that implies, "I can manage. Leave me alone."*

> *My heart is breaking for her predicament. With each step she takes, her crippled foot forces her body to undulate in such a way that her spine pushes her face into the dirt, as though she is forced to eat dirt. She comes up with dust on her nose and mouth. I begin to feel the courage and integrity to her experience. Helplessly, I stand by, letting her manage as best she can. She doesn't need my help, and she most certainly doesn't need my pity.*

This black child is suffering, and at the same time, she is holding her ground and insisting on being in charge of her experience. I note that her thoughts cause a heaviness that serves to her detriment. At first, I am paying more attention to the white child, but in the end, I sympathize with the black girl and recognize that she deserves recognition and caring. Yet she also has the strength she needs to make it on her own if necessary.

"Speak to me of my darkness. I am la prieta, the dark one, which probably contributed to my status in my family. Bad enough to be a girl, worse, to be the 'dark one,'" I pray. These are the thoughts that are weighing me down, and it's important to accept them and deal with them.

In this dream, I am dark, innocent, and determined. What is dark? In the dark, we find gravity, the power of creation. I'm reminded of Coyolxauhqui and her intuitive nature. We have a source within that has a power of its own to create, expand, and heal. I like that. I'll take that. I am black and have a wisdom of the ages.

Sin Dios Y Sin Esperanza Dream

> *The chief throws the dice and counts off the spaces. Whoever gets to the end of the line is out of the game— safe. The players look like pawns on the board, and the sinister method he uses heightens the fact that they are prisoners under heavy guard. I can't bear the thought of my brother's being selected for the sacrifice, for that is what is happening. His pawn is coming toward the end of the game. If he is out of the game, it means freedom, if not . . . one, two, three . . . you're out. One, two three . . . you're in. Toward the fire? Or freedom? The anxiety mounts as the*

players thin out. One, two, three . . . Thank god, he makes it off the board, safely.

It's rumored that a dark-eyed woman with a thick black mane lost at the game and was killed and eaten by the tribe, a virgin sacrificed. I think of the woman and wonder if she whispered, "Madre, Madre." Or screamed for the Father, "Padre, ten misericordia." Father, have mercy. For whom she called is important to me, yet I wouldn't have blamed her if she had been knocked unconscious and moaned when the flames devoured her, "Padre, Padre."

"Mother, save us," I pray. "Don't let her passing be in vain. Help us in this struggle. Give us courage." Later, still worrying about these ghastly events, and not very far from the death pyre myself, I try to warm myself while I wait for my husband to come home. It seems that I wait the long night, shivering from the cold. At dawn, I begin having doubts that he is returning and think that perhaps he has gotten caught and thrown into prison.

I wait with friends. A Caucasian woman wants to use the phone and tells me to get it for her. I hand her the phone, and then her partner commands me to do something for him. "Do it yourself," I respond. What surprises me is that I feel no malice toward him. I just don't like their entitlement to push me around. But, with this, the waiting and thinking about the victims, I feel alone and friendless. There is no place to turn to for comfort; I am a stranger in this land where laws and gods have been abandoned. Tell me the truth and tell me who I am. Bring me to simplicity. I need not the superfluous. Spell it out and comfort me. Have mercy on me.

This is a dream that brought out issues of my culture. It brings to mind sacrificing on the pyramids and the fear that lies deeply within. I also note that interacting with the Caucasian couple brought up racial issues, and the mixture of the two brought on tremendous anxiety and feelings of marginalization. How can I put them in the context of now, here in

Hawaii? Perhaps I see more of the racial than I've been acknowledging in my waking state. Maui feels old to me. Something ancient and unspoken, a presence that lurks around corners all the way to the bottom of the sea. But it too was stolen away from the Natives. Hm. It follows me wherever I go, this feeling of being the outsider.

Blue Light

I am current. I am energy. I am health. A blue light flows through my body, and I feel a surge of power like a rocket. I'm in a large building with ceilings two and three stories up, with lots of natural light filtering through the opaque glass, reminiscent of an old library. The feelings of wellbeing are as clear as being held in the palm of the Creator. I turn and walk toward the light. People at random extend their love. I am in a world at peace with myself, and there has never been a time when I was frightened in my dreams or waking time, or a place where I had to hide for safety.

The blue light intensifies, and my mind is whole, my body vibrant; a feeling of tranquility comes over me like Mirror Lake in Yosemite on a warm summer's day.

During the past few months, I have been dealing with issues of abandonment, not belonging, feeling marginalized, and attempting to regain the strength that I need to make my life meaningful. Perhaps being in Hawaii, surrounded on all sides by deep waters emphasizes the eternity of the soul; it also brings to mind again a separation, of having traveled far from home. I think of the Hawaiians and how they'd lost their lands. I know what it must feel like to have their lands taken and used by others. Whatever the issues, this dream in particular synthesizes the feelings and integrates those that initially were at war with each other. The blue light invigorates me and brings peace.

The storm is passing, and I stand here. I pray, "Thank you for showing me the way, for guiding my path and bringing me to safety." I dare not ask what these words mean, for I would then have to question the meaning of history—what happened in the Americas, what happened here in the islands. Is there really peace after colonization?

Leaving the Islands

The Damaged Airplane Dream

I'm in Mexico, maybe Guanajuato, and getting ready to take a plane. I don't see people around me, but I have a feeling I don't belong here. People are meeting in the next room, and I am not part of the group.

The feelings are becoming more intense. An airplane with parts of its side blown off appears, and a Native American man in a light tan business suit approaches me and says that I will be taking it home. Other people arrive and are going to take the plane, but the man is directing me to my place that's right on the edge of the plane, where there is no wall and nothing to hang on to. I look at him; he is smiling as I assess the situation. It isn't a friendly smile, but more like a taunting sneer that's daring me to take the bite. I look for other means of finding a flight out of the area. Perhaps if there were bars I could hang on. Even that prospect would be challenging to my strength and endurance. I check again for bars or hooks to hang on to. Taking the plane is certain suicide.

The imminent danger and the sinister quality of the dream wake me up.

This dream leaves me with a feeling that is very familiar, that is, anxious and with a sense of alienation and marginalization. It's morning. I pick up my journal to process the dream. I have no idea where to begin. First, I'll find out who the Native American guy is and go from there.

Me: So who are you?

Man: I am Ocelotl. I've come to remind you to open your ears and listen. Your life has a specific purpose. You are terrified at the slightest movement in your consciousness. The danger presented in the form of a damaged airplane is the perfect vehicle to challenge you to wake up after the years of indifference from your family. The families you lived with were indifferent to your spiritual needs—your real needs. You got used to being in a limbo-like place, and learned to mistrust yourself. You've experienced isolation and loneliness, but you will see, this does have advantages. I am glad to tell you that I am here as an ally. Wake up and remember that you and I are committed to the same goals.

Me: Ocelotl. Ah, yes, of course. You feel familiar, but seemed rather ungracious and I didn't recognize you. I do remember you from other dreams. What am I forgetting?

Ocelotl: An agreement to meet destiny and help others meet theirs.

Me: I made an agreement?

Ocelotl: In your soul, you are a dreamer, and have lived many lifetimes as a dreamer. You've been using your dreamtime to awaken within the dream of life. Stop investing in these feelings of alienation and loneliness and don't believe in them anymore. They are so far from the truth of who you are. Right now as you write, sit for a few minutes and breathe and let in new memories. Anything is possible—destiny is much more forgiving than you realize, but courage is essential.

I sit quietly, breathing into my belly, relaxing my shoulders

Me: What is the thing about the airplane? And what am I trying to accomplish in this dream, as you say, to remember who I am? Who am I, really? Why do I feel like an orphan?

Ocelotl: That's a good question. You get scared every time you start experiencing rapid growth, but there is no need for fear. Oftentimes, when you appear to be standing still or even moving backward, you are actually moving forward. Your values in this world are upside down to the spiritual. In your waking time, the growth is subtle, but in your dreams, you can change at the speed of light. You are giving yourself the chance to remember other lifetimes and the agreement you made with others and me. There is no loss. There is no fear. There is no *you* who can be destroyed. Try to remember a dream where you meet the gods and agree to come back to this world again. Wake up. It's that simple. You know the answers now, so stop acting out of fear.

Me: I've had many dreams with divine beings.

Ocelotl: Let the memories come. You will begin to see the pattern. Allow yourself to remember your commitment. I will give you a dream when you are ready. But there is something else. You are leaving the islands.

You will not be alone, and you will not be with your husband. This dream has several layers of information that you will have to decipher for yourself. That's what is terrifying you.

My dreams are telling me that I'm leaving the islands, but on a surface level, I am not planning anything. There is something deeper that my consciousness is attempting to grasp.

After writing my dream down, I take some time to just relax and let the memories roll across my mind. I'll pay more attention to those in which Ocelotl appears to me, or I have some memory of him. The trick is to allow them to happen as they bleed into this dimension. But first, I must face today.

I come out of my room and go to the kitchen. Holden, looking up from his paper, takes his glasses off and greets me with a smile.

"Good morning. There's some French toast in the oven. Have some," he invites me. He's sitting at the long wooden kitchen table where the tall windows meet at the corner. I serve myself from the small stack in the oven, bring them to the breakfast nook, and sit next to him. He leans on my shoulder lightly and kisses my cheek.

"Did you sleep well?' he inquires.

"Like a log. If it hadn't been for the francolins and their ruckus coming through, I'd still be asleep." I love that about Maui, the gentle natural life that surrounds us. The francolins remind me of wild turkeys, and I love their daily stroll through the yard. They sound like kids on their way to school, only the birds are noisier.

"So what time's your flight to Seattle?" I ask. We had discussed my going, but I want to stay behind to work on my book. That's odd, that I don't want to go to the mainland with him.

"Six o'clock," he answers.

"I'll take you. But you know it's Grandmother's birthday party this weekend. We should have taken that into consideration. I'm sorry you will be missing it."

Holden is very low-key, and the slow pace of life here has been amazingly gentle for both of us. Our plan had been to open a retreat center. Problems with investors and other difficulties arose, and we have not yet met the building codes to engage in such an enterprise. We're not actually stranded here in the hotel. Some repairs have been made. The kitchen, though quite large for a family of two, has been fixed up to resemble an exotic estate with pale green marble counter tops, big windows, and a goldfish pond in a lush side garden outside the window. People come and visit for short periods, but we avoid attracting the attention of large groups. We've gotten to know people in the area. We brought in a piano, and I've been practicing scales. Holden's business of selling medical equipment takes him to the mainland and places in the Pacific Rim. Sometimes I accompany him to visit my brothers and my friends when he goes.

Grandmother's family and I have become *comadres* and *compadres*. I go visit, and they come here. The back door is always open, and they know better than to knock. At their house, it's nonstop action. We've managed to visit one another at least a couple of times a week. I love going over there evenings when everyone is home from work. It's an easygoing feeling, just sitting at the table in their garden.

After breakfast, I make coffee and come back to write. Alone again, I think on the drabness of our conversations. It surprises me that the garden that has been a source of inspiration looks vacant and inactive. Nothing seems to happen that tweaks my interest or stirs within as it once did. Something is off.

Opening *A Course in Miracles* at random, I come to the topic of atonement. I look the word up in the dictionary: "Restoring, restitution for a wrong done. Harmonizing." Is *A Course* saying we owe restitution for separating ourselves from the divine? We sleep, and in our dreams assess accurately our state of mind. Sometimes we are in fear, other times, we see the truth—what we're not willing to admit in our waking time—clearly. Or we revel in it confidently with delight, only to open our eyes and forget what we have seen. Then, we distance ourselves and become strangers to this elusive paradise within.

It occurs to me that this curtain that separates us from the divine needs an intentional pulling back, or exposure to the weather, to let it get old and threadbare until it falls of its own volition. That's what I would like to see for myself: I want to be so focused that there is no curtain. That with my eyes open or shut, I am aware of the truth, the truth that runs like a laser beam throughout my consciousness and is the fire that alights my activities with the splendor and wonder of my true likeness of the divine. This is the lamp I want to guide my path to focus on love and mercy; to inspire me toward the golden innocence, so my mind is as clear as the rays of the sun that light our world.

In prayer I begin to reflect: I want the consciousness that banishes the thought of sacrifice or punishment or sin from my mind and brings me to the altar of strength and wisdom, where my consciousness and awareness travel on the same beam of light, instead of being static and stagnant in darkness, waiting for the spark that may or may not ever arrive. I want that effortless communion with the divine, where I am ever present in the moment; where power from you is at my fingertips, at the tip of my tongue, and instant healing is the norm. However I have pulled away in the past from your awareness, I am committed to being present and letting you be the lantern for my life. I am committed to stepping aside and letting your light shine upon my mind, to be used for your intents and purposes. Yes, this feels familiar. Let the curtain dissolve. Let me remember.

The Party

Three palm trees that appear to stand in the middle of the road are markers that tell me that I am nearing Grandmother's driveway. A curve in the road points the way to the entrance. I turn into the short gravel driveway and a wide blue ocean opens up, extending from the edge of the lawn. Huge poinsettias that will be in full color in a few weeks surround the yard. Evening casts its long shadows, and the rays of light radiate from behind the West Maui Mountains on the left side of the garden. I see the streamers, lanterns with paper shades, and white cloths over the dining tables, adding an atmosphere of formal celebration.

I park the car behind a navy blue CRX and let the door shut quietly. I've just dropped off Holden at the Kahului Airport, and I'm mulling over the coolness that has settled between us. It's a puzzle to me how I go from hot to cold in relationships. Try as I may, I can't find that magic button that makes me want to stay. I've stayed in other relationships long after the bonds were gone, but this time, there was no cooling off period, just a snap of the fingers, and a cold wind blew through my heart. I can't recover from it.

My dreams of looking for a new home and the dream where I travel throughout the night seem to be telling me that on some level, I am thinking about leaving. I feel sad, and even scared when the thoughts crystalize, but I'm not giving them a lot of weight. I don't want to turn my life upside down. I like my room, the garden. It's peaceful. I gather my overnight bag I brought in case I'm too tired to drive home, my purse, and Grandmother's present, a crystal to hang in the kitchen window.

The three easy steps from the car through the garage to the kitchen door help me refocus my attention on something more appealing. I'm looking forward to coming into Grandmother's grace and welcoming spirit. I hear boisterous laughter, and tall Joe, the first of Grandmother's three sons-in-law, greets me when I step into the kitchen. He's on the telephone. The stove is loaded with pots, and there's a clutter of spices and vegetables on the chopping block in the middle of the kitchen.

"*Comadre*! How are you? I'm so glad to see you," he hugs me with a warm welcome. I always feel received with his show of affection.

"Where's everybody else?" I inquire about his wife and her sisters, picking up a lid of something simmering on the stove. "Wow! What's this? It looks Mexican."

"It is Mexican. Grandmother is making something in your honor. She thought you would like some chicken in *mole*." He returns to chopping up generous portions of chicken he's preparing to put on the grill in the patio.

I take the stirring spoon, dip it into the sauce, and let it drip on to the palm of my hand. "Mm. This is good stuff," I comment, licking my hand. "Real good, and hot."

A native man comes into the kitchen, asking about getting some music on. He has a southern accent, which is rarely heard on the islands.

"We recorded a session at the Hyatt last weekend. The tape's in my car," Joe tells him. They appear to have an easygoing friendship. No please or thank you necessary.

Ray is his name. I've seen him on many occasions. He's always smiling and friendly, but flirtatious—a big flirt. We've never been formally introduced. He leaves through the garage door. Joe and I continue catching up with each other since the last time we met a couple of weeks ago. "Have you been playing a lot lately?" He's a guitarist in a popular trio that blends jazz with popular Hawaiian music. They are remarkably good. Ray returns shortly with a couple of tapes.

"So, Joe, who's the pretty lady?" he asks. *Pretty lady?* what a line. He has dancing dark brown eyes, a curl to his dark hair, and stands slightly taller than myself, maybe 5'7". I've seen him at church on Sundays, and know for a fact that he's Native American. We've never actually spoken, though I've heard him making quirky comments in conversation with others that have made me laugh aloud. Through the grapevine, I've heard that he's a traditional medicine man. I feel a little intrigued by this bit of information about him, though approaching him directly about it would be socially out of bounds.

One could say Ray and I are meeting for the first time. Maui is a small community, and gradually all information about newcomers goes around to everybody. We've had a couple of group meetings at the house—we call it "the house" now, not the hotel—so people know something about us, and they've each formed their own opinion about what they know. I assume he must know something.

"Hello," I say, embarrassed with his over-enthusiasm.

I see Grandmother through the glass sliding door in the garden, and I go in that direction. I slide the door open. Her favorite traditional Hawaiian music is playing on her tape player. It's nice to hear the singing in another language. I like the ukulele, and it changes my mood instantly. I forget my musings about my marriage.

I come up to her and put my arm around her shoulder. We're both facing the grill. "What's a nice girl like you doing in front of a stove?" I ask. "Don't you know the Hawaiian police will come after you for working on your birthday?"

She looks at me smiling. "I can't leave you with this. That's a nice pink silk blouse you're wearing."

"So you don't trust me!"

"You do know how to twist words around," she retorts, laughing.

"The guys will be here in just a minute. Let them do it. I'll stand guard until they come out. By the way, I saw what you did with the *mole*. It looks mighty fine, and I tasted it—mm . . . mm . . . mm!"

The door slides open, and I turn around to see Ray coming toward the grill with a plate of chicken. "Ah, relief has arrived," I remark, encouraging Grandmother to take her leave and go rest or get ready for her party. We put the chicken pieces on the grill, and take the cooked ones to simmer in the *mole* on the stove. I go back into the kitchen with Joe.

It's just like Grandmother to choose for dinner something that would please someone else. Everyone's leaning back on their chairs, full of enchiladas and Mexican beer. Joe brings out his ukulele, and Kaela directs our attention to the gifts that have been piling up on one of the tables. The kids want to guess at the gifts, so she has a contest to see who comes closest to describing the gifts inside. Grandmother isn't particularly interested in the game, but she tolerates the girls—thirteen- and fourteen-year-olds—and their playfulness.

Joe plays "Somewhere over the Rainbow," which Grandmother loves. Hawaii is often referred to as the land of rainbows. Standing atop a knoll overlooking Pukalani toward the West Maui Mountains on an afternoon of light showers, I counted seven rainbows. Going up Crater Highway, I often see rainbows through the lavender blossoms of the jacarandas, and they're not just ordinary rainbows, they pop up everywhere. Once, and only once, I saw a rainbow at night caused by the light of a full moon. Hearing the song in this context gives new meaning to the lyrics. I feel like I'm privy to the secret places where the Mother Queen bathes and the enchanting stories that go with the locations. First he sings the song by himself, accompanied by the ukulele, and then we all join in.

The first gift comes in a flat box that could be a blouse or light sweater, in ordinary Macy's-type wrapping of pink metallic paper with matching bow and silk stem rose.

"I know, I know!" one of the girls shouts out enthusiastically. She holds it to her chest, closes her eyes, and puts her ear up to the box. "It's something flat and soft with pink flowers," she remarks with enthusiasm.

"It's a white blouse!" shouts Paul, Grandmother's other son-in-law, a Hawaiian man in his mid-forties. Someone else added, "It's an antique frame for photographs."

"Okay, let's see who's right." Kaela concludes.

Grandmother opens the gift, and it turns out to be matching napkins and place mats with a soft pink floral pattern. It was Chanah who guessed, but consensus among the kids is that she had prior information.

"She cheated," shouts her elder brother Akau.

Turning to Beth, Kaela's younger sister and Chanah's mother, she asks, "Well, what is it? Did Chanah know?"

"Actually, I hadn't said anything to anyone, and I had the gift wrapped at Macy's in Oahu."

"Let's try another one," Kaela continues. She picks up a rectangular box wrapped in silver paper with a navy blue bow. "Who has an idea?"

Ray quietly offers, "I see a young man, like a fisherman."

"A pair of tickets to Dad's gig next week," Akau jokes.

This one turns out to be a newly framed photograph of Grandmother's husband in his early years, no older than thirty, coming back with the fishermen after a day's work on the boat. He's wearing a plain white T-shirt, shorts, and boots up to his knees. The men are bringing the catch of the day off a fishing boat and onto a dock in large round gray aluminum tubs.

Joe leads off with his ukulele a song in Hawaiian that everyone knows (except me), and he shouts the lyrics ahead of the music. It's quite nice. I can join in and actually feel that I am singing this old favorite.

Ray comes over and puts his hand around the back of my chair. I feel like he's being a little presumptuous. He doesn't drink, so I can't blame it on the booze, but he puts me at ease by talking about his work and a new program for teens. He's the director at Mahalo House, a recovery program for alcoholics and drug addicts. I don't know anything about recovery, but he says that he needs someone with a master's as required by the grant and thinks that I would be a good fit.

"I might be interested. My work has been slow," I add. I could use the money, but I don't want him to think I'm desperate.

"Come by on Monday morning to formalize it. I have some ideas on how we can get the program off the ground." It's settled, and I agree to be there at ten in the morning on Monday.

Around midnight, I notice that Kaela is starting to clean up around the edges of the party. Joe's music is slowing down, and it's a matter of time before they all begin to pitch in. I go to where my things are in one of the bedrooms and put on something more casual. On my way back, I stop in the kitchen and pull out a large plastic garbage bag from the drawer. When I return to the patio, others with babies have left; the girls have ducked out to listen to their own music in one of the bedrooms. I'm surprised to see Ray helping out. I start collecting the remains of the birthday cake plates and forks. He comes over and takes the plastic bag out of my hands.

"I'm rather good at this. Besides, you shouldn't get your pretty little hands dirty," he says, laughing. I walk away without commenting.

After everyone's left, Grandmother and I sit talking on the lawn chairs, and she cautions me, "You'd better watch out for this Ray guy. He's sweet on you."

Tossing my head back laughing, I dismiss her warning and say, "Ah, he's just a flirt."

"I'm warning you. Watch out for him."

Feeling quite complimented, I then add, "Besides, I'm married, and I am not looking for a boyfriend." It's late, the kids stayed over, and it's time to drive home. Grandmother and I leave the garden and the gentle sound of the ocean lapping against the rocks not too far away, and she walks me to my car.

Decided

I've lived an erratic life, beginning with being shifted in and out of my family while my mother worked outside our home as cook in the *brazero* asparagus camps around the Stockton Delta. I, the only girl in the family with three brothers, was devastated by the constant disruption throughout my childhood, tossed out without phone calls, visits, or letters from home for months at a time. My brothers had each other; when I was at home, I would listen to their conversations that flowed seamlessly about school, tests, and teachers. In being away alone, I had no one to hang on to and listen to my thoughts, reflect my strengths and triumphs. Then I was pulled home to resume the role of dutiful daughter. There were striking differences in freedom once home. My movement was restricted from a tradition of nineteenth-century Mexico where I needed to be chaperoned in an activity as simple as going downtown to Kress's five-and-dime.

In a sense, I am validating and giving myself permission to claim my very existence, but there is a place within of self-hatred and alienation that I don't understand and can't heal. As an adult, when I seek therapy to be restored from the ravages of poverty, I come up against a paradigm that cannot accommodate my psychospiritual needs. There is no connection to our legends of the Mother and the God of Duality. Instead, I am encouraged to be angry at my parents for imposing the travesty of uncertainty upon me. As a dreamer/psychologist, I need to find a system of beliefs to re-parent myself and teach myself a way of walking through life with integrity and self-respect. Were I to be closer to my culture, I would probably do it in community and ceremony. That makes more sense to me. But, for now, I'll just have to trust what appears to be the logical next step.

When does one wake up and say, "All right, today I pack my bags and leave," and have it be final, with no more debate or discussion? After all the nightmares and half-baked thoughts and pain of trying to make something work that's gone offtrack, something in me has shifted. Yet I haven't been thinking about it. I haven't been staring into space secretly daydreaming about another life—I took that job at Mahalo House three months ago.

Something snapped in me yesterday. I walked into the video store to rent a movie as a married woman, and I walk out a single woman. It was that clear and direct. A microdot in time, nothing earth-shattering.

"What does the G stand for?" The clerk was asking a simple little question—about my name—to make idle, friendly chit-chat. Without missing a beat, Holden answered, "Gloria."

I turned my head slowly toward him, not believing my ears. Granted, the name started with the same letter. But other than that, the case is shut. the abyss between us has broken open. It's over. He answered with his ex-wife's name. And that wasn't the first time. He called me by her name last Christmas while we were cooking dinner, and another time at the beach when we were having fun together. For some reason, this time I'm not willing to ignore it. I'm in a mood for taking up a pair of red boxing gloves.

We got into our blue Mercedes, and he said, "I'm sorry, I don't know why her name came out." I looked straight ahead and kept my silence. In that moment, there's no need for sharing my feelings. I had no interest in talking about them. I preferred to drive home in thick silence.

When we arrived home, I looked at the building and the place where I've had a room of my own for four years. It looks into a peaceful garden of plumeria, mango trees, and the lush lawn watered by reliable Maui rains. I walked into the living room, looked around as though seeing the arrangement of my life for the last time, and noticed the sofa with Polynesian flowers in pale shades of pink, blue, and green leaves. Everything began to take on new meaning as though I was silently saying goodbye to the familiar

This morning, I feel as if I've already broken the news to Holden. I'm making up a dream from where I left off in the endless train ride, walking through new neighborhoods looking for a home. The sense of being groundless that's so familiar begins to churn within my stomach. The naked panic as though I'm on a collision course on a plane. I hadn't articulated my thoughts because I wasn't prepared to launch out on my own. Am I making this up?

The situation has become more strained between us, Holden and I, and I don't know what to think. There is a mismatching of energy between us, as though he's on a bluff across from where I stand, and we occasionally wave at one another. Holden has been silent for several weeks; there is no intimacy, and I can't remember when I last saw a sign of life in him. At the Matsu in Kahului where we went for dinner last night, our feet accidentally touched under the table, and quite reflexively, I jumped back as though I had bumped knees with a stranger.

Grandmother was right. Since I was hired, Ray has been relentless in breaking the barriers between us. I don't remember how it started, but his presence seems to be pervasive. We lunch together as a group, and he seems to find his way next to me often. I came home with some music he gave me that he picked up in Hilo at a conference. I've been playing it over and over.

"Holden," I say, approaching him when he's returning home with groceries, "We need to resolve what's happening between us. I can't stand the silence any longer. What is happening?" The discussion goes downhill from there. I suppose that for starters, my choice of time and place is ill-appointed—at the front door. Neither of us knows where to begin. He isn't happy, I'm not happy, and admitting our thorough frustration isn't proving productive. It was instant chaotic admissions interspersed with counterattacks—not exactly fertile ground for restoring a broken marriage.

"I am not a good communicator, and you're running a close second behind me," I say. "To me, it seems that this goes back to when you let Cynthia sleep in your bed, and I was left out in the cold for weeks. It's always bothered me, but I seem to be more aware of it now than ever before. I can't let go of that resentment. You let her sleep in your bed for three weeks, and treated me as though I was the other woman. We were never the same after that." Perhaps it's the extended silence, or the dreams, or Ray's proximity that prompt me to speak out.

Breaking the silence after a few moments, he confesses, "I didn't know I loved you. I'm sorry, I didn't know I loved you."

That's an honest answer, but a jolt to me. All this time that I've had trouble believing I am in the right place at the right time, there was something to my confusion after all. This is probably the most honesty we have spoken in the past several months, but I'm shocked, and can't continue much further. It's too painful to think that he lied to me and that she was there because he had arranged it, not as he had described. I can't articulate my feelings, and he can't stand my silence, so we stop there. I go for a walk through the neighborhood all the way down to the water.

It's been three weeks since my last conversation with Holden. I've been thinking we "should" take the time to do counseling, but these are just thoughts that weigh heavily in my mind, and I don't have the will or the desire to follow through. We discussed it months ago, but nothing came of it. Finally, we are calling a halt at an odd place in our relationship, but the lack of communication makes it unbearable. I've moved into a room at work, and I haven't said anything about Ray's waiting in the wings.

This afternoon while I'm in my office, I hear the diesel engine long before I hear the sound of tires running over the gravel in the parking lot. I turn my head from my work and see the blue Mercedes pulling in. It's inconvenient to have to deal with a discussion of whether I should return home. My stomach tightens as I see Holden coming toward my office. He knocks, and I open the door. He hands me an envelope. He isn't communicative, so why would it be different? I'm glad to not have to say what's happening for me or answer questions of any sort. Things have gotten more complicated with Ray, and I don't feel like investing my emotions in pretending I'm interested in saving the marriage.

Opening the envelope, I pull out a stack of papers. I note that he put his name as the plaintiff and left the rest for me to fill out. I remember his last words to me, "I didn't know I loved you." The punch of rejection: divorce papers in front of me. Maybe he wants to be the first to say it. I'm puzzled why there's been no effort on his part to reach out. I feel like I've been kicked in the stomach, but he won't get any reaction from me either, no show of pain or angst. He's right, I conclude, why go through the motions? Better to spare us the trouble and sever the strings now, rather than after dragging each other through months of bickering and arguing in front of a marriage counselor.

I haven't had the stamina to get a program off the ground for recovering teens here at Mahalo House. I feel very lonely reaching out to people in a community where I am a stranger. I don't have anyone to discuss outreach with, and it progresses slowly.

Perhaps I can get out of having to face these emotions with another opportunity that has surfaced. There's nothing here to hold me back, and I haven't been happy anyway. Grandmother believes that people come here to heal. When the healing is done, they've accomplished what they came for. She thinks I'm getting ready to leave. I would miss her and the family, but maybe it is time to go home.

Departure

News has just broken that San Francisco has been hit with a huge earthquake and that the second level of I-580 collapsed. A few of the treatment center residents (and former residents) are from California. We gather in the large conference room for processing, and this time Ray, being the director, decides that people are feeling unsettled with the news and that we will have a native ceremony to allay people's worries and concerns and to pray for the people of San Francisco.

It's nine o'clock in the morning, it's overcast, and people are trickling into the room in twos and threes, dressed casually in jeans and T-shirts and sandals. A few Native Hawaiians, Caucasians. Even though it is overcast, the weather is comfortably warm, and the sun may come out later in the day. There is no table in this room, just large fluffy navy blue pillows around the floor, and we begin by standing together and joining hands. A drummer beats the drum softly, as though imitating a heartbeat. After a few minutes, Ray begins by saluting the four directions, starting by thanking the sun to the east. "Father sun, for the light that illuminates our path and gives us life." I am standing in the position of the south. When he stands in front of me, I get an internal nudge, and a woman begins to speak to me from within. I can't imagine who she may be, but I see her in my mind's eye, and with a wave of her hand, she makes it plain that she is his grandmother, and says to me, "I want you to take care of Ray." Now, I believe in the ancestors, and I believe they can communicate with us mortals, but I'm not sure I agree with her having the right to direct my affairs. After he has given thanks in all directions, he begins his prayer for the day—for the people present, for those distressed in San Francisco, and for those in early recovery.

For people newly in recovery, this is a welcome opportunity to admit their powerlessness and surrender or call on their higher power to begin their day with the strength and the power to carry out God's will for them. It's my first time in this larger group, but others seem to be familiar with the order of the program. There are two circles, owing to the number of people that have arrived. I am on the outer circle.

The drumming continues, and a woman speaks, "Kai and I are having problems, and he's back to drinking this morning." Someone else leads a prayer for the couple. "Spirit, guide Shana, bless Kai, and show them the way. May they walk the road in peace." Others say their prayers aloud, and this continues until there is only silence, other than the drum. About forty-five minutes later, we sit down on the pillows and do some reading from *The Big Book* of Alcoholics Anonymous. After that, people begin to share. It's noon when the meeting is concluded. Thrown off by the message I received from Ray's grandmother, I can't wait to speak with Grandmother to see what she thinks.

After the meeting, I stop by Ray's office to comment on the events of the morning, and he invites me to go out for lunch outside the compound, which is a rarity in itself. Staff always eats together. We stop in Paia to pick up some sandwiches at the new deli and head for Baby Beach. I'm dressed casually, but still in business attire—beige slacks and shoes and a smooth blue cotton blouse. We find a table at the far end of the park and sit down to eat. I look around under the shade of palm trees, and notice it's such a pleasant and beautiful beach.

"Well, so what have you decided? Are you coming or not?" He's referring to his invitation to leave the islands with him. I wasn't aware that he had asked me previously, unless his telling me that he was leaving on the sixteenth, which wasn't far off, was his invitation. It wasn't his romantic side that appealed to me, but because he was playful and jovial.

"Tell me about your grandmother," I ask.

"Why do you ask?" he answers.

So I tell him about the message I received.

"That's interesting," he said. "I was sorting through pictures last night, and I set hers aside, to have her blessing."

"This is so sudden," I think aloud. "What if it doesn't work out?"

"We'll be civil about it. I won't try to hold you back. If it works out, we'll see what's next."

"It seems so easy. Jump on a plane together, no strings attached. Okay, let's try it."

It is that straightforward, and even as I write, I can't believe I would be so offhand about my life with Holden and leaving without him. His serving the divorce papers without consulting with me seemed like an aggressive act on his part. But who knows what's fair? It ends with a lack of clarity just as it began with a lie.

I call Grandmother to give her the lowdown on my life, and she pauses for a moment. "I really don't trust him." I remember about his grandmother's words to me, and mention this to her. "Hm. I wonder why he needs protection," she muses aloud.

"Is this unusual?" I ask.

"Yes, of course, but we'll just have to wait and see why she is speaking on his behalf."

I call Holden to let him know I'm picking up the rest of my clothes and leaving everything else behind. I will take some books, but only a handful. Before coming to Hawaii, I gave a sizeable number away. It hurts me to think I'll be leaving my LPs that I've collected for many years. The *Brandenburg Concertos*, Mozart, a piano jazz collection, Hampton Hawes, Chick Correa. I even have Mendes and Brazil '66. I hate to think I'll leave behind my writing. I know he doesn't want it, but I have a couple drawers' full of papers and short stories, mostly papers from Cal Berkeley and San Francisco State University. I'll be at the house when he's out. That's when I have access to the Mahalo van, though I'm sure it's not to be used for that purpose.

Holden gave me a baby white cockatiel for my birthday a year ago. I named her Pinky for her huge pink cheeks. I hand-fed her the first three weeks, getting up during the night. She ate every three hours. She thinks I am her mother and follows me wherever I go. I dread the thought of having to leave her. I brought her to Mahalo House, but I don't feel comfortable with having her here. People come and go through the building. I'm afraid someone will release her, and she isn't used to being in the wild. So I am taking her back to the house.

I walk into the house for the first time in several weeks. The last time I was here was to pick up my clothes when I moved to the office. The silence is noticeable. I feel as though I'm in a morgue. I take Pinky back and put her cage in her old place. All the sadness of leaving the marriage and Hawaii are concentrated on her, but I ignore the feelings and set about quickly gathering my things as though I am running away from home. In some respects, I suppose I am doing that. I haven't mentioned to Holden that Ray and I are leaving together.

Things seem to be happening so quickly, that I haven't had time to digest the changes. Ray had made plans to leave before we got together, and we came together because his impending departure broke down the boundaries between us more quickly than would have otherwise happened. For now, that's all I can do. He's coming out of a relationship. I don't know why his ended, any more than he knows what happened between Holden and me.

I am leaving some nice pieces of furniture, a couple of antique tables, but I can't think about that now. I hear Pinky wanting my attention and wanting me to come and pick her up, but I can't bear to look in her direction now. I'm just going through collecting belongings I need or want to keep. I have Diana Marto's *Ancestral Mountain*, which I haven't had framed yet, but definitely don't want to leave behind. It doesn't take much to collect my personal belongings—most of it was done when I moved a few weeks ago.

Pinky's chirps are more insistent, as though she knows something I haven't advised her of. I leave, shutting the door quickly and quietly. I can still hear her when I reach the driveway and get into the van. I take one last look at the house and drive down the driveway back to Hana Highway.

In the weeks that follow, Ray and I intermingle our worldly goods into shipping boxes and have another round of deciding what goes and what will remain behind. This time, I part with my papers from Cal and SF State. My living quarters are rather rustic, and it becomes more convenient to stay at his apartment, since there are just two more weeks left before leaving.

Most of the packing is being done in my room. I have about six large boxes, so Ray tells me he will take them to the post office in Paia and send them to his daughter's in Texas, where we will be stopping for a short visit.

"Shall I go with you? There are quite a few boxes for just one person," I offer.

"No, no, I can manage. I can ask one of the guys to come with me," he adds. So I go back to my office and watch them load the jeep and drive off.

Three, four hours go by. Finally, I think this unusual, and I get into my orange VW bug and drive down to the post office. There is no sign of them. I think they must have stopped at the nearby coffeehouse. They aren't there either. Puzzled, I return to the office.

Two hours later, they come back. By then, I'm thinking something is fishy. "What happened?" I ask in an indifferent tone of voice, if such a voice exists in these circumstances.

"Oh, the clerk said we had to tape the boxes better, so we went to look for some tape." Now, I am not about to push the issue, but this sounds fabricated to me. I let it go and stop thinking about it.

I submit my resignation addressed to Mr. Ray Becker, as he requested, and give the date of my last day of service. The remaining couple of weeks pass quickly in an atmosphere of slowing down—an almost vacation-like approach to the job, going to different restaurants, and enjoying relaxed tropical evenings.

Holden traveled with his business, and experience conditioned him toward being efficient and organized. Packing was done early. The day of travel was not exactly relaxed, but definitely not rushed, with time at the airport to buy a magazine or lunch or a cup of coffee before boarding. I am pleasantly surprised to see that Ray has the same approach to travel: tickets purchased with plenty of time, bags set out the night before. I am just amazed at his efficiency and control of the situation. We are flying from Kahului to Honolulu, and from there to Los Angeles.

"We have a reservation at the Hyatt. I got some tickets for the cultural museum in the morning," he tells me.

"We're staying at the Hyatt in Honolulu?" I ask. I didn't think of staying a night in Honolulu and going to the museum before our flight at 1:00 p.m., but Ray did. I am highly impressed and feel well cared for. I can easily get used to this.

"It's so sweet of you. Thank you. It's very thoughtful of you to think of this." I swoon.

We arrive at the hotel and leave our bags in the room to explore Honolulu by foot. The beach is only a block away. I want to walk along the water.

We stop at Aki-no-No, a Japanese family-owned diner on King Street, and I order what I always order, donburi.

Returning to the hotel room, I admire the "His" and "Hers" luxurious bathrobes and run a hot bath. Ray is making some phone calls to the mainland, and I scan the radio dial for music and catch a classical radio program playing Brahms, which I listen to as I lean back into the water. As I luxuriate in the warm, soothing bathwater, I think on all the blessings I have and what an elegant lady I am.

Ray has been talking and joking on the phone. But I notice that his voice has become quiet and subdued, and this catches my attention instantly. When you hear racket and laughter, and suddenly there is quiet and whispers, something feels amiss. I get curious and my ears stand at attention. I notice, but I'm not alarmed. I hear a soft chuckle, and that gets my attention. I get out of the water and put on my elegant robe and come out into the room. Whispering, I ask, "Who's on the other end? Are you talking to a woman?"

In a most unfriendly expression, he retorts, covering the phone, "Yes, I am, and it's none of your business."

Hurt and confused, I turn back to continue my bath. My head is in a wild spin. He gets off the phone, and I demand from the bedroom, "What's going on, Ray?"

Still in a rough tone, he answers, "Hey, I have the right to my feelings. Quit being so nosey." He leaves the room and slams the door as he walks out.

While he's gone, I try to remember any hints of his feelings, and I remember the day he went to the post office and gave such a flimsy reason for taking four hours to find shipping tape.

I lie on the bed, staring up at the ceiling. *What are my options?* I ask myself. Eventually he comes back in a better mood, but I'm not sure I am willing to pick up the battle. I will have to wait until I've collected my things in Texas. In the meantime, I am going to enjoy the trip between here and there, and we shall see what happens next. Who but an idiot of a man does that in front of a woman?

California

After retrieving Ray's Jeep at Matson Lines, in Los Angeles, we venture out onto the open road. The ribbons of freeway and desert roads roll endlessly beneath the car. Ray's continued private telephone calls with his ex tend to keep me annoyed. I look back on Grandmother's warning that fell on deaf ears; the dream of the shot-off airplane is quite telling in that it points to a half-baked, half-cooked plan with no resolution, and, even worse, no happy ending. I had neglected looking at the material side of the dream. Ocelotl tried to warn me as well. I'd forgotten about the sawed-off airplane—all this is clear now.

The vastness of Arizona and New Mexico stretches out like a movie in slow motion, without any side excursions to Anasazi pueblo sites or places like Canyon De Chelly or others of historical interest. It's fascinating to note that migrations that took place more than a thousand years ago, where cultures settled selectively, are all aligned on the same meridian 108° south—Aztec ruins, Solomon sites, Chaco Canyon, and Casas Grandes in Mexico. I would have loved to see these sights, places now mostly famous for their continuous pottery traditions. It isn't possible so as to preclude the appearance of taking a vacation between the islands and our final destination, be it Texas or Oklahoma, Ray's home state and where his brother currently lives.

Texas

Arriving in Texas, where Ray's daughter Maysie lives, the weather is cold, the sky a pervasive, thick, heavy gray. I feel scattered as some of my pieces of art arrive weeks apart, and other personal belongings come through the mail. I can't remember feeling as ungrounded as I do this moment.

Oklahoma

We travel on to Oklahoma City, and we settle into a one-bedroom, ground-floor apartment with a small patio. The area is pleasant, but I am feeling like I have one foot tethered to a post while trying to navigate with the other. I get a part-time job with a recovery program, but before I start, I bail out and leave for California.

California, Again

It hasn't taken long to realize I'm not leaving exactly as I promised myself to leave. In fact, I came back by myself, and Ray is joining me this weekend. Being among my people again, I feel the burden of being with someone when I actually want the freedom to make my own decisions.

I pick him up at the airport and pretend to be glad to see him, but it's over, and it won't be long now. He gave me a reasonable, tangible reason this afternoon when he proceeded to call old girlfriends and flirted with them the way he used to flirt with me—"Hi, pretty lady . . ." I see Grandmother's teasing eyes telling me, "I told . . ."

After a few days of seeing my family and friends, we settle in Sacramento. I have no idea why I am here—I know no one and have no job connections. But we've found an apartment in a complex with gardens, fountains, a swimming pool, and even a workout room with equipment.

I suppose he is as fed up with me as well. I stop engaging with him and have very little to say in the course of our conversations. The point comes when I give him the silent treatment that Holden gave me. It worked for him; it will have to work for me.

My excuse is that he began to behave like a dry drunk, talking stupidly on the phone with women and driving erratically this afternoon. While he is at an AA meeting, I call a friend in Hawaii and tell her what's happening. She suggests I head for a women's shelter.

"Brilliant idea," I say. I hang up and get the number for a women's shelter. I explain to the intake worker that I am traveling, away from family, and homeless, and she decides to take me in.

When the intern picks me up at a Shell gas station at ten fifteen at night, she tells me the shelter is just a couple of blocks away. I get to bed right away and am fast asleep before long. By morning, I get my bearings and call my friend Tara who lives in Novato, north of San Francisco, and she offers to pick me up in a couple of days. Tara is a nurse, has three kids, and has been divorced for a couple of years. I know her from the healing center, where she was a client several years ago. I end up renting a room from her for a few weeks.

I receive a letter sent to my brother's house from Ray; he says that this is his last if I don't respond. He encloses a color photo of himself. I hold it in my hand, thinking it over. I made my friends swear not to give out a phone number or address. I don't feel any bonds binding us together, and I throw the letter out. Would that be called getting even? I mean, all those times I had to strain my ears to listen to his hush-hush telephone calls! I just disappear without so much as a "thank you" for bringing me this far.

Getting Real

I've gotten into a pleasant routine. I return to the center for family support of people with life-threatening illness. I'm living with two women in a lovely Eichler home in San Rafael. The house, surrounded by several tall oak trees, is all glass in the back and is nestled into the hills. The owner of the house has a heart condition. She tells me about it over the phone, and being familiar with life-threatening illnesses, I agree to stay with her. I can handle this. My other roommate is an artist. I like the atmosphere of the home, and I am happy here.

A couple of weeks ago, my therapist Betsy suggested I start attending twelve-step meetings to explore my feelings toward relationships. After failure number three, I can't very well claim ignorance of my part in the crashes I keep having. I can see I am perching myself to find another partner. Two years of mourning and no dating ought to be enough. I am not an addict. I do need to interrupt the cycles of madness and find a peaceful way to live. How can anyone blame me when I was the abandoned one? How could I look critically at my family when we were the victims of a classist, racist society? I can fix myself on my own. Betsy can help me if she wants, but that is as far as I am willing to admit guilt. After the session, I go to a bookstore and find a book called *Looking for Love in all the Wrong Places*.

Today, I hold my book up proudly when I meet with Betsy. The book suggests that I need the highs—food, wine, sugar, romance, sex, or any kind of drama—to keep me going. I still say I can do it on my own, even though the book describes my dysfunctional behaviors squarely on my head. Looking at me patiently and quietly, she says, "No, Gracia, you've got to go to meetings and get involved in a program. You've got to humble yourself to something greater than yourself. You cannot be in charge. Your best thinking got you here."

"It's not like I'm a plane going down in flames," I retort.

"Well, what would you call it?" she asks demurely.

I look at the clock. It's time to stop. I write the check out in silence, hand it to her, and leave, muttering under my breath, "This is bullshit."

That was a couple of months ago. Yesterday I picked up the phone and inquired about a twelve step meeting, and then I called Betsy, my therapist, to make an appointment. Someone mentioned that sugar keeps her off balance, and she is going on a sugar-free diet.

I come directly home after the meeting, my head spinning and feeling overwhelmed. The first thing I do is go to the phone to see if I have any messages. Nothing. I rely on the flashing red light to tell me someone out there loves me. That's creepy. I come into the living room and sit down on the rocking chair. I rock myself to sleep. That's all I can manage. Incredible how one could need a little flashing light to affirm one's existence. All of a sudden, my life, it turns out, hasn't been so exciting, but merely a series of ill-thought-out reactions to my childhood pain.

Admitting Powerlessness

Betsy has been telling me to get a sponsor and start doing the steps. I'm not in any great hurry to start the steps. Who wants to admit she is "powerless"? That seems counterintuitive. I notice that any tiny bit of kindness from a man opens my heart and exposes a gaping wound. I feel so raw. I do need a guide through this process, but I can't imagine having to answer to someone for what I am doing and how I am doing it. In this program, one would consider that I have no boundaries and that this is what gets me into trouble. It is a good thing, I think, to set boundaries. I have none, when I really stop to think of it. I didn't have any with Holden when we started. I could have set limits to starting our relationship when he was having the woman from Spain coming over. I could have walked away. I could have taken any number of directions to keep my distance, but the thought didn't even cross my mind.

So how do I go about setting boundaries? The program suggests "setting bottom lines." This program isn't as easy as it looks. It seems so inflexible and dogmatic. On the other hand, my life is totally unmanageable, I am seeing that now. I am powerless over the wounding of abandonment, and I will do anything to end the loneliness and pain. Working the program gives me a sense of groundedness, a sense of self-respect. If I want integrity, I need to take the program seriously. That would be step one, shared with a sponsor and checking in to report my thoughts, feelings, and behaviors.

Learning to Say No

I'm ready to consider looking for a sponsor. There are some who are rigid about it—full disclosure, no secrets. "It's my way or the highway," they'll say. I can't stand those big egos. I can barely get myself out of bed in the morning, how will I please someone a hundred percent of the time? There are some people who cosponsor each other, so I am looking for just such a person. It might be like cheating. No pain, no gain. Maybe this will work for me. There's a woman who is open and honest about her process yet has a sense of humor, and she's been around the program for a couple of years. We're having lunch tomorrow.

I've been noticing a tall skinny man with a thick black mustache. He seems kind and gentle, but since I am new at this system of thought, I've kept my distance. I haven't been staring, one of my favorite bad habits. I've just kept to talking with women. But today, I'm not sure how it happened, we bumped into each other as the meeting was breaking up, and we talked a little. He said he liked my share. That was all of our conversation, as a guy came up to him and started talking. Since I've been allowing my vulnerability, anything will open the wound; anything will make me fall in love. On my way home, through the oak trees on Fifth Street in San Rafael only a few blocks away, I began to think about him. Nope, I said to myself, this ain't happenin'. I won't go back to that meeting. I looked up to the pretty blue sky and said a prayer, "Mother, if you want him in my life, you're going to have to bring him to me."

Saturday, I met with Rose, the woman I want to cosponsor with me. We decided to make some collages to get visual images of our feelings. She's been doing this a while, and she immediately went to the pain of her relationship with her mother. One image she chose was a woman with a stern face, long black hair pulled to the side of her face like a spray of water out of a fire hose. The woman was wearing a red dress, stretched out between her knees, and she had her hands on her hips, as though saying, "Don't mess with me, you . . ."

Mine were random pictures of shadowy figures and musicians in a dark smoky nightclub. Another picture was of a house turned upside down and floating in space.

I brought the collage with me to therapy. It turned out, that's how I feel about my brothers, people I can't really see; and the house, my lost home after my mother died. I seem to be looking for my family and the community that rejected me. As I contemplate on them now, I feel a heaviness settling around my heart; a dead silence. That gives me some perspective on what I've been doing. I'm not a kid anymore. I'm going toward fifty years, and I seem to be looking for a life most people find during their twenties or thirties.

Other Programs

I've decided to check out another program, food, to see if I can stem this need for sugar that seems to create havoc for me. My system can't tolerate sugar, yet I'm like an alcoholic that keeps ingesting wine despite the chaos of its results. It's hard for me to believe it's the sugar. I want to blame circumstances and justify my mood swings even when I see there seems to be a connection.

I went to a meeting where we talk about food and feelings. I keep trying to resist sugar, but I'm putty being around it. After listening at a few meetings, I am realizing that I seem to be starving myself to keep thin, and then lacking the resistance and binging on sugar to satisfy my hunger. I'm also keeping myself dehydrated because I forget to drink water. All this sounds like a form of self-punishment. I gathered my courage and shared honestly about the day-to-day pain I am in.

Also, Rose, my cosponsor in the relationships program, says that I could benefit from the money program as well. Now, that's going too far! I'll stop right here . . .

Higher Power

I haven't heard any great confessions from Rose, nor has she from me as part of our step five. I mentioned this in a meeting, and someone later said that "If you keep telling Higher Power what you want, when you want it, how you want it, and where, it is going to assume you know what you need and want." Some people can be truly annoying. When I heard this guy's remarks, I had to admit something rang true, but clarity took a while.

I did go to the money program, and I've been learning about taking better care of my money. I'm no longer broke three days after payday, scrounging around for pennies when I have an unexpected expense. Things have changed considerably in that department. I even have money in a savings account—now, that's unheard of for me!

Rose has her own qualms with God. She believes in spirit, but the god of her childhood was too exclusive and restricting. The same is true for me. Nevertheless, I have to admit that we are only doing the steps half-assed. So I've been looking for someone who is a little more traditional. We'll see if I can have the best of both worlds.

My understanding of "surrender," though I may not always practice it (I include "Thy will, not mine" and "Thank you for directing my thoughts, words, and actions" in my prayers, which I write out every morning) is to take care of the actions and things I need to do, and let the results be what they will be. That's hard to do because I still have my own notions of perfection, and I am nowhere near it. So I am willing to try another way.

So what is Higher Power? Is it an entity that watches what I do and decides, "Okay, she's behaving, let her have what she wants"? Is it listening to me? If I turn around and face it, will it be there? Gradually, my thinking has changed. I'm less compulsive about things, I'm not as ruled by the outside as I once was. I try to stay out of harm's way. So there are many ways in which I have changed.

Higher Power has become a relationship within that I listen for—that "still small voice" that whispers when I focus and still my own mind. Its wisdom comes to me as though through the ages, like from a distant star, and then appears in its fullness. It guides me silently, yet it is ever present.

In my rational mind, it is the gravity that holds everything in the multiverse in place, whether a moving planet, a star, a galaxy, a flower in my garden, a bird in the tree outside or within the cells of my blood and marrow. It lives within my ancestors. It is self-intelligent and duplicates itself to keep everything within the universe alive and vibrant. It resides within a painting or musical note, and is the power that guides my hand in my writing.

Higher Power is my personal guardian angel that cares deeply; the spirit and soul that courses through the veins in the cells of my blood. There is nothing it does not know about me; it protects and provides my smallest need. It is my first and primary relationship before my mother, father, brothers or friends. It loves and adores me. My relationship with it is perfect.

Elsa's Death

Recently Elsa, my roommate, applied for a heart transplant. Her diagnosis has been something that is hardening her heart. Her parents were survivors of the Holocaust. She looks about six months pregnant, but these are signs of her liver and kidneys failing. Yesterday afternoon, she got word that the team of doctors determining her fate turned down her request.

Yesterday, I went with her to a doctor's previously scheduled appointment for a second opinion or method of treatment. He read the medical reports and examined the lab results. We waited quietly to hear his decision. I held her hand as she cried when she heard confirmation of the other doctors' conclusion. There was nothing to be done.

This morning, Elsa reported a dream to me that appears to indicate a major change. She is happy and smiling as she describes it.

> *"I'm in the basement of the home I grew up in. Water is coming in and rising quickly. At first, it frightens me, and I am trying to get out. Something shifts in me, and it's okay. It's as though I surrender to it."*

Something about the dream seems to be comforting to her, and she appears to accept the outcome. The signs point toward allowing death to come, and I think she also knows that. The deluge of bad news hangs heavy in the air, but I just smile at her, and she walks down the hall toward her bedroom. I'm not sure if I made the right decision to remain silent about it.

When I return from work in the early evening, I see a note. "Elsa is at Kaiser Hospital." I eat dinner and run out the door to visit her. Apparently, her kidneys are failing. Her daughter is with her, and I stay for about a half hour. I think of her dream and promptly dismiss it.

It's nine o'clock when I reach home again. Linda, my other roommate, has just come home from work. We talk about Elsa's condition, and she leaves for the hospital a few minutes later. Shortly after midnight, Elsa's daughter calls on the telephone and tells us that Elsa's heart has stopped, and no emergency treatment is able to bring her back.

The courage I had at the beginning of my meeting Elsa is gone. Grief is cumulative, and all the sadness from all the losses I've ever had have found their place in me, and I fall in. I'm completely overcome with sadness.

A couple of months later, Elsa's house, where her other roommate and I lived for the past eight months, was put up for sale by her children.

Another Home

My dreams are changing, and I am noticing that wanting and needing love is a matter for other realms. Loving something greater than myself is different than saying, "I want this here and now." These dreams are beginning to shape areas of my life, to contribute to my being able to trust myself, and to enable me to appreciate these gifts. As they shape my experience, I've given up trying to control the messages they convey, and surrender to eddies and turns in the river of life.

Keeping in mind that I am still an addict, if a guy gives me a piece of See's Candies, I want to bake a chocolate cake out of it. The insatiable need for love lurks just below the surface, and it's only through the grace of heaven that I am tending to business, going to work, going to meetings, and keeping a neat house. I want to read into these dreams what I want, but there is a broader picture at work, and I have to stay open, not to what I want, but to what spirit wants for me.

I found a job in San Mateo as a social worker, coordinating group homes for youth, about twenty miles south of San Francisco. This job offer necessitated my moving from Marin County, just north of the Golden Gate Bridge, to San Francisco. The pay wasn't generous, but it got my foot in the door for something better later. A friend from the center where I volunteer as a facilitator had a room for rent in his house in San Francisco, which I decided to take. I had no idea how long I would stay in this in-between state, but the job decided for me, when cutbacks were made in the organization twelve months into the position.

The Light within Dream

I come upon a house that's been renovated and painted from basement to attic. The walls are painted entirely white, and the house is empty, ready for the next occupants. I check the doorknob and find that the house is unlocked, and I walk in. I notice that the railings of the stairs going to the bedrooms on the second floor are smooth and spotless. It's a charming old house with lots of windows to let in sunlight; the floors are a light maple, the windows sparkly, and there is light filtering through the windows, ushering in a lovely feeling of peace and serenity. I take the first step toward the second floor and breathe in a delightful essence that seems to be light—not light from a lamp or man-made source, but a graceful, soft, inviting ray that comes from above, perhaps from an alcove or maybe even the attic. It is love, and I want to rush up and wrap my arms around it. Through the dream, I wonder if this is addiction playing a trick on me—that I've found love, but will awaken in the morning empty-handed. It doesn't matter; the expectation will suffice, and my needs will be met regardless. I realize this is the home that has been waiting for me and where I belong. This is home. I belong here.

Yes, I have found a new home in Marin County again after being away for over two years. It's a lovely one-room cottage with barely a tiny space I call the kitchen, right on the edge of a creek that runs directly under the cottage in Fairfax. It's painted white, but it does not have a second floor with lovely light filtering down from a loving higher source. But it's mine, and I adore it. The sun comes into it in the mornings. A forest preserve runs along one side and gives the illusion of being in a secluded world, while on the other side, just a block away, is a cinema and a row of restaurants, coffee houses, bars, and breakfast spots. Other houses on the block-long street are 1940s wooden-frame houses, charming with quaint rose gardens. But returning to the dream, there is a luminosity that cannot be described in earthly terms. Now, in the past, I may have insisted that the loving presence was a foretelling of something good to come, a special enduring relationship, and that may be so, but the message for me today is that there is a measure of peace that I am attaining that was not there in the past. I'll hang my hat on that without further embellishment.

Today at the center, where I continue to facilitate a support group for loved ones with life-threatening illnesses, a new member attended who felt vaguely familiar. He was there because his brother has cancer and is close to dying. His name is Robert.

Eleanor Barron Druckrey, Ph.D.

Pathways on Mother Earth Dream

I'm discovering new emotions within, a sense of trust that I am not in this world as a solitary molecule lost and adrift, but rather as a part of something greater than myself—a being in community, a participant in a larger drama than the one I've created out of my experiences of being alone and the fear that this loneliness will endure forever.

> *Other couples join in time to the music as my husband and I lead the dance off with a two-step. I pick up the beat easily and glide around the floor as free and light as a feather. I love that about dancing—the sense of freedom and the way the music feels flowing through my being.*
>
> *We leave the dance floor for fresh air and to survey the expansiveness of the land. I have a sense that the community we are in has a commitment to consciousness to decide together what, where, and how crops will be planted. Everything is thought out in detail so that the food supply is carefully stored and replenished when the current one is exhausted.*
>
> *I notice that there are huge houses sprinkled throughout the farmland and surmise that these are solar houses used to grow special vegetables and fruits that could grow abundantly in controlled environments.*
>
> *I hear the newscaster Walter Cronkite announcing the weather report, predicting heavy rains and that some of the roads will be closed during the heavier rainy season. A governmental inspector comes onscreen and advises taking only certain roads because "these particular roads run along the longitudinal lines of the world." I look in the direction of the roads and see that threads of energy run parallel to each other on both sides. Apparently, these lines are strong currents that keep the flow of humanity running smoothly; they have the power of healing so that all organisms, trees, crops, rivers, and oceans, if between the lines, align themselves spiritually as well as on a cellular level.*

This dream, the celebration in the dance hall, the "fresh air," the "expansiveness of the land," and the "sense of community" speaks to me of harmony, spring showers, and renewal. Wouldn't it be lovely if we could all get along and forget about borders between countries, between yours and mine, and just allow surplus to be decided by need? What's mine is yours, what's yours is mine—the perfect marriage throughout the world.

As always, dreams offer the opportunity to create change within the dreamer; this is an opportunity for me to delve into the ways that I fail to set the boundaries in my life. Is it possible for me to be generous with myself and offer a safe haven in the community? This dream defines the difference between service and giving to get something in return, i.e., the difference between generosity and greed.

What I take the longitudinal lines to be are what I consider power as it flows through the human body, the power that comes from the earth, gravity, and magnetic fields that hold the world and its inhabitants together and give shape and form to all life on earth and throughout the universe.

The Beloved Dream

My beautiful Beloved and I fly parallel to the shore high above San Francisco like Lois Lane and Superman. The sun shines brightly, and we can see the sparkle of sunlight dancing on the bay. As though we're at an Arthur Murray Dance Studio, we're waltzing with freedom and lightheartedness, holding hands, flying to higher levels, and swooping down and laughing, like two children in love.

Feeling the safety of his protection with his arm around my waist, I turn and see a group of monks in brown robes coming toward us with lit candles. Their unexpected appearance startles me, and suddenly, I become aware of my back resting on the mattress. I wish to recapture the bubbly, happy sensations and am curious about the message the monks are bringing.

This feels like a double-edged message. On the one hand, the divine is prominent in this dream; and in the flying, I experience feelings of exquisite beauty. The sunlight dancing on the waves of the bay is another indication of love and beauty. In the past, I would have attributed these feelings to the security of an earthly being, but now I know that the beauty within is the message. On the other hand, not getting carried into fantasy is crucial.

"Still crazy after all these years," the lyrics to the Simon and Garfunkel song are on my mind this morning. I've been talking to Robert, the new member of the support group who, it turns out, is the same person I prayed to the Mother to send to me if she felt it should be so when I walked away from the other meeting a few years ago.

The Wedding Gift

I feel uncomfortable when I receive the feelings inherent in this dream. They are light and airy. I could easily get lost in the feelings of love, but there is something deeper that these dreams are attempting to demonstrate for me—a necessity of grounding. As I've seen in the recovery programs, addiction can be cunning and baffling. I would rather explore the deeper feelings that are being revealed.

> *I spread a sheet of tissue paper over the dining room table and run my fingertips over its smoothness. I study closely the inlayed 14k gold swirls, feeling their richness. Patsy R., a materially wealthy friend, is remarrying after the death of her husband. She had the special tissue paper made for wrapping gifts that she is giving to her friends. Each one is individually painted with ink from a silk paintbrush.*
>
> *I admire the paper and watch her use it generously for a gift that she is putting into a small gold box. I haven't seen the gift, but the generosity with which she uses this exquisite paper makes me think of delicate crystal.*

At some point, the gift must be received and recognized. The gift is the soul, a celebration of the awakening and marriage with the divine at last. It gets tricky to not fall into the trap and go off into fantasy.

Vestido de Novia Dream (The Wedding Gown Dream)

I experience a sense of fear when I begin diving deeper into awareness, like a vibration that is calling my attention. What is this blackness that has been labeled "evil"? Am I willing to plunge into it to discover its true value? The following dream sets the stage that begins to redefine what the feminine and Coyolxauhqui mean to me. It's time to examine and trust the answers I get.

Preparations for the wedding are stopped midstream. We've both gotten cold feet, so we mutually agree that going our separate ways is for the better. The moment the decision is made, we both recognize the insanity of the separation and that we really do want to be united in marriage

Nothing is said, however. Some people know that we have broken up, but others are still planning and assuming that all is well. Even between us, there isn't a clear statement of ending or committing. I venture to say something like "When we're married" to him to indicate that I am still committed and that I will proceed with the wedding preparations.

His mother is one of the people that just ignores our drama and continues to plan for the day. She goes shopping for my wedding dress and returns excitedly with a beautiful white box.

"Try it on," she says, handing me the box.

I open it and feel the smoothness of the expensive silk. I run my fingers over it, such smoothness it sends me into ecstasy. It leaves me breathless.

I wash my hands to avoid spoiling the dress. I undress and slip into it gently, slowly fitting myself into the skirt through the back zipper, and then my arms through the trim long sleeves to try it on and look at myself in the full-length mirror on the wall. I turn around to check out the view from all angles. It is a beautiful tea-length sheath that looks stunning on me.

The beauty of the dress and the fact that it looks tailor-made for me convinces me enough that I should, indeed, be married in this beautiful garment. It's simple yet elegant. The more I gaze at it, the more I realize its magnificence—a dress that commands awareness of the divine feminine. By shutting my physical eyes and opening to the inner stillness, I come into the wonder of silence and depth.

"Mother, it's black," I comment, puzzled at her radical departure from tradition. "A black wedding dress," I repeat, still dazzled, not only by its beauty, but also for its symbol of the feminine and wisdom. "Wouldn't something lighter be more appropriate?" I ask, still attempting to diminish the immensity of the gift. As I ask the question, night falls, and I begin to stretch my arms in the direction to which I am being carried. I am floating in space in awe of the magnificence of creation. Yes, this is where I am going, I marvel. I am carried gently, gently toward the feminine, a depth and richness of knowing I've never before witnessed. This is the gift I've waited for.

The wedding is only a month away, and I make up my mind in that instant. Without a doubt, this dress has impressed upon me that full commitment is a necessity. The Mother awaits my surrender. Life without her is certain obliteration.

The black wedding gown calls me to abide in the wisdom; to avail myself of the magnificent power inherent in the dark spaces of the universe—the power of the motion of the Milky Way, extending its fingers; the wisdom of the moon when it is in its dark phases; the spaces of seeming emptiness that are instruments to bring us back to the one consciousness, of which all of us are a part. There is no emptiness. Darkness defines power. I am hers.

A Test, Dream

Dreams will always turn things upside down, move events forward, move them back, and foretell them. This dream comes at the time of my twenty-fifth wedding anniversary. I still wobble from spiritual/emotional insecurity, but I have learned that there is only one true love, the divine, who never fails me. Yet there is still an important lesson to be learned.

I am on my way to work, carrying a basket I have woven. People are celebrating a couple's twenty-fifth wedding anniversary with a formal dinner and entertainment provided by my employees. The basket is a gift from me to them. I see that my husband will be there because his navy blue 2002 Toyota Corolla is in the parking lot. I feel extremely uneasy facing him since he has been absent from home for a few days, which might indicate that he wants out of the marriage. I have all the signs of heartbreak—palpitations and knot in my throat—even though I have not heard directly from his lips that he's leaving me. My feet are heavy and barely able to move, and everything in my body is resisting going to the party. So I look for a smaller group of people. I find the bookkeeper busily at work with a donor, which is far less inviting than any party.

When I walk toward the gathering, I hear the beautiful sound of a flute, rich and full yet ever so sensuous and soft. I realize Robert is the musician—I did not know about this side of him. When I walk into the room, I see that a young woman in a soft blue silk sari is dancing and has attracted the attention of the group, which has formed a circle around her and Robert. I have only a quick glance of her, but notice that she has an air of young innocence and sweetness reflected in her small delicate features, lovely pink lips, dark sparkling eyes, and dark hair down to her waist. She's not even into her twenties. The waft of her hands, hips, and feet are as graceful as a tropical breeze.

> *She looks divinely happy. It's obvious she's in love with him and they are on intimate terms, for how else could they have rehearsed this performance with such sensitivity and sensuality?*
>
> *My hackles are up, a dark rage surfaces and induces me to break up the party and expose this affair. To hell with what people think or say of me. To hell with appearances of tight coupleship. I get ready to pound on the nearest wooden tabletop to flip it over. My head is hot and I want blood. Just as instantly, I stop. That's not really what I want. If he's left me, I can still have my dignity. I feel the cold knife of betrayal slitting my chest, but why be the fool? I hold myself back.*
>
> *Other people have joined in and are dancing to the music. I see this was no planned feature at all, but simply a spontaneous response to sway and feel the smooth celestial flow of the wind. There is no intrigue—just my mind playing games with me. No one seems to be aware of my quandary, and I don't seem to have anything to say anyway. I come up to Elena Romano who is sitting at one of the large round tables, put my tulle basket down, and whisper in her ear that I am stepping out momentarily. "Al ratito vuelvo," I tell her. So I leave quietly through the same crowded areas I came through. Once outside, my composure returns—the fear passes, and I stand composed on solid ground. Feeling revitalized, and with great relief, I return to the celebration. Upon reentering the group, it hits me—this party is for Robert and me! He continues to be my husband as he ever has been. Then, I see the truth of this dream: I allowed fear to separate me from the divine. How easily I forgot; how easily I stepped away.*

Ah, what fear of abandonment will convince me to believe. I would believe nasty things about myself: I'm easily forgotten; I'm not worthy of commitment and fidelity. How easily I will sell my soul as dust in the wind. I would weaken my connection with the Mother. Fear, a familiar companion, will destroy me; will destroy my beauty, and leave me in hell. I have no hope if this hideous disease that destroys the container of life consumes me; it destroys my trust in the hand that is eternally extended to me, ready to lift me out of despair. How can I go on without my skin to hold me together? How can I wander with my veins and muscles decaying, hopeless and afloat without faith? These are the questions the dream invites me to ask, yet reaffirms my faith in what is real and true. In resisting the temptation to be angry. I have triumphed over fear. I've made a choice. It's been a long, slow, and hard journey.

Let's not overlook that the musician is my earthly husband, who has cherished me, and I him, for twenty-five years now. That the prayer I spoke softly reached the Mother's ears and brought him to me.

As I reflect on the legends of Coyolxauhqui, I see that she represents faith in the dark moments of life. The presence of fear (and thereby, being in the dark) is an indication that I have stepped away from the divine and lost faith. Coyolxauhqui is the reminder that when I have "forgotten" about her, she is still with me. I am never alone, she is always with me.

The Dalai Lama Dream

Here is a dream in which responsibility for "remembering" is placed squarely on my shoulders. The Dalai Lama tells me he has had a dream of me, and proceeds to engage me in the unraveling of sacred tools and tasks that will take me into committing to truth.

I am on retreat in the woods behind Christ the Victor Lutheran Church on Sir Francis Drake outside Fairfax, California. I'm orienting myself to the people, but generally, there is silence. We've gone further into the woods, and the Dalai Lama has joined us and is leading us in meditation. He arrives with an armful of yarn for a large blanket he is weaving, and sits down on the ground near me. Other women are sitting nearby. He says to me, "I had a dream of you."

He puts the large bundle of yarn on the ground, and I move closer to him. I ask, "Please tell me about it." The women, and there seems to be only women, make a semicircle behind us, and I invite them to join us because I want them to hear the dream. "This dream belongs to everybody," I say, for all to hear. The Dalai Lama is concentrating on the yarn, so we all gather around him. My dream sister Yana is there.

The yarn is not just a pile of wool; he's been praying and using it in ritual for a long time. It has meaning, and he is now ready to take the blessing to another level. "Help me do this," he says. "Pull the string that will reveal the wisdom." It looks like a huge ball of mixed-up yarn in bright shimmering reds, browns, blues, and greens, but he encourages me to trust myself, and I begin to pull on a bright yellow cord. The ball is getting tighter, and it looks like I'm just making it worse, but he sticks his finger into a loop as I keep pulling slowly. Eventually, it becomes obvious that this was the right cord to pull, and the ball of yarn unravels into a visible design of an elongated, stylized cross or ankh for the blanket or shawl which will be woven and used only for meditation and ritual. Its function keeps shifting as thoughts float through my mind and attempt to determine what's happening. In one instant, I feel the immensity of the universe, in the next, the grandeur of our spirit. Attempting to pin down one thought or feeling is pointless because the message is beyond human comprehension. For the time being, we will have to just sit in awe of the profound beauty and immense implications of what we are experiencing. What we witness is beyond human comprehension; amazement at the transformation of what seemed to be commonplace is now neatly laid out in solemn order of dazzling color, light, vibration, and unfathomable wonder and veneration.

It's time to pick up camp, and I am going around gathering things that have been brought for the retreat. I put back items that belong to the retreat center. It's night, and I am walking around the campgrounds in meditation, wearing my white thermals. Ocelotl appears and, with a nod, leads me to a path. I follow him away from the campground and end up in a kitchen in the woods, a peaceful, serene, quiet spot where the women are at work. Long spoons and forks are hung neatly on metal hooks and have the appearance of bright, shiny pink metal piglet baskets that make me chuckle. I walk slowly toward a large boulder and sit down, not quite in a daze, but in meditation. Jamie, an Asian woman I just met, looks intently at my face as though puzzled by what she is seeing. Still looking at me with her forehead wrinkled, she says in a voice meant for the women in the kitchen to hear, "Gracia is in Samadhi." I grasp what she is saying, yet conclude that if she is right, it must be the future she is seeing.

What needs to be unraveled? If the ankh is turned on its back, it reminds me of the Milky Way in another stage of forming. The ball of yarn symbolizes the ego, which needs undoing, unraveling—no small feat. The Dalai Lama has given me the key to step beyond duality and into the Mother's arms. When I awake, I am in awe of the gift I've received, a new way of being in my body and feeling the peace and serenity I've been seeking. I have received the gift of meditation. Yet I do not work alone, and I am ever grateful for that truth; I continue to be surrounded and guided by my earthly mother and father's spirits, the ancestors, and the Goddess.

Then, as though hit by a lightning bolt, I remember Ocelotl's promise, "I will give you a dream when you are ready." This is the dream—to awaken, to dream with my eyes open. The ancestors have been orchestrating this all along! A promise from more than thirty years ago has come to pass. At long last, the full moon shines into my life, and I can awaken to the reality that awareness is my one true hope.

In the following dream, I am shown the power of the sacred Dark Goddess and its availability for stepping beyond duality.

The Sacred Dark Feminine

The temple is deserted when I walk in and sit down midway to the altar. A dim glow as soft as the full moon shows the slight outline of engravings on two heavy large stone tablets in the background of the stone platform. As my eyes adjust to the dimness, I see hieroglyphics that I can't read. I wonder what the message might be. I hear a voice from behind commanding, "Stretch your consciousness." I turn my head to see who is speaking, but I am alone in the temple. I imagine what "Stretch your consciousness means," and manage to create a small circle of awareness around me just slightly beyond my body.

"No, little one, ¡Héchele ganas!"

I expand my consciousness a second time. I hear an explosion—the roof blows off, the walls crumble, and the floor blasts out from under me. I'm traveling in the Milky Way toward the center of the sun and past the stars. The rubble of what had been the little dot of my personal space disintegrates into millions of specks and creates a thick cloud of dust around me that quickly settles. Everything dissolves, including myself. I drift blissfully in the vast silence of pure, dark energy.

Chapter Three

La Curandera: Hearing Coyolxauhqui's Call

Coyolxauhqui Speaks

Pierce my heart;
Lean your ear against my lips, and listen carefully.
I will tell you all you need to know for your travels through time and space.
I will take you to that point beyond duality.
I am subtle, and though I speak plainly, this message for you is also written on the far side of the moon when I am in the dark and I draw closer and cover you with my protective cloak,
for it is only in the dark that you will see the light within.
Listen to me and know that I speak to you, and you alone.
Set aside your fears and worries.
The path to me may be difficult, but I promise to lead you to nothing short of truth.

Some say I am wicked and cruel.
I remember the day my mother discovered she was heavy with child.
My father had succumbed in the underworld and there was no explanation other than treachery.
How could she defile his memory?
She, who wore the necklace of skulls and hearts around her throat,
her serpent skirt, all as weapons against cruelty, injustice, and deceit!
I wanted her blood.
I wanted a confession, a thorough and comprehensive admission that she had failed the letter of the law.
When my twin brothers were born, answers came to light.
Huitzilopochtli, with sword in hand, awed us with his forthrightness.
I was too young to understand the ways of magic—the ways of the gods—that can produce the mysterious with ease and finesse, and

confound the opposites that stand in the way of truth.
"Kill her, kill her!" I shouted, demanding her damnation for her most base affront, as though spirit can be trapped and held for ransom.

Before my conversion, when there was only water,
I lived aimlessly in the ocean of life,
indiscriminately devouring everything within it.
Necessity called for the separation of heaven and earth.
My brothers, opposites of one another, had their own interests.
When they saw the urgency of dividing eternity from matter,
they took it upon themselves to be rid of me.
If I wanted my mother's blood, since I blamed her for this travesty of duality imposed upon your world,
then, surely, they must have conjectured,
I could wait in the wings of dark spaces, unseen and unheard, for them.
They pulled me apart.
They pulled and twisted me in half, one with my left leg and right arm, and the other with the right leg and left arm.
The vines and muscles that held me together were torn asunder in one sweep of power.
I was strewn across the universe and
transfigured into the Milky Way, my head remaining as the moon.

The gods grieved at the loss of Coyolxauhqui, as they call me.
However, there is more wisdom than the eye beholds.
Spirit and matter cannot live side by side, and
it is I who chose to be the heaven to divide them.
This cataclysmic event caused heart and mind to become distinct and separate. In this stretching and pulling apart,

*I produced the necessity of the human being to define face and heart; and
for the soul to seek its true home
on the other side of infinity where
it is united with the one consciousness.*

*Knowledge of the Milky Way is elusive—
the depth of magic to birth your dreams is hidden from view in the dark and unpredictable spaces of the universe.
If you choose to seek my wisdom,
you will see and feel my presence in all matter,
when you step into the unknown and faith is your only ally and companion.
I am not recognizable to the naked eye, but
I am always in your dreams where reality abides.
Look for me when you feel the sharp sting or
indistinguishable prick of rejection;
when you feel the pain of insult and loneliness caused
by distorted perceptions and other cruelties of this vale of shadows.
Seek my wisdom beyond the opposites and illusions you will find here.
Between my limbs are the secrets of wisdom you will need.
Beyond my fingertips, you must see the stardust that enlivens consciousness.
My presence weaves throughout time immemorial,
cutting like an obsidian knife through illusions.*

*Pierce my heart, blast through it;
become the light you are meant to be.
Just as I was torn asunder to sharpen consciousness,
the path toward transformation was laid open for you to travel in balance.
My force abounds in your life;
you must decide between the aspects of matter and soul to find me.*

*I reside at the far edges of time, and
in the blood that flows through your veins.
Look for me beyond duality
in the light of the full moon,
in the stillness of the darkness within.
I am always at the edge of the precipice
where you can find your way home,
to the one consciousness where
truth abides, and
all creation derives.
Find me.
Let me guide and care for you.
Truth waits.*

Eleanor Barron Druckrey, Ph.D.

Held by the Grandmothers

At this stage of my life at ninety-three years, there is not a day that goes by that I don't contemplate on death in some form or other. Death is a daily companion that sits quietly on my left shoulder and reminds me sweetly, "It will be your time soon." There is not a day that I open my eyes and I don't think that this may be my last. So I come to the computer this morning and wonder what you are thinking—you, my descendant, my reason for preparing to leave something for the next seven generations. I would be remiss, incomplete, unfinished were I not to leave you with some thoughts to ponder.

I have the honor of being called *La Curandera* by my friends and community. This hasn't always been so; it was quite late in life that the name came to me. Today, after doing my practice of cleansing with sage and saying my prayers in the early morning, as the last quarter of the moon shone its light and Orion was high up in the eastern sky and the stars prepared for their day, I picked up a copy of *Not Always So: Practicing the True Spirit of Zen* by the famous and beloved monk who wrote *Zen Mind, Beginner's Mind*, Shunryu Suzuki. I am struck by the introduction written posthumously:

> Shunryu Suzuki Roshi died on December 4, 1971. His students at Tasajara Zen Mountain Center had begun a *senshin*, a week-long meditation intensive on December 1, while in San Francisco where Roshi was staying., Aa *senshin* began at 5:00 A.M. the morning of the fourth. As his students settled into the first period of *zazen* [sitting meditation] in the *zendo* [meditation hall], upstairs in the company of his chosen successor Richard Baker Roshi, his wife Mitsu, and son Otohiro, the master left this world. He had waited to depart until most of his students were meditating and would be meditating for several more days. That was a parting gift. (Brown, 2011, p. vii)

As I read the introduction, I cannot but help thinking about my own mortality, and my mind drifts off to thinking that not only had the Roshi chosen who would surround him in the end, but he also chose when he would leave and how. I consider that am I going through a period of letting go. I've been doing a practice of breathing deeply, holding my breath, and affirming, "I am that." It is a practice to reclaim my natural state of being, the clarity of mind that leaves behind what others think of me, and ask the Creator to bring me face-to-face with truth of what I am, what all of us are. Actually, the denial of truth is a huge challenge and one that is not given up willingly. At least, I am not willing. Not only am I not willing, but I hold on to these old self-concepts as though my life depended on them. The thought crosses my mind that this is like the final struggle of letting go of breath—a gentle tug of war of not wanting and wanting, and not letting go though the end is imminent. I think on that. I am holding on to the old ego that is ready to go, yet is not entirely surrendered to letting go of its position. This would engender "change." Oh no, not change. Let me change, but not now. So, after having been up since 3:00 a.m., it is now 7:00 a.m., and I decide to go back to bed for another hour. Then I have the dream that pushes me over the edge.

Facing Death Dream

My father has just left the room, and I am left with two children: a lovely little three-year-old girl and a boy of about five years old. I also have a dog that is as sweet as a newborn pup who loves me. The children love me, and I would give my life for them if needed. A young man with a daughter of his own asks me if I am the children's mother, and I hesitate to say, thinking that they will be taken away from me if this is known. But I confess, "No, they are not mine, but they are dearer to me than life itself." He's not fazed by my answer, but I continue to hold them close to me, nevertheless. Even the puppy is dear to me, and I would not part with him under any circumstances.

For some reason, I take the children and the dog with me to another area of the spiritual center situated on sprawling grounds. I climb a hill and enter a building (like a zendo), and come out the other side where I must walk

> *down a pyramid, carrying the girl and making sure the dog is on a leash and that the boy is walking close to me.*
>
> *As we are walking down the steep incline, I notice that my legs are swollen and have developed a disease that may be incurable. I yell for help, but it's just too late, and the only recourse I have is to lie down and take my last breath. I feel myself falling into a deep sleep. The boy is beside himself, not knowing what to do, and I am falling into a dream, a gentle slumber like no rest I've ever known. I must let go of life, and I surrender my breath, the very last one. A woman comes by and sees my predicament, and begins to clean my aura, restore my energy, and remove the disease. I can feel all the shifting she is doing, and I am tempted to continue to sleep, knowing this is not my time to go. I force my eyes open and gaze into her piercing dark eyes, and realize I have another chance to correct my life. I commit to keeping my eyes open, to being awake and letting the ego die instead.*

As I awaken, my husband's innocent, childlike smile makes me feel grateful, and he welcomes me into the day with a heartfelt kiss. The dream has shifted something in me, and I feel resolved to make every moment count. I recommit to the calling I've been dealt. I can't say that in the dream I had very much choice in the matter of dying an undignified death on the cold, hard pavement, but I didn't fight it. I allowed death to come over me, and allowed the falling, falling into blissful surrender. I speak not of dying, but of making the choices to live consciously, dream consciously, act consciously. This dream is not as much about a physical death as it is about resistance to change, or perhaps death of the ego. It suggests I take a softer approach toward death. It prompts me to allow a new experience to color the essence of my life—living by truth, in all levels of consciousness.

As I get into my day, I attend a meeting on money. A speaker reflects on his life and talks of his frivolous spending of time and other follies he has committed. At the end of his talk, someone asks him, "How are you or how have you been accountable to your vision?" I mull the question over in my mind, and begin thinking of my own misadventures.

Leaving the meeting, I feel mildly unsettled with the realization that writing has always been vital to me and that I could have exercised more caution pursuing a professional license that distracted me from writing for several years. The meeting is held in a church at the foot of Mt. Tamalpais, where I am now among redwoods and birches. I have the choice to remain here or come down the mountain and stop for a while at a favorite spot off Tiburon Boulevard, where the water forms a slight cove. From there, I can see Mt. Tamalpais stretching languidly along the coast north of the Golden Gate Bridge. Inland it reveals an image of a goddess in repose. In fact, that is the way the Miwok saw her.

The day is like early spring even though it is now September. A slight dreamlike haze subdues the colors of the sky and trees, and I have an amazing view of the mountain, Sausalito, Mill Valley, and Tiburon, all intermingled with trees and shrubbery that hide evidence of thriving communities. I find the vantage point where a retaining wall with a wooden plank over the top serves as a bench, and I sit down to eat a spinach and chicken salad I've brought. I let my feet dangle over boulders at the edge of the water. Behind me, four ancient cypress trees sprawl their branches high above and hang over the edge of the shore. The trunks are bigger than one set of arms could stretch around. A soft sea breeze blows through my hair, and the water hits against the rocks with the tempo of a quiet ritual drum.

I breathe in the fresh air, the crisp smell of the sea. One of my *comadres* mentioned to me earlier today that Clarissa Pinkola Estés believes that old deeply rooted trees are grandmothers that teach us about standing firm and having thick skins as we go through changes in our lives— more about endurance than having the final say. How comforting to be among these ancient beings and feel the restoration slowly seeping into my consciousness. My sharpened senses absorb the healing properties of the ground and the beauty that surrounds me. I may have stumbled, been careless, and faltered thousands of times; I may have worried that others thought me foolish. All that matters nothing in the glorious reverie of this moment. I can live with my answers to the question posed to the speaker. I haven't been consistent with my writing, but certainly consistent enough. The inquietude that plagued me earlier begins to loosen its grip on my mind. I feel the tranquility and the calming effect of the consciousness of the grandmothers bending low, murmuring softly, "Surrender."

The efficiency of the universe gives me pause to think that when it looks like I am offtrack, I am only momentarily stepping away. A *curandera* doesn't need permission to write, heal, or dream. What she needs is to listen, and be prepared for death at any moment's notice. The rest takes care of itself. The significance of a professional license to practice a craft pales when viewed in the context of reality.

Remembering

I was sixty-six years old when I finally began to experience more clearly the unity of the interior with the outer. I became one with humanity. Not that all suffering ended for me, but at least I had a glimmer of understanding of when I was causing myself sorrow and had the choice to live in it or opt for something more rewarding. The struggle to allow the secrets of my dreams fly in the face of science exploded into a galaxy of opportunities for integration. The blend of mind and matter became a calm ocean with grace of movement, soothing to my spirit. I felt a quiet assurance that my silent prayers were being heard throughout many worlds. In short, I began to understand the delicate balance between practicality and faith. I began to feel patience, self-love, appreciation of my gifts, and appreciation of everything that walks and breathes upon Mother Earth—friends, trees, flowers, the oceans, the blue sky, our four-legged relatives, all of which play a unique role in life. At the same time, I would choose to doubt what I had been shown.

The evening of this balancing, I went for a walk along the Bay. The twilight was still and comfortably cool; the sky, a cobalt blue; and the sun's rays spread like an aura above the head of Mt. Tamalpais. In this reverie, I could hear gentle waves quietly swirling around the rocks, chanting their nightly ode for the stars to appear. The lights of San Francisco across the Bay were beginning their twinkle. With the Mother in her reposing silhouette at my back, a fleeting but profound thought crossed my mind: this is peace. This is the balance I've waited for, as opposed to the conflicts of duality pulling within me. I felt a spaciousness surrounding me that I'd never felt before.

Don't misunderstand me. This wasn't a lightbulb that went on with crystal clarity, where suddenly I had a three-hundred-sixty-degree view. It wasn't that simple. I was brought to this point with thousands of starts and stops. From the beginning of my journals, I had dozens of dreams where I could see flashes of inspiration that dismally disappeared with the coming light of day. Nevertheless, with each instance of seeing the glimmer of reality, I was brought closer to this particular moment of realization, this evening, which marked a turning point for me.

I can see that two years prior this memorable event, I had several dreams that alerted me to the coming of something spectacular. I began a game of wait-and-see, the sacred not being a gift handed over easily. I wondered if this was a trick of the mind—like quasars going off and on—or whether I was chasing a light that would dim upon turning a corner. But this was different. When the star drops into awareness and creates ripples throughout our being, it's here to stay if we want to believe in it. I became aware that we protect this moment of knowing by remembering we are the light. It's in our consciousness.

After many years of conversing with a group of elders, I finally connected with one, and he identified himself as Ocelotl. But it is difficult to explain how this paradigm finally became my reality. In this North American culture, there is little doubt that the linear, time-sequential paradigm we believe in is held to be the true reality. I needed help from both sides of the curtain. With Ocelotl's support, I seamlessly developed into a new awareness that confirmed what the dreamers of the culture predicted hundreds of years ago. Not only did it expand my awareness of existence in other dimensions, I was able to integrate travels into past, future, and simultaneous lives. I began to reinterpret my experiences on both sides of the curtain from this new awareness.

I've looked through my journals and found a series of dreams contributing to this awakening. I liken the transformation process to a house being renovated, with dust flying, old plumbing, insulation, wallpaper, and sheet rock being stripped and gutted out, and then starting over again with construction on a new building. I would never be able to fully describe the sound and color; the words conveyed by my dream teachers; the pulling, stretching, and reshaping of my beliefs; the patterns of emotions and reactions that impacted this massive project over the years. But gradually, painfully, meticulously, I was thrown through a training or treatment that continues to this day to guide me toward wholeness.

Love and Wisdom

The lessons in love become apparent when I remember the wisdom imparted through the death of loved ones. Try as I may, I can't make my life go in a straight line. But I have learned through dreaming that dreams don't happen randomly. I have found that love is not what I once thought, because it includes more of one's being and becoming one with all creation than just mind and body. Sacred gifts fall into the mix, and the chemistry becomes more complicated. Loving my sacred gifts, my sisters and brothers on the path of life, entails committing to a practice of believing in the greatness within all creation. Commitment is vital to understanding. Love, loyalty, compassion, and kindness are not something that wells up from within and manifests effortlessly, but rather a practice and a vow that is achieved with daily practice. What is more, I've seen that love is practiced throughout our travels from one life into another as our consciousness expands into the one consciousness.

Love in a committed relationship, as love with all humanity, is a lifelong achievement. The illusion of life will bring confusion and present countless opportunities to send us off course. In this addictive world, where much passes for love, it takes a conscious commitment to honestly bring love and compassion into the smallest of tasks or moments, and to make them tangible by consistent demonstration. I certainly have had my share of illusions of love.

Many friends from this lifetime have passed on to their next life and have returned in my dreams to show me how they are doing. The lessons they have taught me vary, but it also makes me think of a template or pattern as in sacred geometry, and a broader picture comes together for me. The messages my friends have left seem to need no explanation; they are simple and straightforward. They are lessons in being present for the occasion and observing the feelings as they linger a moment and then flow through. I remember the constriction of my consciousness and the almost juvenile notions of love I held, but more importantly, I am coming to understand that the process of learning to love happens over extended time—many lifetimes. I know now that over the centuries, Grandmother, Ocelotl, and other ancestors have visited, along with others of my peers also from other lifetimes, and they have all left messages to strengthen my resolve for this lifetime. For example, on one occasion, Grandmother visited me and gently whispered, as I lay in my bed under the blankets with the full moon shining on my face, "If you want love, learn to love unconditionally." Now, I can be very dense, and I must admit, I had not even a clue as to what she was referring. This announcement came quietly, and then joined itself with others that then together created a roar, and I finally received the unmistakable message.

The following dreams are of friends and relatives in this lifetime who have passed on. The one that follows, Claudia, addresses the power of thoughts and the importance of treading lightly with them, of not grasping. While on earth, my friend struggled with loneliness and ambivalence. The lesson of not grasping was unmistakable when viewed with the long string of other lessons over time.

Claudia

Claudia comes to me the way she would call me on the telephone—insistently, urgently, and telling me of the events in her new life. She's in a relationship with a man with whom she has little in common. She has a list of complaints, and I stop her. "You're stuck in this dimension. I'm going to pray for you," I tell her, and I begin, "I love you. I love you. I love you."

My words surprise even myself, but as I am praying, she begins to rise off the ground and disappears into another dimension. By the time I finish the fourth I love you, she has disappeared completely, and I consider my prayer answered.

The impressions this dream left me were that love was not about grasping, because she had, in fact, elevated into another dimension. I, as spirit, facilitated her healing as well as mine.

Matt

I met Matt when he was grappling with the diagnosis of AIDS. He had just moved from Philadelphia to his sister's in San Francisco. We became friends, and his family adopted me as a new member. We took many walks along the beach, and when the ravages of the disease overtook him, we spent many hours in silence observing the subtle movements of the trees outside his window. I had the honor of being at his bedside with his mother when he took his last breath. A few months after his departure, I had the following dream.

> *I'm at the front door of a "world bank" in a quaint seaside town nestled at the mouth of a canyon. I look down the hill toward the ocean as I am ready to open the tall glass door, and I hear my friend Matt's voice saying, "I love you." I hear his voice and it immediately registers in my consciousness, and I turn around to face him. I am so happy to see him and reach out to hug him. But he holds me at arms' length, indicating we should not touch. I've missed him terribly, and want to know how he's faring. He leaves quickly. The memory of his love lingers and leaves me feeling very happy. The quiet village where he has chosen to live tells me he is at peace.*

This is such a vivid dream, and the feelings of affection and longing to see him are so clear that even forty years later, I can recall it clearly. The feelings of joy are exquisite. I am also noticing the expansion that envelops me when I experience his love, and not only do I feel this expansion from his presence, but also from the environment, ground, and sky. It's as though everything serves to convey a language of love. This dream redistributed my sense of love to include all matter.

C. S.

My friend Charlotte had cancer, was cured of it, and, twenty-five years later, was diagnosed with a different type of bone cancer. In the last three years of her life, I had the good fortune to spend time with her, going to movies, art openings, lunches, and dinners. We often spoke of death, and we seriously/jokingly promised one another that whoever left first would return to give the other a report. As her life narrowed to a wheelchair, we spent more and more time in meditation. In the early hours of the morning on the last day of her life, I held her hand in meditation. Her bed facing Mt. Tamalpais in Marin County, the greenery of the trees in contrast to the dark blue of the sky, we sat in meditation, and she gave me a parting gift that I savored for a long time—a sense of communion and harmony. She had kept her promise.

Little did I know that she would also literally fulfill that promise of returning to report on her new life. She came to me in a dream.

> *I feel Charlotte's presence as I sit with a group of friends in conversation. I turn to see her and speak directly with her. She is vibrant and smiling. I ask, "Well, what's it like being in your new life?" She only smiles, but closes her eyes and transmits delicate feelings of joy and love to me, which I drink in slowly. I smile back and say, "Not bad." We start giggling, just as we did when hanging out at the Crepevine in San Rafael.*

Christopher

The morning my nephew passed away, I had a dream where some images kept repeating. I only had a sense of confusion. The feelings woke me up, and it was very early in the morning. My brother had asked me not to call too early, so I put off calling, since I would be reporting a dream and telling him to go check on his son, who was in perfectly good health.

Later that morning, on my way to the San Francisco Airport for a conference in Los Angeles, quite spontaneously I began to chant, "I love you, I love you, I love you, I love you." Initially, I did not make the connection between the mantra and the dream, which by then I had forgotten. In some respects, it felt as though I was saying it to myself, but in other respects, as though I was chanting for the world. Either way, the chanting began to expand my consciousness beyond my little self to include all living beings, whether human or animal. The mantra continued throughout the day and for the next couple of days until my return, when I was told about my nephew's death.

I know Christopher had given me a clue to the great puzzle of life. He practiced meditation, and we often spoke of its benefits in his life. It would only make sense that he would share his new experience with me. The lesson was not conveyed in one full picture, but stretched over time and with other lessons contributing to it as I chanted, "I love you, I love you, I love you, I love you."

Roar of the Lion

In the dream that follows, I distinctly have the impression that the lion is a highly evolved consciousness. He is disguised as a four-legged relative that leaves its mark emblazoned in my soul to such a degree that it expands a sense of the aura around my body and my consciousness. It leaves me feeling that I live in a vast awareness that has no limits.

> *I'm at a train station where the trains are coming and going. I'm standing on a platform where I can see several lines of tracks, and decide to walk toward the outside of the station to examine a line of cargo cars loading circus animals. I step off the platform and onto hard-packed ground, and walk toward them.*
>
> *I come face-to-face with a caged, fully grown, muscular lion. He's not happy about his present condition and conveys his thoughts to me in a resounding roar that creates a rumble below the ground and makes the leaves shake off their trees. I jump back in terror and shock. He's standing now and looking away from me as though to assure me I am safe, but something in his roar has reminded me of a commitment I have to him from lifetimes ago.*

In dreams, thoughts are conveyed through sounds and music as well as through movement. They may not even be complete thoughts, as though leaving a question lingering. I am amazed at the significance of the lion's message. In the lion's roar, I am "told" to lift myself out of my human limitations. Power and intention travels across time, and the lion's roar is an example of how this may happen. It's the message of a chant, a repeated sound in prayer. The call is definite and compelling, and I am left with thousands of little gnawing questions. How does one acknowledge the implications? And how real are they? Life continues with its irritations and annoyances, and then here's this gift! Translation from spirit to the mundane requires artistry and agility. We receive the gift delicately and humbly. There's no other way to put it because the gift requires our dedication to do the work we've agreed to before entering into this lifetime. Even if we deny that we know it, the reminder persists with the steadiness of a jackhammer. Somehow, the truth wants to slip away unnoticed, uncelebrated, and we deceive ourselves by pretending we are not worthy of receiving such messages.

To excavate deeper into this message, during my morning writing, I asked the lion to spell it out for me detail by detail. These are my process notes from the writing years ago:

> "I hear your roar echoing throughout the universe. I feel a bond between us, a definite connection that binds us to an agreement I have with you; I am committed to answering your call. But what *is* the call? Who are you?"
>
> The lion responds,
>
> "You must understand that your participation matters and is vital to the plan. Your part in it is to remove the encrustations that prevent the shining star that brightens the universe in numerous ways to simply be. You and everyone else who takes on a human form come into this world with many gifts and the agreement to heal the world. Be glad for the challenge, and don't shrink from it. It's time you turned loose and accepted reality.
>
> "Your primary responsibility is to transcend the illusions of this world. To do so, you must remember the light from which you come, prior to your birth. Imposing shadows on others are obstacles not only upon the object of your thought, but also upon yourself. These thoughts also obscure and confuse your light and vision. They become your personal stumbling blocks. Likewise, your visiting wholeness and compassion upon others will result in benefit to you. What you focus your thoughts on manifests in your life and environment.
>
> "Ages in the ancestors' calendars can be bunched in twenty-eight years, half a century, five hundred years, a thousand years, sixteen thousand years, twenty thousand—there is no end to the repetition of the cycles found in the universe. Responsibility to the gods requires your

attention in consciousness. When the Great Star emerges through the heart of Coyolxauhqui, the event will offer the opportunity to transcend all that holds you in duality. Face it, and allow the consciousness to seep through your being. Consciousness transcends dimensions. Can you suspend judgment to expand awareness beyond the opposites that hold you prisoner? You decide.

"My roar frightened you. Actually, it is as powerful as the light from a thousand suns, which shines within all humanity. Shed the pretense that you don't hear or see it. Teach what your heart yearns to learn. If you are inclined toward music, then become a musician and impart the vision of the light through sound and beautiful chord progressions and melodies. If you are a healer, then give healings through your eyes, voice, hands, heart. This is as natural as drinking water. You agreed to remember truth. My roar is a vehicle expanding your consciousness.

"Because of your vulnerability, you have suffered insults and ridicule. The book of eternity calls only for your dedication. You cannot fail. You think that the lies you heard or assumed about yourself as a child were real and that you must atone for your mistakes. There are no scales to balance. Remember that in the spirit world, there are no sins or wrongs, only human moments of absentmindedness that are easily corrected. There is no need for penance, never a cause for guilt. Be gentle with yourself and discontinue feeding mistaken information to yourself, and by your actions, to others. Release illusions and look beyond them—breathe through them, dance them away. A life of freedom without these encumbrances is your natural inheritance. Enjoy yourself with beautiful sunsets, music, friends, family. Enjoy yourself. Spend time in nature often. Do creative projects. Shadows appear, they are not real. With a tiny shift in your thoughts, you can be restored to the consciousness that is your true nature. Any obstacles between you and truth are mere illusions.

"I caged myself to highlight the misguided thoughts holding you back. There is no cage—it's created by illusion. I am spirit. I am free, and so are you. Freedom is yours. Walk with me. Happiness is yours simply by assuming your innate power and living by truth. What you think is my strength is within you as well. There is no separation between us. There is no separation among all creation. Everything is one.

"In this world, many opposites abound. What is seen as 'good' carries meaning only because there is something that is considered 'bad.' Look beyond them and become the gift of perfection. The perfect reflection of this gift would reveal the light of eternal peace, your recognition of the oneness of all creation, and your willingness to be guided by the light from within.

"Open your heart and return to truth, for it is only in living it that you will be happy and understand the call. Your role is simply to be happy and serve the universe with your strengths and gifts. Remember the light, remember love. Go back, far back, to the beginning of innocence. Believe it, and you are there."

Here is another truth for me to grasp the star that can carry me over the chasm, between sleeping and waking reality, beyond good and bad, beyond duality. The challenge lies in trusting. What seems fantastic only appears so because I am measuring it from my pitiful, frail material vision. Learning to love is crucial. Intuitively, I understand that the answer is to love unconditionally. It's time to take the lion's roar as my personal sound of the universal om and love everyone and everything.

A Dream Map to

Power

Other examples of announcements prior to and after that moment evening come from the following dreams I had that added to the surge of oncoming energy once I acknowledged it. These dreams gave me a broad platform on which to stand to remember my tasks and remain committed. The boost was not exactly honey and sunshine, but rather a torch that came through to singe the useless fuzz in my mind.

These dreams emphasized the gifts that are innate to us beyond time and space—in the memory of the consciousness of those who came before us and attained a great measure of clarity and knowing. Power is abundant throughout the universe, including ourselves. What does it take for each one of us to remember them and access them? Remembering the gifts is one answer. The answers are encoded in obvious places in our dreams. Remembering that we have lived before is another answer.

Removing more obstacles in my seeing and remembering, these dreams signaled that I was getting closer to my purpose. These dreams came in close succession, which held up "the promise," stating, "reach for them, and you are home free," removing or recognizing the trance that prevented me from seeing beyond this lifetime. There was something deep and intense that spoke of the dream traditions the ancient ones speak of: an awareness of consciousness far beyond the body, of past lives, future lives, and a reality that envelops a "multiverse" rather than the one universe, though great in itself, that our eyes see in the night sky; or a narrow band of time and space commonly believed to be the range of our existence.

The following dreams jarred my memory and expanded my consciousness to drop to another level of truth that I had been reticent to accept. Who was I, a mere *chicanita,* to challenge the precepts of the world? My father's pragmatism comes to mind; he was the most pragmatic man I have ever known, yet brilliant in his spiritual vision and understanding. If I could just take an ounce of his wisdom and bypass the negating voices in my mind, I could stare truth in the eye and know beyond doubt that I was right. And that's what these dreams gave me: permission to shed the cloak of timidity, guilt, shame, and doubt—deficits that kept me glued to my chair, hidden, silent, in fear of being seen.

...ey, Ph.D.

...ble of Power Dream

...rk at Forty-second and Seventh Avenue ...treat in Mexico. The directions I carry in ...very complicated, but my niece Rosy has ... and will come with me as my guide. The ... concrete buildings as we walk through this ... anyon feels soothing in the morning air. As we enter a building, the marble walls make the temperature drop several degrees.

We walk onto a knee-high, tub-like elevator with no ceiling or walls, just a tub that takes us up forty floors. We walk out onto a busy lobby of a hotel in Grand Central Station, and take a train to the hotel next door where we will then take another elevator another forty or sixty floors down into the earth.

When we emerge from the second elevator, we come to a train station at surface level and take a train for Mexico City. We arrive promptly. I've left my phone book at home, and do not have the phone numbers for my cousins, which is probably just as well. We do not have time because another train leaves for Teotihuacán immediately.

Rosy tells me the old ones will be there to conduct the ceremonies. Experienced pilgrims will enter into a trance and be shown or taken to the grand teacher. We board the train and travel the countryside, passing ranchitos, small farming communities, acres and acres of corn interspersed with dry land, and the highway that also runs to the ancient city. At the church, we will be given further instructions. When I come out the front door of the train station on the ridge of a mountain range, I see a small speck of the church miles down a narrow dirt path.

We walk through the narrow streets of a pueblito, adobe walls on both sides of us. Once outside the small town, the dirt path is easy to find. We walk through more fields of corn, and surprisingly, quickly arrive at the church.

The church is a huge one-room structure with tall, thick, wooden doors that are cumbersome and heavy to open. The building is quite deceiving from the outside. When a native man in white shirt and trousers pushes the door open for us, we see that the part of the church we see from the outside is merely the dome of a temple that reaches many levels down into the earth. Upon entering, we find a grand marble stairway that circles around the complete structure. Parts of the stairs are for seating, but the levels keep going so far down that people are barely distinguishable from where we stand. I see that many areas of the temple have been filled. People are wearing loose-fitting white garments. No longer wearing street clothes, I am now in a plain blue cotton gown.

Rosy explains that the select few elders who have practiced for many lifetimes will enter into a samadhi-like state and impart power. The power they will manifest is available for the open-hearted devotee who is willing to give everything up to hold in hand only the essence of truth and love. A strong feeling of commitment and devotion hits me in my solar plexus, and I can't help but embrace the grace the elders generate; it humbles me to be in the presence of this grandeur.

The stairs are steep enough to require a chain alongside, reminiscent of those on the Pyramid of the Moon on the opposite side of the valley from this temple. I reach for the chain and feel the heat of those who entered before me on their way to the inner sanctum.

An elder comes down the stairs in a great hurry, not noticing he's pushed my hand out of the way. I feel tentative about what this ritual is because he seems so unconscious. My worst thought is that I may not want to participate, for this appears to be a hierarchical network of "good ol' boys." The thought makes my stomach tighten, but I let him pass and keep my eyes on the path. I must learn to be resilient and less identified with the body.

Now people are coming down the stairs in droves, and I wonder whether there's room for everyone. I get to the bottom of the stairs several stories down from the entrance and look back. There is yet plenty of space for everyone, and for those yet to come.

The deeper I descend into this temple, I notice that the number of people thins out behind me, and I am able to take in the surroundings to assess what's to come next. The little church I saw from the top of the hill is even more amazing than I first thought. Looking back, I see I've descended through a rotunda. Many corridors travel through the multiple levels of the underground structure. At this level, light is barely visible through the stained glass windows at the top. Torches are used to light up this part of the temple. The concentric circles of stairs tighten as I continue downward.

I find a side chapel, a small enclosure where an elder is waiting for me. I kiss his cheek, and he tenderly returns my reverence with a blessing that reverberates throughout my already alert and heightened consciousness. His warmth and welcome soften my heart with gratitude as though the rose of La Virgen has touched my heart. Out of the corner of my eye, I catch a glimpse of a cross at the top, eye-level to the entrance. I hadn't paid much attention, but at this level, it has a powerful emanation. Instead of the body of Christ, there's a huge round bouquet of blue flowers. A force from behind me begins to lift me toward the cross. I relax into the ascent, realizing that the spirit of the cross is taking me toward it. With the thousands of people, the temple becomes silent, and all eyes are upon me. I am honored; I have been singled out, and begin to cry from a deep well of compassion I've never known before. The movement stops and holds my body along the length of the cross. As I acknowledge the stirring of joy through my tears, the force multiplies and begins pushing me away from the cross and toward the underground caverns of the temple. The caverns are the inner dwellings of power, resembling lava tubes where devotees and initiates train.

I'm flying at tremendous speeds through these canyons, and behind me are many initiates following. I slow down for sharp corners so as not to lose any of my trainees because the tubes extend in so many directions that staying together is essential. The force and balance required are astounding, but we take the challenge in stride by keeping sight of each other and maintaining the group in one whole to complete the journey as anticipated. I come back to the elder who originally gave me his blessing on my arrival. He introduces me to a strong black man who says, "You are under my protection. Remain in this temple until the elders move you on." By now, my body is pulsating at the speed of light with the spirit of the cross.

I wake up, and the charge of energy continues to surge throughout my body. I've been to another realm, and I'll need time in this dimension to digest it. I pull the blankets back and wait for my body to become still.

I close my eyes and begin another dream.

Keeping It Simple Dream

I'm working in an office as a counselor. I have lots of freedom to accommodate my writing and private practice. I notice that my desk is as big as the one I had in high school and that other psychologists have separate offices with huge dark mahogany desks and smooth black leather executive chairs.

I want to be one of those people, recognized and held in high esteem. I want a flashy life instead of this lackluster condition I'm in, with only a handful of students and at poverty's door. I ponder these feelings when a woman steps in front of me and says, "Remember, Gracia, you chose not to join them. Your decision was to keep it simple." Without responding to her remarks, I watch her walk away. I really do remember that I said that. I did say that. Yet

> *here I sit in jealousy and diminished confidence. I rack my brain, trying to recall the real essence of my conviction. A dim light begins to glow within. Thankfully, the memory comes back to me—I simply want to be a healer. I chose not to complicate my life with superfluous or meaningless possessions. I chose prayer and meditation because that is what matters most to me: prayer, meditation, and surrender.*

The first dream, "Rumble of Power," is duality showing itself, together with its direct opposite, the power of one, which is manifested in my rising toward the cross, a literal elevating, as though being presented to the universe as its servant, a symbolic baptism. In the magnitude of the temple, the training of the novitiates, and the blessing from my teacher, I see spirit calling. I also begin to recognize that I've done the training before, I have taught before, and it compels me to do so again, culling the teachings from previous lifetimes. I hear the rumble that is reconfiguring my universe; I am being reconfigured, reshaped, reformed, and born again. My awareness is expanded, stretching across the centuries and the universe, obliterating my body and bringing me face-to-face with creation. The sensations of rising toward the cross and flying through the lava tubes became an experience that stretched my sense of reality and gave me a view into truth, a reminder of the consciousness I saw in the "Roar of the Lion" dream. In this dream, I found a direction, a promise.

In the second dream, "Keeping It Simple," I am dazzled by the implications of power as I see it in the first dream, and confuse them with definitions of power and status I hold in the waking state. How could I bring myself to the other side of this confusion where the contrasts between spirit and the material plane clang against one another? Swinging from one extreme to the other needs a softening and acceptance from within, a becoming quiet and serene that takes time—days that each stretch into months, years—and patience. The contrasts of the dream juxtaposed against my waking self serve as examples of my attachment to duality and the loss of my true identity, being light, spirit. I am shown that I have a vested belief in the size of a desk and acknowledgment from others. It may be of value to some, but here I am being shown a contrast in the two realities. Which would I prefer, the big desk and status? Or would I choose awakening?

There isn't simply a *decision* to make. I must be tempered by spirit to be led to the life destiny requires of me. But first, there were these little conflicts and annoyances that dominated a huge chunk of my consciousness, such as learning to forgive the global history of oppression, colonization, racism, etc., and my own constructs of antidotes to these challenges—all the things that kept me small, wondering where I could get permission to become what was given me to be. These were confusions of the ego, for its existence was threatened, and it wanted to distract me with mundane challenges.

The answer is in the reminder to keep it simple—just pray, meditate, and allow humility to touch my heart. I certainly cannot do it alone. But I quickly get the opportunity to test my resilience or flexibility in letting go of my thought processes to understand what "forgiveness" looks like. It becomes an unraveling of perceptions and emotions to reveal the truth of what lies beneath the obstacles to peace. "Keeping It Simple Dream" is the light that provides the golden opportunity to fully step into the role as agreed long before this lifetime. It provides the clues: I sit stewing in jealousy and envy of others' fortunate status and symbols of success, the fine furniture and private offices. The woman reminds me, "Remember, you chose not to join them. Your decision was to keep it simple." Yes, I want to keep my life simple, but I also want acknowledgment and recognition. I want what they "have," tangible, concrete chunks of evidence that indicate power (of a sort), proof that I've "arrived." I can only sit in feelings that diminish my stature as a human being, and overwhelm me with a sense of inferiority that blocks gratitude, the antidote to remove the ego from its perceived place of power. Which will I choose, true power or the manifestation of the ego's dictates?

What a *curandera* needs is the courage to step from rainbow to rainbow, listen, and be prepared for death at any moment's notice. In my earlier years, I would awaken from these feelings of expansiveness and confuse my identity with the feelings of despair and hopelessness when juxtaposed against the frustrations of my waking life: manifestations in the smallest of slights, as standing in line or getting into traffic. These were small irritations that I hung on to because I still believed more in the needs of the ego than in the power of spirit.

Eventually, I came to accept the truth and realized that leaving the values of the world behind was a choice to make. The choice was mine. I couldn't claim ignorance anymore. That auspicious evening marked the beginning of new resolve to walk the path of power knowing that we humans are much more than the pitiful little creatures we hold ourselves to be in common belief.

Spiritual Training

In attempting to recreate a paradigm within myself that enables me to live by the tenets my dreams have shown me about my culture, I have also found other sources that somehow coincide with the truth that vibrates within. For a time, I was associated with a Buddhist meditation center in Berkeley. I've studied various world religions that have given me a clearer understanding of the myths and legends I've uncovered in my travels. Apart from my culture, my brother gave me a set of books that became the foundation of my spiritual practice, *A Course in Miracles*. The books have taken me through a long, arduous journey that set my mind right side up from the illusions of this world. For over thirty years, I've practiced its curriculum of 365 daily lessons, and have gained clarity of the meaning of duality in the ancient religions of the Americas as well as other religions.

As *A Course* outlines the curriculum for students and teachers, it describes the choices to be made. Essentially, it states that there are only two emotions: love and fear—choose one! I remember the first time I became aware of a dynamic relationship occurring: it was on a sunny spring Saturday morning as I walked through Pacific Heights down Vallejo Street in San Francisco. I saw small coffee tables and other light household items in a sidewalk sale in front of a lovely tall ivy-covered wooden fence. It wasn't the sale that caught my attention, it was the open door under an arch that lured me in. I must have walked past this mysterious door hundreds of times, always imagining a magical garden behind it. That was the only time I ever saw the door ajar. Inside, I found an immaculate, old-fashioned white rose garden shaded by several sprawling oak trees. The fragrance from the roses jolted me as I walked through the door. At the back of the garden, far from the street, stood an elegant Victorian mansion with heavy curtains closed in all the windows facing the garden. Walking through the door and finally having a glance at the house I'd always imagined seemed surreal. Perhaps the owner had died, but whatever the reason, small tables and chairs lined the sidewalk, and inside were items too big to permit passage along the walkway. My eyes were riveted on a vibrant plain purple carpet that had been rolled up and left partially open for display. "Notice the color," I heard a voice instruct me. The carpet seemed to be vibrating in its vibrant color, and try as I might to normalize my vision, the more

I studied the carpet, the more electrifying it became. I closed my eyes, opened them, and the color kept intensifying. I drew closer to it, observing my breath to steady my attention. I was dreaming awake.

That evening, I came to realize that *A Course* was the instigator of this personal little theater I had witnessed in the garden. The voice became a constant companion over the years, and I came to rely on it for direction and guidance in moments of distress and, as in this case, a mini mystical experience. I have stopped trying to figure out which is from which domain—the course? The ancestors?

There Is Only One Consciousness

The lessons from *A Course In Miracles* themselves are masterpieces that gradually have been correcting my vision from seeing the world as reality, to the illusion that it is. The Last Judgment was transformed from an event in which the world would hear trumpets, see the heavens opening, and all God's children would see his face; but the poor, miserable unbelievers would be left singing a sad song in hell. Instead, the Last Judgment has been redefined as taking personal responsibility to find peace within myself and recognize the unity of my being with all creation. There is no guilt. There is only love, the recognition of peace and compassion abiding in all living things at the level beyond the body. There is only one consciousness, completely changeless and forever pure and whole.

Grandmother, Ocelotl, and others have guided me through the maze of dreams and teachings from my culture. Between the two practices, as well as those of other major religions of the world, I've come to have a better understanding of the role of duality and finding the one truth. This one central idea, and my part in this awakening as a modern woman attempting to fathom these truths, is to allow my points of reference to be corrected— let go of resentments, anger, fear, and all thoughts that diminish in my eyes not only myself, but also the stature of my brothers and sisters on this planet. If I want to be whole and awake, I need bid everyone else welcome in my quest for truth. No exceptions. Guilt is nonexistent.

Here is a journal entry that speaks to the meandering of consciousness that brings home to me the concept of one consciousness:

Rain today. The trees outside my window stand with droplets of water like tiny bubbles resting on their bare branches. The sky is a heavy gray, and there is no wind. Only crows conversing with one another are heard outside. All in all, an ordinary early spring day.

The past weeks have been intense. Two months ago, I descended into hell as the cycle of grief griped my heart for the second time since late November. My mind grabs at something it thinks is real—the past that appears to have been a travesty upon the native cultures. But as I feel the anguish of loss, I realize that my feelings are merely looking for a source at which to point the finger. When I examine the feelings under the microscope of meditation, I find nothing I can actually blame for the fire within but my own sadness. I must just sit with it and invite the pain of loss until it burns itself out.

In my dream "Going to Tlalocan," my friend is mentioned as "CS." In life, she was one of the greatest sources of comfort to thousands, myself included. In that dream, I stop at a cafeteria on my way down the east side of the pyramid, and come upon my friends from a job forty years ago. My mentor JJ hears my voice and comes over to see me and says, "I heard you were having trouble sleeping, and I found something gentle to help you rest." I take a small handful of green seeds, smaller than sweet peas, which he hands to me, and I continue on my way down the hill.

Twenty years later, the scene played itself out with a slight twist—I give my friend the seeds to help her rest. In the weeks leading up to her death, she experienced tremendous pain. I was one of the last people to be with her while she was still conscious. Her husband, son, JJ, and friends from the center gathered around her in her final hours.

As I write, I pause a moment to remember her and think of how much I miss her. In my last moments with her, I sat very early in the morning of November 21, a day very much like today, exchanging blessings with her and holding her hand in meditation as she lay in bed.

My parents passed on many years ago; my middle brother, Carlos, and my nephew, Christopher, in recent months. I was certain I had worked through all those levels of suffering, but here they were again, nagging and prodding me to dig deeper once again—self-loathing, depression, a car accident were events that forced me pick up the spade once again and keep digging. I had no other choice.

My thoughts and feelings of loneliness and isolation are put through a ringer over and over until I am left spent, without a rudder, but with the willingness to start again, trusting in what I know to be true.

Forgiveness

I've always thought that forgiveness is something we do when we think someone has done something mean-spirited to us. "You did this to me, but I'm going to be bigger than you and forget about it," I'd say. In blaming, I am abdicating power to the ego and forgetting that the oneness of our existence cannot ever be marred. The self cannot be made to suffer injury or be diminished.

Duality has many faces, and the need for forgiveness is just one of them. In the pain of insult, injury surfaces as a need for healing. Our thoughts have bypassed the sum of our wholeness, and momentarily, we believe that there is need of an apology. As I till the soil in my spiritual garden, I begin to realize there can be no wrong done to me; it is separation from my true identity that leads me to believe someone has caused me injury. I've traded "injury" for the undeniable certainty of truth.

I gradually begin to see what held my breath for a moment: beauty and strength surround us, we experience them in the smallest effort we make to manifest and behold the grandeur of truth. We often overlook the results because we wonder, who am I to claim such greatness? Power is subtle, safely tucked within us. The ability to create and develop our sacred gifts grows in us steadily every time we choose to live by truth. Power comes with our dreams, and the more we use this power, the sooner we discover our natural relationship with it. We feel its texture and color in myriad ways. We know it's there, we know what needs to be done. I've begun to understand that forgiveness itself is not necessarily a confirmation that someone did something "bad" to me. Rather, the injury was not intended, since there isn't a reason for someone to do me harm, and the other doesn't perceive any intent on my part to cause harm. Ultimately, we are joined at the source, and there is no mistake.

Duality, in cultural beliefs, brings the flicker of contradictions and plants the seed of doubt. It presents itself, and I feel as though I'm dancing with my shadow, unable to shake free of it. Transcending duality is a necessary step in achieving my life's purpose. The four directions are full of opposites and contradictions aimed at helping me fathom the messages sent, and help from the gods is ever weaving in and out of sight. In the Chicana/o culture, an opening in space and time exists that enables us to live in a pool of ever-helpful entities that want to and can give us bits of wisdom beyond our human comprehension, be they ancestors or other beings. As I have found from dreams, help abounds if I but listen, take note, and surrender to the whole truth that lies within. The point is to believe this and truly avail myself of the help.

We live in a basket of psychic energy. Simply in living, we are surrounded by power, but in order to allow its free flow, we must be still and calm. It's within, it wants to flow through our art, music, movement, and healing capacity with every little endeavor we undertake to make manifest what is ours to give.

Coming back to forgiveness, my relentless teacher. In my younger years, my plan had been to speak to large groups. I wanted to give away the wisdom I was receiving through dreaming. I could teach about movement and transformation because I felt that people needed to claim their strengths by expanding their awareness through mind/body union. I wanted to be knowledgeable about processes and to understand the workings of transformation. I wanted to feed the spiritually hungry. In the end, the dream extended the hand of wisdom and gave way for forgiveness to take hold because events and outcomes didn't happen the way I intended them.

Ancestors Live in Our Dreams

It took me years to figure out that the people I met in my dreams included my ancestors and others who have lived before and are available as a source of wisdom and strength. They are not random characters the mind makes up to distract us from our suffering, but rather a source of wisdom to abide by. They have a purpose in our dreams, and if we listen, we benefit in this lifetime. They can also be reminders that we have lived before.

Seeing the magnitude of the self once again as I see in the following dream—the energy from flying through the dimensions—reminds me of the urgency to stay ahead of the thoughts and feelings that make me want to fall unconscious. I ask myself why it is important to transcend ordinary time and space. I argue with psychology yet believe in it because it is a "science" to be reckoned with in this domain. I need something more concrete to convince me that there is more to life than living by arbitrary rules that aren't sustaining and significant in the scheme of reality. Coming back to the teachings of the past serves an important function in recognizing my true mission in life and how I may profit from the ancient wisdom available.

I come into an auditorium like in a school or university. I hear Father William talking about my arrival, and he is directing people to step back a little and open the circle to make room for me. Waving his hand, he motions me to come stand with him in the opening he has made and begins his teaching.

Three elders that I've met in other dreams arrive at the front door. I recognize Ocelotl among them. We can see their silhouettes against the morning sun, and I get the sense that they are there to help me in this endeavor. Instantly, I leave the circle and am flying through dimensions. I am leading, rather than following along. Again, I feel as though we are traveling through underground caverns. We change speeds, moving at high speeds, and then slowing down to almost a standstill. We fly through thin lines of demarcation between dimensions. I'm doing the exercises easily and effortlessly, and I begin to feel that I've done this before in other lifetimes and am no stranger to these teachings. The space opens up, and I am sailing through the air on a swing, my hair blowing in the breeze freely.

When we return to the auditorium, we come back to a small dark room with a two-way mirror. SPT, a mentor at the Center for Attitudinal Healing, steps through the large square plate glass. It occurs to me that she has faced some tribulations, and this spiritual development of stepping through dimensions is a result of her efforts. I am confident that I am experienced enough to relax and just proceed as my meeting with the elders continues.

I run out of dreamtime and find myself back in my bed with the cells in my body vibrating from the experience.

Feelings are convincing enough to make us experience the sting of insult or rejection. But if I examine this dream closely, I am certain that I have been in these places before, lived in relationship with the teachers, have been one myself, and am one in my dreams even now. Transcending duality is the answer. I must return to the "Roar of the Lion" and the "Rumble of Power" to remind me that suffering is not real and that consciousness lives forever.

The Wounded Sea Raven

I keep coming back to the fact that all consciousness is one. And we give it so many names: forgiveness, love, power, and other forms of the divine. Another avenue I discovered that shows me these qualities, and causes me to think of love or power, abides in nature.

At sundown, I go for a walk along the water as is customary for me. The water is agitated with white caps and short, choppy waves beating against the rocks. As I look up and take in the deep blue sky, there is a calm, with light still reflected above in the last rays of the sun and on the bay. At the tip of the peninsula where I live, there is a rock in the water not more than fifty feet away from shore. A platform was built around it with a footbridge to connect it to land. This is Elephant Rock. I like to go there to let the wind clean my aura, and get a new perspective on things. The sky and the setting sun behind Mt. Tamalpais create a stunning, serene atmosphere at that time of day. Approaching the bridge, I am puzzled by a persistent, worrisome chirp of a bird, and think that perhaps a baby is waiting for its mother to return to the nest with food, though it doesn't sound like a baby and the trees are further away. When I get to the platform, I look for the source of concern. My own desperation and helplessness mounts as I see the waves furiously tossing about a poor little creature. I'm not sure what type of bird it is, but it could be a cormorant, a sea raven, birds I've seen in the area. He is out of his element under the deck of a three-story house that extends over the water, definitely not accessible if there could be any help. When she tries to lift herself out and falls back, I dart my eyes around, looking for a solution. I can't imagine that the fire department could be of help, but a thought comes to mind: give it reiki. I chuckle inwardly, but I begin with the first symbol. My efforts seem so futile standing over the waves. So I say to it, "Come on. Fly, you can do it." With mouth agape, I observe her feeble attempts to rise, expecting her to fail. Instead, to my amazement, she begins to lift herself out of the water. She is wobbly, looking surprised herself. She gets the wind under her wings, rises, flaps her wings, and flies toward me, tenuously at first, and then rising higher, wavering, still squawking with alarm. She turns her direction and flies more assured above the house, and out of sight. Soon, her desperate peep fades, and she is gone.

I stand there for several minutes, unable to take in what I have just witnessed. A part of me wants to deny that this little wonder of nature has just occurred, but the memory of the sea raven's cry for help is testament in itself to me that something extraordinary just happened. I look in the direction of the setting sun. The blue is darker and deeper, the evening stars are slowly appearing, and the quiet of the area is marked by the absence of the sound of the beautiful sea raven in distress.

This experience with the sea raven caused me to stop to integrate my feelings about big and small, all and nothing—opposites, duality. I thought about many years before when I witnessed in the "Power of the Mountain" dream. In that dream, I had a visceral experience of the enormity of the universe. The dream started first with a view of the rock, which gradually revealed its immense power. I saw its ferocious strength, and I crumbled inside. Still, I held my ground, and it gave me reason to trust. With this opening, the power I was seeing reached out to me and took me with it on a voyage across the universe where it rearranged my orientation and reconfigured my sense of reality. The experiences of the dream and the sea raven in this moment cause the same sensations within me, but this time, forty years later, I am dreaming in the waking dimension, and there is consistency in my awareness.

Power is a wisdom that can be seen and felt like the phases of the moon and their impact on the tides of the oceans and rivers. I am not speaking of intensity we can measure, but rather of the effects that it has upon our lives. It comes to all of us because we are part of the unseen source and carry the power within. I often say we live in a psychic basket of energy, and we are one with it. So when I notice its influence, it is important to learn to flow with it, because it wants to be in relationship with me. Power can manifest itself dramatically, or quietly awaken a memory, a secret within that yearns for expression. If I can fathom the depths of the gift, I will have a moment of illumination and feel a sense of satisfaction that I've reached the vein of gold. It may seem elusive, but when the time is ripe, I come to terms with all these contradictions and frustrations, and come to a resting place where I've stopped measuring, questioning, criticizing, or dismissing it. The antidote to frustration in understanding the ways of power is in accepting challenges as they arise without question or doubt.

Eleanor Barron Druckrey, Ph.D.

Fire Ceremony and the Moving Stars

I receive an invitation to attend a fire ceremony and have the privilege of meeting a teacher from Mexico. We met Don José, a makarame from the Huichol tradition, last evening at a film screening of artists discussing their work and spirituality. Don José was present to extend his blessing on the project. A makarame is a person in good standing in their community who is selected for a period of seven years to conduct ceremonies and represent the spiritual community. I drive to my friends Dana and Steve's home in Sausalito. Dana, an artist I've known for many years, Steve, and I are driving together to a fire ceremony held this evening in Pescadero. Crossing the Golden Gate Bridge, I look over the ocean and think of how we are already connected to our destination, some fifty or sixty miles south along the coast to Swan Ranch where the ceremony is held. It's about four o'clock on a September evening, and the sun's rays are coming from the west. The sun is still high in the sky, and beginning its descent.

In preparation for the ceremony, we've been advised to bring a white candle in a container, plenty of blankets and warm clothing, food to share with the group in the morning, and lots of chocolate. After driving down Nineteenth Avenue and coming to Highway 280 for several miles, we take a right at I–35 toward the ocean. It begins to feel like we are out of the urban and into the rural areas of California. I sit in the backseat of Dana's small burgundy Toyota SUV, and enjoy watching the change of scene from freeway to trees and finally to the blue sea on one side of the road, with rolling hills on the other.

We've reached the ranch, which is situated atop a yellow bluff overlooking the ocean. The grass is dry, it being early autumn, and the rains have not begun. The owner leaves wood at the partially enclosed area for the ceremony. People have already begun selecting their places on the opposite side of the opening—some with sleeping bags, others with blankets and heavy coats. The gods love chocolate, and throwing it into the fire during the ceremony assures answer to one's prayers.

One of the participants, the friend who invited us, tells us that her cat has been ill and her daughter is very sad about it. My kitty has just died, and I can sympathize with the child, and we talk about kitties and how loving they are.

Don José arrives in ceremonial garb, handwoven cotton designed with flowers, birds, and butterflies in reds, pinks, and bright blues. The fire is lit, and the ceremony begins exactly at sundown with prayers and chants. The tone of the event changes, and people have gone inward in response to the prayers. When the sun sets, there is a marked drop in temperature, but it is nothing compared to how cold it gets once mother night has covered us with her cloak. Temperatures must have fallen to the lower forty degrees Fahrenheit. Don José is in a cotton shirt and pants. He stands in front of the fire, facing toward the water. A half-moon rises, and he lifts his handmade violin to his chin and begins to play and chant.

As time progresses, the atmosphere becomes relaxed, and people break out their own music, wine, and chocolate, consuming great amounts and throwing enough into the fire to warrant acknowledgment from the gods. I'm at the door of the enclosure. The wind is hitting the back of my legs, and I feel the chill down to the marrow. Fortunately, I've brought extra blankets, as others have as well, and Don José has become benefactor of this forethought, and I don't have to feel guilty for keeping my spare blanket. He is securely wrapped in coat and blanket, which also makes him look a few sizes larger. A few children are present, and they have drifted off to sleep, snuggled up in their sleeping bags. Don José continues his singing with the violin for quite some time, and at about ten o'clock, he stops for a rest. I am looking at the stars, and I notice their gentle movement, ever so slightly, but they definitely are moving or swaying. I lean back in my chair, listen to Don José's chant, and observe. I look to the fire of unearthly brilliant colors and note that I hadn't witnessed such beauty ever before—it's mesmerizingly, stunningly vibrant. The singing starts up again, but this time, it is the participants that are singing traditional Mexican songs, favorites of the group. At one point, it becomes a duel between a boy singer and a girl singer, improvising.

A story develops where the boy is complaining that the girl is not making her pretty little self available to dance with him. She explains that she is with her parents and they have a string tied around her waist. The topic of the lyrics deteriorates into insults and counter-insults, and would I be able to convey the humor, I would attempt. But the group is in stitches, and it finally ends up with the boy threatening to throw his guitar into the fire if she doesn't assert her independence. Then, the truth comes out:

she is not interested, and the boy's allusions to his disappointment in her coquettish behavior are as funny and poetic as the similes to flowers and beauty that caused us to believe love was in bloom.

Meanwhile, Don José is ready for another round of chanting, and the night passes alternating between the groups of musicians improvising and playing old favorites. The stars continue their vibration. At one point, the group joins in individual prayers, aloud, at the same time, and for several minutes, I have the feeling of being in my fundamentalist prayer meeting, where everyone is in a personal reverie yet praying aloud to god, some with hands raised. The voices settle down, and Don José does another hour of chanting and playing his violin.

At the first hint of dawn, praises shift to the glory of the sun, the blessings received, and the beginning of a new day. Don José calls us into circle, and we each describe our experience. One young man reports the changes in his life since the last ceremony—marriage and graduation from college. I report that nothing happened except for the moving stars, and he remarks that the stars have acknowledged my presence. The blowing wind makes other reports difficult to hear.

We stand with our blankets wrapped around us, the fire almost extinguished, the chill of the morning air still penetrating through. Clarity of mind and heart causes us as a group to smile more openly, bringing in a joyful timber into our voices. Within myself, I can feel a dramatic letting go of a position of holding myself apart. The friend who invited me to the event shows me photos in which exposed candlesticks glow around people's faces, and even an image of her frail kitty is reflected above the fire. I notice that the divisions created by egos to identify us apart from the group that existed before sunset last night has melted, and a palpable joining of the hearts occurred. Definitely, an internal shift happened for us.

The Sacred Gifts

Over the years I've allowed my writing and music to be my meditation. The journey has taken me far and wide, but there was a point when I felt that I was imploding and seeing life from the bottom up, feeling only emptiness and isolation, an eerie sense of being alive and not being seen nor heard. I had disappeared and my shadow remained behind. I came to realize that the true struggle was being at odds with myself.

I took a meditation class I asked one of my sister dreamers to help me come back to meditation, and she suggested a practice of slowly breathing in and out, holding awareness of the breath and, reciting a mantra, "I am that." Bringing the breath back to complete the full circle. Instantly, the breath brought me into awareness of the trees, the birds, the sky, and the eternal self. The word "awareness" summarizes it succinctly. It is home.

This morning, getting ready for the day, I feel the "chorus" or "community" of guides and spirit with me. Why would I need acknowledgment from the outer world when I am surrounded by all this support? I hear Canadian geese outside my window as though honking in agreement.

Writing Dream

I stand at the blackboard in a classroom with tall windows along the north side of the wall and my notes in hand, outlining the structure of a class. I am teaching Autobiography 101 at UC Berkeley. I am an instructor, a professor of autobiography.

Although I started writing in my teens, I was a young woman in my thirties when I had this dream and writing appeared as a significant contender for my attention. In an ideal world, I would have welcomed the depth of knowledge, but at the time, writing did not seem like a viable choice. Teaching writing at the University of California at Berkeley seemed unrelated to my life. I couldn't fathom myself as a writer, much less an instructor. In hindsight, this dream suggested that I presume the role of writer of autobiography, and a teacher of courage, trust, and wit. The dream guided me to write more, and I began the process of writing down my dreams each morning. When, according to my standards, I had acquired a sufficient amount of experience, I began to write and teach, not as a conventional teacher, but through writing about the issues of life that most mattered to me, addressing psychological homelessness, creative process, and spirituality. Not realizing it, this dream groomed me without my consent or knowledge to become a writer. I say "without my consent" because I was unconscious of opening to something I enjoyed and only faintly becoming aware of something bubbling within that merited commitment and hard work. Writing became a vehicle by which to describe my experiences and observations. My dreams opened up the wide expanse by which I could be in relationship and harmony with the past, the present and the future.

Forgotten Baskets

Driving down a busy thoroughfare in a hilly city like San Francisco, I come upon some beautiful, well-crafted baskets a woman has left on the side of a busy street. The baskets are large enough to serve as luggage, but their weave is also tight enough that they could be used as caldrons for cooking or for boiling water when birthing babies. I wonder who could possibly leave such precious jewels carelessly abandoned and at risk, but I figure she will eventually come back for them. I admire the intricate design of yellow grass and the fine stripe of brown leather woven into a Navajo design, and still can't image why such beauty has been carelessly discarded. Slowing the car down to a crawl, I drive past them. I am glad to see in the rearview mirror that they have remained undisturbed. Traffic is backing up for several blocks; I feel the hopelessness of the baskets ever surviving the onslaught of traffic.

I come back the same way a couple of days later, only to find that the woman has not yet reclaimed her belongings. But now the baskets are scattered, and traffic is at a complete standstill. A heavy sadness overwhelms

> *me, seeing these precious items still unclaimed. My breath becomes irregular, as though I am suffocating, and I awaken with my heart palpitating.*

The topic is the things forgotten, and things I've yet to remember. In part, I am alluding to cultural collective memory, the psychic energy that is woven into baskets. But in a larger sense, I am referring to the universe that is a basket of psychic energy. There is something greater that life is about that I've neglected; I've forgotten why I have come here. I've made excuses for leaving my baskets strewn carelessly out in traffic and run the risk of having my creations scattered.

A dream weaver doesn't forget from lifetime to lifetime. She picks up the threads from the past and continues weaving her basket of dreams where she left off. In this dream, I've left my memories strewn about, taken on a new identity, and pretended to forget my true commitments. I didn't forget, however. I am here and must begin re-weaving, not a new basket, but from where I left off, and finish the story the baskets want to tell.

The answer to remembering the greater picture lies not solely in the discovery of secrets and underground treasures, but also in the recognition of duality. There is an abundance of love—the energy that permeates all matter, along with power. Love abounds and erupts from the weaving of baskets, the movement of dance, the creation of art. As I researched the feminine, I found that throughout the ages, this energy has often been recognized as the power of love from the Mother. The dream of forgotten baskets brings this correlation to my attention, but I have also seen it in a myriad of dreams that demonstrate a force greater than myself that can be found in music—the sound of the piano, the flute, light, trees, water, rock formations, meditation, and love for the beloved. In short, there is nothing outside this sphere of the power of love.

This dream is recovering my memory about something to which I committed, something valuable that will set my life aright and in touch with destiny. The dream has triggered a kinesthetic process that tells me that something needs to come together. These feelings have taken me to the story of the dismembering of Coyolxauhqui, and how parts of her are strewn across the universe, becoming the Milky Way, her head remaining with us in the moon. In our human condition, we are just like her, and it's up to us to recover the pieces and bring the fragments from all our lives back together.

The assignment for me has been to *remember*. Remember what? Yes, I've been recovering the memory of the agreement with dreamers. That's been difficult and vital. I identify with that group. They are a source of inspiration, and being in touch with them has given me meaning and reason for my life. Yes, I safeguard my sacred gifts, music and writing, and ensure that I sharpen them. But there is something deeper and more essential. In Aztec Mythology, Coatlicue is the Mother of the universe, of all creation, beyond Mother Earth, the moon, the Sun, even beyond the Milky Way. Maybe even the billions of solar systems that exist. But the point of Coyolxauhqui's violent tearing apart, as told in the story of our culture, is to bring forth consciousness, identification of the *nagual* and the *tonal* (spirit and matter), and ultimately, giving us the option to recover the memory of Coatlicue, our connection to all creation. On the one hand, we create activities to distract ourselves while here on Earth, especially identities invented by the ego. We ignore the real self that is truly immortal, the self that never dies and reigns in the substance of light and darkness and in the power of creation. I think that's what indigenous religions are all about, and that's what other world religions are about, which brings all creation into unity. This dream calls me to remember that.

Let me explore the legend of Coyolxauhqui a couple of steps further to illustrate this point. Coyolxauhqui's mother becomes heavy with child, a pregnancy that began with a tuft of feathers. The pregnancy comes to full term, and out come a pair of twins, opposites of one another—the dark Huitzilopochtli and the light Quetzalcoatl, the dark being warring, and the light being peaceful. Quetzalcoatl's destiny is to demonstrate compassion and love. Huitzilopochtli is born in the armor of war with a sword in hand. In the end, their objectives are the same—to awaken us—but their paths are distinct. In reality, they are acting out by the promptings of spirit, and we humans have taken this story at face value and assumed that Huitzilopochtli is a god of war with the destruction of life in his plan. But what if we examine his creation through our spiritual eyes, from which all myths come, and see him as bringer of truth and slayer of all that is unlike it? He brings forth the sword of truth, and the twins as a unit bring the confusing effects of duality in the material plane to point the way for us. It would be a mistake if we humans were to take this story at face value and assumed that Huitzilopochtli is a god of war with the destruction of life in his plan. We have a choice as to which side we choose to enact, but if we choose outside of both? What will we find?

At deeper levels of reality, even our dreams can confuse us in unraveling the opposites of duality. It may seem impossible, but we author our dreams, even though the ancestors point the way out for us. We can choose to starve the dreams that lead us to believe we are victims, that we've been forgotten, and worse yet, those we've created in the context of duality. We dream figures like Huitzilopochtli who torment us, despise us. We ingest lies. However, this is duality at its finest playing itself out.

Coyolxauhqui too plays her part in pointing out the necessity of going beyond duality. She starts out happily swimming in a boundless ocean, devouring everything in sight. However, she agrees to be torn asunder in order to bring the message of consciousness. In this fragmentation, she becomes the Milky Way and bursts forth from sameness to create spirit and matter. The moon is an aspect of herself to guide us back to the self. As the Milky Way, she is the instrument through which the Great Star will pierce Mother's center, giving us the moment to transcend duality. What greater gift could be given—a sacrifice for all eternity?

Returning to the dream process as influenced by the dream of the forgotten baskets: at one level, the ancestors are guiding my music and writing, and they are showing me that all creativity is an avenue toward transformation that matures in response to a deep, abiding devotion. The baskets left in the street serve as a reminder that conscious tending—slow, gentle, consistent courtship and wooing—run as deep as the oceans, and as high as the stars. They are tools that enable us to live full lives. With this tending, love surfaces and appears magnificently, unannounced, a light that casts itself across the horizon. But the bigger picture is that it reminds me/us that our true identity comes from the eternal soul. Being the dreamers, we can choose which dreams to live by. We choose from a wide array of choices and support. There is no end to the dream. In "reality," our dreams and our decisions add confusion or greater substance to the dream of creation. It takes patience and steady digging to understand which dreams keep us in illusions—believing we are victims and at whim to the tides of destruction and chaos—and which dreams lead us to the other side of duality, to truth.

Connections

I can say in all frankness that allowing my life to unravel, as destiny insisted, was my grandest stroke of genius. I think of Grandmother as La Virgen de Guadalupe, the Mother. She has woven in and out of my dreams since I was a mere child. Once, she appeared to me on this side of reality by visiting me as I was coming out of a meditation. I heard footsteps and turned toward them, and there she was in the middle of my living room, bigger than life, extending her compassion in wave upon wave of love. I am certain that she is far more than an aspect of myself as psychologists would claim. When I take her lessons into my being, I must say that I feel the boundless regions beyond this world and myself. The history of all humanity has taught us to be small, to be subservient to the "state," to look upon each other as paltry, untrustworthy beings. My practice has become one of stopping the lies and being willing to see the light. Every day, I write to her when I first wake up, even if I only have one minute before I need to run out the door. My simple prayer is "What did you say? Keep reminding me throughout the day. Use me. I love you."

Here is an example of one of my communications with her: "Grandmother, thank you for your presence in my life, for your guidance and love. I commit to being your vassal. I realize that I've not seen you in your grand beauty and the goddess that you are. I am yours to reflect your greatness and wonder. I stand before you eternally grateful. Tell me what I need to hear."

Here is one of her replies: "You have been listening. Take each dream and examine it again and again. Here is reality spelled out for you: open your eyes and let the power that's been given you blossom. You know its source, let it come forth. The physical eyes can deceive because this realm is full of contradictions and suffering. Doubt stands between us.

"Trust your heart, and let the light shine forth. Faith is all that's needed.

"Love yourself. Your ears have heard many negative things said about you. You've witnessed too much sorrow. This is the suffering of the world. Duality is a basic tenet here. Go beyond it. It's as though you were trying to pass a huge trailer truck on the freeway while driving a Mini Cooper. The displaced force of air would stop you, but at the same time, there would be ease in coasting. This ease is deceiving because coasting along is easy, but it is stagnation. Get in front of the truck. Learn to ignore the forces that scrunch your heart, seal your eyes shut, and keep you coasting.

"Beyond the darkness that you see, many events of light have shaped and molded you—events in your dreams, in other lifetimes, and in the simultaneous lives you live. Focus on these, the light. You've seen how the dream is easily forgotten. You've seen how power and love can just as easily be dismissed and overlooked. It takes determination to hang on to reality. Rev up your motors and pass the forces of resistance. Move into the silence beyond duality. Your mind is ready to move forward. Train it to stop exploring the meaningless and expecting to find the light.

"The light is within you. Invite it to guide you and be your ally. Take the final step and move through. You've done it many times and then fallen into forgetfulness. You're ready to step through and retain awareness if you are willing.

"Bind yourself to Coyolxauhqui's multilevels of being. She is the light and darkness that leads to the edge of consciousness. Let yourself be led to the precipice, where the leap is easy and certain. Beyond this world, you find what your heart truly longs to embrace. By piercing her heart, you attain true awareness. Trust your blind steps toward the point where your psyche meets its soul."

I don't believe there is an end to the searching one must do to awaken from our illusions and cling to the eternal. We must walk a fine line to remain awake. It is possible to do so. The following dream of finding community reminds me of finding a home, a spiritual community where there is safety and trust. We need such a home to flourish and thrive. We can always find the place within that will speak to us of arriving home

Going Home Dream

I want to investigate a new living space, an area where my people live, and where I can be at home with my thoughts, feelings, and people with whom I feel comfortable. A man in traditional medicine handwoven trousers and shirt tells me of an indigenous artistic community high up in the mountains inhabited by highly evolved beings.

He warns me that the land naturally shifts and shakes frequently but that I would flourish spiritually as well as artistically. My curiosity is tickled because I've heard elsewhere that artists thrive in this environment, so I want to see for myself. The only way to get there is by chartered bus, so I organize an excursion and start packing my bags.

When we arrive, after winding on a rickety bus around the mountain for an eternity, I find that everything I've heard is true. There is something electric in the air, and the shaking of the ground is especially remarkable in that as the ground is trembling, I feel it restructuring my brain to the smallest cell of my consciousness, reversing my concepts so that what I've considered reality is turned upside down. I look around to see how people manage this constantly shifting ground, and they don't seem to notice. There's nothing but space and silence in my head. I lose my reference points for feelings and everything I thought was concrete and real. The terror of being in a vacuum and having no reference point for myself stuns me. I have no recollection of anything familiar; the future is a vacant horizon, and each step is a complete act of faith never before imagined. I hold my breath, hoping that something, something concrete, will reappear for me, but I know I am here because I have chosen to experience the profound nature of the land; to be a nobody, to be nothing; to have no past or future. Just blank. I brace myself and commit to seeing it through.

It becomes apparent to me that we've only stopped halfway up the mountain. The artists live still higher up, and if I want to meet them, I'll have to come back without attachments and belongings, naked for all intents and purposes. Everything disappears—tourists, friends, everyone. Now I must take the final leg of the journey alone. I begin walking up the rugged terrain, and when I reach the community, standing on top of the world here, the natural beauty astounds me. Under the open sky, beautiful works of art, etchings and statues in wood and stone, reveal striations depicting the history of humanity. It is a universe with a magical quality I could never have imagined. Blankets radiate emanations created from the colors, all vibrant and stunningly beautiful. It's as though I have X-ray vision and can see into the genetic makeup of the wood and chemical composition of the dye of the woven carpets. I touch the wood, and it feels alive with a consciousness of its own. The colors in the fabrics have a vibration that is enlivening and informing to everything in its field of vision. I can't believe my luck at finding such a welcoming place to live. I have found my home. The people have been waiting for me. In fact, I have met them before—in other dreams—and it begins to feel natural to me, familiar and normal on an exquisitely higher plane.

This is home. I will stay here and make these people mine. Their gods shall be my gods. No divisions, no separation, no withholding. I will leave the world I thought was real behind. This is home at last.

When I wake up, I realize that heaven is within. I see that being in communion with all living beings, including the trees, surrounding land, and animals, is the joining of breath and awareness. There is surrender in allowing myself to join with nature and community. The consciousness traveling into other worlds is as real as that of our waking world. I become aware that the community in my dream is a community I have been a part of. How long, I am not certain, but knowing this becomes as solid as the hand I hold up before my eyes. The beauty and higher vibration of the creative process is a result of surrendering to a higher purpose, and letting the ego die its natural death.

We dream our lives, and our travels into our dreams bring forth the substance of creation in waking time. The friends and families we meet in these travels are ours. They are as real as our waking communities, and they too participate in the forming of our psychological and spiritual experiences. These types of dreams, of meeting community and finding home, can help us find our footing in this life. More importantly, they are the very foundation of our spiritual quest.

Coyolxauhqui's Gift

I had met Coyolxauhqui in many dreams prior to my encounter with her on the morning that the stars and planets were aligned for the first time in twenty-six thousand years. This was the momentous event that we awaited—the end of a great cycle and the beginning of a new, a new day of enlightenment and transformation, the day of the Star of Venus, the Great Star, piercing through her heart, the Milky Way. When December 21 signaled the change in consciousness from the *tonal* (waking) to the *nagual* (dream state), I'd been waiting for it at least fifty years. Yet I found myself before going to bed hunting for sunrise time in the computer the night before. I had talked with friends about gathering a group, but nothing had materialized, and here it was—the night before and I had no plan.

I decided to get myself atop a surrounding hill before dawn to greet that magical moment before Grandfather Sun's arrival. Nothing complicated, just a decision to take myself to the top of the hill before dawn. To my utter horror, I awoke in the morning to the sound of the rain pounding on the windows, the wind blowing the trees to their roots, and the temperatures that had dropped considerably for the winter, perhaps even into thirty degrees Fahrenheit. Questioning the wisdom of my plan, I lay in bed with my eyes closed, and I argued with myself whether or not to put my feet to the floor and venture out. I often feel physical signals from the spirit world that I need to come to attention. I felt such a nudge in the middle of my spine, and I knew I'd better get myself going. I set one foot on the floor and then the other, and commanded myself to trudge out into inclement weather regardless. I got dressed and went to my silver 2001 Honda Civic.

I circled the town looking for a lookout point, but there was no other solution than to head up the switchback road and hike a trail to find a spot with a three-hundred-sixty-degree vantage point. As I drove upward, I could see an orange strip of light in the horizon, telling me to hurry before the light came. I finally reached the top, the end of the road, and I headed for the trail. Instantly, my fingers froze. At least the umbrella held up. I kept going and going, complaining inwardly. I didn't stop until there was a reasonable opening behind a large boulder that lent protection from the wind. I stopped the groaning and directed my attention toward meditation and prayers of thanks.

In front of me, the sun appeared with a display of moving orange clouds and an unexpectedly clear view of the Bay Area with the Golden Gate Bridge and even the Richmond Bridge, east of where I stood. It couldn't have been better. I waited at the top of the hill for about forty-five minutes. I've always been amazed at how the spirit will grab my attention, quietly at first, but in this instance, there was a quality of insistence. Strangely, slowly, and subtly, I became aware of a presence behind me. I followed the feeling for a few moments. It wasn't human, I knew that much, but I thought it might be a bobcat, which are often spotted in the hills. Then I heard the sound, a soft vibration within my being. My hair stood on end. The sound reached far beyond the limits of my physical body, a stretching of consciousness beyond this world. Under the protection of the umbrella, I could only see what was immediately behind me. The rain had turned to a light drizzle, and I put my umbrella down to investigate. There she was in brilliant colors—two magnificent rainbows, complete, electrifying from horizon to horizon. My awareness expanded, and I wasn't just my little human self but a full-blown consciousness stretched high above the clouds, behind, in front, above, and below, glowing as brilliantly at the rainbows. I stood there dumbfounded, ecstatic, savoring the feelings and sensations of this expansiveness. In a moment of this magnitude, I didn't stop to question how long it would last, but it continued to endure. The enchantment and glory of those moments stretched into the day. I was as light as the mist that surrounded me. And, in the days that followed, she spoke to me through "Coyolxauhqui Speaks" that defined her place in my new cosmology. The entire experience was an unmistakable communication I will always remember. It was then that I realized that she had precipitated another level of transformation, that the imprinted memory of her was another avenue through which I would be reminded of her reality.

As the days and weeks passed, with the new consciousness brought on by the double rainbow and Coyolxauhqui, I received further revelations that were essential to this new consciousness. I saw that I duplicate my thoughts, just like patterns in nature are duplicated or repeated. If I focus on a problem, I am adding fuel to the fire. If I send love to the problem, the energy from that thought form replaces the painful thought with love, and I then replace a new thought imbued with love rather than the pain which initiated the first thought, and I am able to return my attention to peace. Equally important is that nature has an awareness of its own, a consciousness that radiates into our lives and activities. It is a protector that guides and imparts wisdom of its own, a knowing and understanding inexplicable to the human mind, but ever attentive and wise.

I try to always remember the power of the spoken word in other traditions throughout the world. Om, being the all-encompassing sound that resonates with the one. In Aztec cosmology, the one consciousness is symbolized by a circle within a square. I love chanting because it brings me peace. Because "I love you," is such a common term, I come back to that to soothe and settle my troubled thoughts. According to *A Course in Miracles*, love and fear cannot coexist with each other. It's one or the other, and if I am going to be duplicating a symbol within myself, let it be worth the while of the universe.

In this frame of mind of expectation and wondering, I had the following dream six months later that gave me further insight for understanding the consciousness that I believe Coyolxauhqui represents within the battle between night and day, when she surrenders to the light of day.

Coyolxauhqui at Dawn

I feel a nudge in my back and open my eyes. I see that I am going down the back steps of my comadre's house in Sonoma. It's a steep set of stairs, so I must hang on to the rail and place my feet carefully. Instead, my eyes gaze upward, and I see the constellation of the warrior. I'm surprised to see the winter night sky reflected here in summer morning before light. It brings a glorious feeling of being delicately off-balance, when suddenly a burst of energy shoots through me, and I see this is the instant in which light of the sun vanquishes the stars. I am glad for this battle in the heavens, for without this battle, there would be no day. It gives me further pause to contemplate on the tremendous energy that can translate into creativity, purpose, and dedication. Without this battle between night and day, where the stars are vanquished, there is no love.

With the passing of time, the ancestors have continued to give me dreams and stories of remembering such as these that have called my attention to the one consciousness. Just as the Milky Way, Coyolxauhqui, has her path marked out to return to her oneness with the Mother, I've come to see that my path is mapped out. I see now that these are the keys to meet any challenge life may present. We all have the ability to remember the story of our lives. We have the ability to choose which dreams to feed and strengthen, or those that will lead us further into illusions. We choose. It's the journey that will define the outcome and what we experience on the way there. In reality, the quest for being conscious is the only route to take. I have found that there is a wide, wonderful world of dimensions upon dimensions within, waiting to be acknowledged and lived. She, Coyolxauhqui's consciousness, and the ancestors await our return. We come here only to dream . . .

Epilogue

The Reunion

"The elders and I have seen this coming for centuries. We've known that the change in consciousness is now in this world. It is here, and we've been preparing for it throughout many lifetimes. The time has come to step into the unknown, where we acknowledge reality beyond this world; where every night, you visit and mingle among the ancestors you know so well; where the nectar of the universe blends with the past, present, and future; where the flight toward the light is magnified a thousandfold to bring forth the textures and subtleties of reality beyond the sharp edges of earthly boundaries. This blending of time and space opens the window of knowing that shows us the vast array of selves that multiply and grow with our breath. There is no static you, only a continual shaping and becoming of power, form, and spirit that extends into infinity."

"Grandmother, wait a second. I don't understand. What you are saying? Are you suggesting that there is more than one of each of us? Or that we can reshape ourselves?" I interrupt, dazzled and bewildered by her conversation. It isn't often that I have Grandmother face-to-face to ask questions about mysterious forces that interplay in our lives, but here she is sitting at our dinette in our remodeled kitchen of the early 1900s, cradling me at age four in her *arms, while I, Aurora, stand leaning against the wall between her and our white Wedgewood stove not even an arm's length away. The window is open, and a soft spring morning breeze makes the leaves of the fig tree outside the window rustle softly and the white sheer curtains billow. "What are you saying?" I ask, leaning forward. I revel in the delicious essence of her presence.*

"Well, remember when you began to write down your dreams when you were in your thirties?" she begins.

My eyes glaze over. "Grandmother, I'm eighteen years old."

"That's right. That's right. Gracia knows what I'm talking about. Let's wait until she gets here," she affirms.

Just then, an elder woman with silver hair wearing a long black sweater, a white cotton shirt, and gray thermals enters barefoot through the dining room door and joins us at the other end of the table. Something about her feels familiar, as though I know her. Right behind her follows a petite woman with dark, deep-set, sparkly eyes, somewhere in her fifties or sixties. Unassumingly and quietly, the elder finds a place on the opposite side of me and sits down to listen. The younger woman is a writer who loves to dance. I'm remembering now—I've seen her at the Jamaica, the open-air bazaar where the women serve food, sell practical goods, and a mariachi brings the guapango on Sundays. I don't think we've ever spoken, though in some way I know things about her, which are puzzling to me. I'm curious as to why she is here with us at this particular time when Grandmother is just about to . . .

Grandmother moves her chair back to open up the circle and brushes her hair away from her face. Addressing all of us, she continues, "Well, as I was about to say . . . I am glad we are here together. I was explaining to Aurora about dreaming and the role it plays in our development over lifetimes. You've been in this dimension many times, especially in early times when our ancestors decided that this time would require experienced dreamers for the task that has been evolving for many cycles now. Destiny has given you this task, and part of my being here is to remind you that it's time to step into the role you've agreed to carry out. All of you understand this task, this function. This particular time is meant for carrying out your part in the reawakening of our people.

"*When the ancestors migrated south, and you were part of that group, you vowed to play a certain part in the drama unfolding since then. You know this, and I don't know why I bring this up now, but . . . you know the elders—you may forget from time to time, but they have been tracking your whereabouts. It's easier for them to remember, since they are in spirit form and not distracted or weighed down by the body and issues of living on earth. They've been luring you forward in consciousness, rekindling your memory. It isn't as though you have to remember everything, or that a heavy task is before you, for you have been doing this for centuries. People need to see themselves reflected in the mirror of eternity, where time is ever present now. So, coming back to your part: your memory is intact at deeper levels, and you've been moving closer and closer to the role you must play, and to each other, for that matter. Destiny has gently been pushing you toward this time. Everything you do helps in meeting this goal, even if at times you may feel it has disappeared or has seemed to disappear in other lifetimes. In the vast and open layers of reality, you remember and know exactly what you must do. The elders have been guiding you. Each of you has been culling your talents to accomplish your tasks.*

"*Remember how it was for you when you began keeping your dream journals?*" Grandmother asks Gracia, the younger woman who just arrived.

"*You mean, that I barely remembered snippets of my dreams and trembled anytime something unusual happened, such as a spirit waking me out of my sleep?*"

"*Sí, you understand,*" Grandmother says, turning around to look at me with a twinkle in her eye. "*But tell us about the real learning and how it happened for you.*"

Gracia goes on, "*I can see this now, though in many lifetimes, I've always felt that something important was happening. But there was a time when I started realizing that I had an array of guides helping me keep track of events once I returned to this dimension. Ocelotl made himself known to me, appearing to me in various ways. Whenever I begin to become conscious of being on earth again, I get scared at first, but after a while, I get used to the heavy feel of my body, and I begin to recognize him, to trust his presence, to have a sense that I have a mission. At first, I remember these sensations and memories dimly, and then they become more pronounced.*

"*In my early travels into other dimensions in this lifetime, there was an experience that shouted, 'Pay attention!' It was on Padmasambhava's birthday. I had just started meditating at the Nyingma Institute in Berkeley, and they were planning an all-night chant to celebrate and reach his essence. I wasn't invited because this was part of a continuing class. A boyfriend was enrolled in the class, and I was quite jealous that I couldn't participate, and I actually thought it was rather rude of them not to invite me. So, the night of the chant, I sat down at home and started chanting by myself. It must have been about three or four in the morning when I woke up suddenly and was flying through doors that flung open by themselves when I came up to them. My flight was quite fast. I came to a space that felt rather invigorating, and I instantly knew that I had joined the group—not in the waking plane, but in another dimension. This may sound strange, but I saw the energy that they were looking for. I felt I was actually in a realm or room with Padmasambhava, but it wasn't as simple as being in a room with him. Rather, that the room contained his energy! I felt cradled in pure nectar of power or something even bigger of that nature. Again, I was pulled through dimensions, doors upon doors springing open in the blink of an eye, but I knew I was seeing something real. I never talked about it to anybody because people could have said that I was being presumptuous. It just felt better to keep quiet."*

"In your terms, you can't prove it, but this is exactly what I am referring to," Grandmother adds. "Dreaming is intensely personal. One has to be disposed to, or available for the vision, but you can't hide from the truth of your true self, and that's what you witnessed that night. How did you figure it out?"

"Year by year, as time passed. When I was living in Hawaii," Gracia continued, "I felt your presence everywhere. It was delightful. But I also came very close to going mad. Maybe I did lose my mind. Some might say I did. I think I saw my thoughts graphically, and there was something that kept teasing and pulling me out of time and space. I had a series of dreams of seeing myself at a younger age, yet I had contact with Aurora, but the setting was out of time and space—it was crazy. The greatest challenge wasn't as much about the energies I encountered, as it was about holding my thoughts and emotions steady in this dimension. But maybe it was the energies that were my nemesis. I felt as though I was juggling a hundred plates at one time. I had medical problems as well as emotional issues with racism and economics—everything, especially men and my mother. Your presence felt reassuring, and that helped a lot. When I look back on it now, it was a process where the obsidian mirror was held up to my face, and I had to contend with the contents of my mind and reality. For extended periods, I thought I wasn't going to make it through the challenges and come out safely. It appeared as though I was holding on to the messages of grandeur as a way of compensating for feeling puny and small, yet I saw that I was being in more than one place at a time.

Just talking about it reminds me of how difficult it was. It took me several years to pull myself together. I lost my memory, which made me lose my footing in my workplace and other practical matters—now that was hard! I was so close to giving up because I was convinced that I was making up what I was seeing and experiencing. It was sheer stubbornness that kept me writing and investigating. I became good friends with pain when I began processing the ravages of poverty, even misogyny within my family and culture. It wasn't easy juggling time and space and multiple dimensions."

"What, would you say, helped you the most in drawing back the curtain of separation?" Grandmother asked her.

"The help I received is incredible, and I had many dreams that softened the road, but a dream that stands out in my memory typifies many others that gave me a new way of being in the world. I was on my way to mass at four o'clock in the morning, and I decide to take advantage of the opportunity to fly. You and my mother are nearby, in the branches of a floating tree. I begin to play with the sensations and float on my back. I turn onto my stomach and do the breaststroke through the air. I land and come upon a man who is making a commercial. He has laughing eyes, even pearly white teeth, dark wavy hair, and broad shoulders. A big man, six feet tall or so. When he sings, his voice is sweeter than a silver bell, and his laughter sends me into a delicate state of reverie. It dawns on me that this is the state of mind to maintain while dealing with this world—a playful, neutral approach, coupled with singing and laughter, a tone I must listen for."

"Do you get it, Aurora?" Grandmother has turned her attention toward me because I'm about to fall back to sleep, and they are laughing at my unsteadiness!

Grandmother goes on talking to the two women. "Ah, she's just pretending she's fainting," she says, tenderly joking. "But that's how it is in dreams and waking. When *something out of the ordinary happens, we want to go to sleep, yet it's very ordinary, very common, and sleep would be so sweet and not worth the luxury. The three of you are facing each other after many attempts on my part to bring you together. Aurora, you are just eighteen years old, and this is you, Gracia, at fifty."* Then, introducing me to the elder who's been silent all this time, she says, *"This is you, La Curandera, at almost ninety. There is one dream where you're in Golden Gate Park and you meet. Gracia is doing tarot readings. All of you come from the same consciousness. You are the same person."*

With Grandmother's words, I feel myself turning in my sleep, wanting to come out of this dream. But Grandmother holds my attention by staring and smiling at me.

Turning to La Curandera, she continues, "Breaking through dimensions is the same as waking up to illusions. The storms of emotions can be scary, no, Curandera?"

"Oh, god! It's intensely terrifying. In its most intense moments of change, it felt like the earth would swallow me. Pain feels so real, so defining of who we think we are," La Curandera says, shaking her head and laughing.

"So what is happening now," Grandmother goes on, "is that you have opened the doors to the dimensions we each come from. You're seeing me, seeing each other, and seeing baby Noni. Nothing to be frightened by, yet quite disconcerting when first becoming conscious. If La Curandera had ignored her intention to expand her awareness in her dreams in this lifetime, none of this would be remembered or even registered in your consciousness now. To be seeing each other is a gift you've worked for. All of you have made efforts in countless past lives and in this one to remain conscious. Just remember how you chose to become awake in that certain lifetime. You and Ocelotl, with other dreamers, agreed to participate in the changing of consciousness. Malinalxochitl, you were called then. It was your decision."

"So what do we do with this knowledge? Life can seem so ordinary and captivating," asks Gracia.

"Humility is a difficult word to explain—breathe through the fear and desire to remain asleep when you experience it. Step into the role you are meant to play in this lifetime. That's how you wake up. You don't have to make a big splash, just remain aware. Consciousness is power that heals and transforms your surroundings. This is the wisdom of the ages. Hold it lovingly, and remain awake to it. This is why it is important to heal from the challenges that are always confronting you, like the pain that comes from you thinking that your parents and your brothers have abandoned you. It's energy that goes way back in time, like dust that has dried on your skin over centuries. You could have chosen physical pain to bring you to attention. The answer is to strive to become that which you are—power, energy, consciousness—and do it boldly. No apologies, no hesitation, no fear. Recognize each other and remain alert to one another—no jealous rages thinking you are competitors because it appears your husband has abandoned you for a younger woman. You are one and the same. The three of you need each other. Everyone needs each other, for that matter. So respect and help one another." Looking at Gracia and La Curandera, she adds, *"Visit Aurora in your dreams and help her awaken."*

"And you, chiquita," Grandmother says, turning to me again, *"you'll need to stand up to your fears. When Gracia dances with a phantom of the past, keep going, don't buckle under. Stand up to her, remind her who she is, let her see who you are—your brilliant innocence, a part of her very Self. When you feel pain of any sort, love yourself through it. Don't let it rule you. Don't let it define you. Be patient with yourself, and let yourself fall through the levels of emotion and fear until you reach the sweet nectar of your tears. Tears wash away illusion. They bring*

you back to breath and provide the opportunity to reach for truth. Don't stay in the pain without breathing, and resist the temptation to become angry at the illusion. Sink down to the tears. What you think you know does not exist, because you made it up. Life is the dream, and you live it one moment at a time, as ordinary as it appears. But don't let yourself be fooled—it is not ordinary. It is magical and full of power. To see, to truly see, you must be willing to be small and ordinary in order to see the true wonder and vastness of reality. Keep your eyes open and stay connected to your breath."

Then, turning to Gracia, Grandmother says, "Here's another example of how consciousness works: in the dream where you see your husband dancing with Aurora, and of course, you didn't know who she was at the time, but if you had continued with your jealousy and flipped the table over as was your first thought in seeing them, you would have been catapulted by the energy into a world so far away that you would have missed the opportunity to meet each other in this lifetime, and maybe even many more lifetimes. The challenge is to have trust in the darkness—love the darkness. Don't let emotions push you over. The four of us would not be sitting here together this moment had you succumbed to the temptation to express that rage. In this lesson, you get to see that consciousness is knowledge, freedom, and joy because you bring together aspects of yourselves. You're not alive just as one person. It isn't often that you get to meet other parts of yourself like this. The more aspects of yourself you come to know intimately, the stronger you become. You stop living out of fear or your weaknesses.

"Everyone is a shape-shifter. Take animo, courage. There's more to life than one dimension. Discipline yourself to expand your awareness. Be firm in your beliefs, don't ask anyone if 'it's okay.'" Turning to La Curandera, Grandmother says, "Remember you travel many

dimensions. You have access to so much wisdom that is immeasurable. I don't have to repeat that it's important for everyone to stay alert, awake, and stop asking, 'Can I?'

"*Of course you can. Remember La Malinche. She was adored, loved, and held in the highest esteem when they first saw her allied to the Spaniard. But when the people saw the destruction that befell their world, they turned away from her. For centuries her memory was defiled, dragged through the underworld where she fought many battles. Another layer of shadow fell upon women. Women paid the price for her part in history, and the condition of their world. Mothers lost their ability to protect their daughters, they lost their power because they turned away from each other and showered their loyalty on their husbands and sons.*

"*But the sixth sun brings another day. Women are recognizing their worth and power. Women don't need approval to take action as befits them. Spirit is never vanquished. The record is set correct. Mothers are no longer beholden to their sons, no longer needing their sons for protection. A mother can at last be loving and tender to her daughter, true to the inner spirit, the throne of power. In spiritual terms, women hold to faith when there is no light. We love our lives through the darkness, we love our sacred gifts through the winter, through the spring rains, and on to blossom time.*

"*Reach deep within yourself. Remember your pact with the dreamers: you agreed to play an important role in bringing truth to the forefront as it has been known throughout time. We, the ancestors, come back to this realm to affirm that reviving dormant memories requires a tremendous amount of concentration. You can, you must, and you are remembering the vastness of space, not only in breadth, but in depth and height. Dreamers from time immemorial recognize that darkness befalls people in this realm. It's common to fall unconscious. There is love in darkness. Perfection exists in the unity of consciousness. Dreamers always anticipate a new dawn, the return of consciousness as it truly exists. You and they, the ancestors, have agreed to bring this change to fruition.*

"Just as you have become aware of each other through focused action, there are many others who have entered into the agreement who are waking up from the dark sleep that befalls humanity. You will meet them, and you will recognize and acknowledge each other. Ancient dreamers continue to bring dreamers in this plane to attention. This is nothing new. Their dedication has been at work in all manner and dimensions of reality for thousands of years. Efforts have been at work from unimaginable realms of reality.

"As contradictory as this may sound, everything is within plain view. Listen, notice, and be still. The veil of doubt is an illusion. It's been accepted as logical and concrete, but it remains an illusion nevertheless. Let the curtain fall. Listen. Seeing truth is your reward for having the faith and courage to let yourself love and trust in the mystery.

"Use dreams as channels for transmitting the message. Assure people of their ability to navigate multidimensional aspects of the spirit. Their guides will then take that wisdom and help them integrate it into their existence. Oftentimes, it's just that we close ourselves off to that guidance, just as it has taken you many lifetimes to accept the truth. Keep your consciousness open. Falling prey to the influence of believing in the linear is deadly. When you trust one another, your consciousness stretches beyond its seeming borders, and your knowing is established in the deeper levels of each other's consciousness. Be awake in the moment, where time stands still, for that's when awareness is captured and takes root. The self-regulating qualities of being will do the work of planting the seed. All you need

do is stop the clock. Go inward, breathe, and remember what's real.

"In the waking plane, keep in mind that you are teaching to people's unconscious levels, and though they will be aware that you are playing a vital role in their development, they may not be forthcoming with direct acknowledgment. Don't let that stop you. Just keep teaching love and acceptance. As your journey deepens, permission to do as needed becomes less important to you. Just do the work! People have their own system of teachers and guides. Power lies within. Just be.

"Live your destiny, you don't need anyone's permission. You have made a wise decision in pursuing truth in this lifetime. Not remembering who you are in reality is part of the illusion strongly built into this world. Face the temptation to split yourself. Hold your attention, and when you open your eyes, keep the memory of where you've been, what you have seen, and what you have heard. Don't worry about the objections of the ego and its need to keep appearances—the ego's needs are endless. The history of people on Mother Earth is a story of remembering our true home with our eyes open. When the Great Star of Venus emerges through Coyolxauhqui's heart, it will be time to step off the precipice. Let the mind rest and reveal its perfection, for that is what you are. Perfection. When you accept that reality, it is reflected when you look into the obsidian mirror, because there is no greater truth. The self is never born and never dies. You will be guided and held. Let the ego unravel. You are responsible for adhering to your own dignity.

"Here is a blessing, prayers to keep you focused. Addressing the four directions, say,

> *'This is a day of reverie for me*
> *You are with me this day as I go forth to help others*
> *I need your guidance and warmth*

*See me through
Guide me
Whisper words that deliver me from the illusions of this world
Smooth the path for me
I rejoice in all your gifts to me.
I offer this day to you
Use me as you will
My attention is still
I walk with you this day
Your power and mercy sustain me
I commit to drawing nearer to you
Holding awareness of your presence.
Contain our space together
Bring the teaching
Provide the tone
I love you, and carry your presence within
I know you are here
Decide for me, and lead me as you will
Thank you for directing my thoughts,
Thank you for directing my words,
Thank you for directing my actions.
I am that
I am that
I am that
I am that."*

Taking her time, she looks into our eyes once more. Then, slowly she disappears, with the baby still in her arms.

La Curandera, Gracia, and I are aware of the vacuum left with Grandmother's exit. "Whisper my name. I will hear you," the eldest of us reminds Gracia and me. "I will keep you both in my heart."

Just then, a man enters the kitchen through the back door. I feel a slight trembling, but La Curandera and Gracia stand up immediately to receive him.

"Ocelotl, Ocelotl, que milagro," Gracia says, with a singsong in her voice I hadn't noticed before. His playfulness is readily apparent in his radiant smile and ready abrazos for them. He looks at me with equally shining eyes.

"What do you mean, 'Que milagro'?" he says, laughing. "You know I wouldn't have missed this meeting!"

La Curandera releases my hand and fades slowly. Gracia fades away. Ocelotl and I are left in the kitchen with only the sound of rustling leaves of the fig tree outside. The vacuum of their departure feels unbearable. The silence is so profound, thundering with each breath. After what seems an eternity, he reaches for my hand and tells me, "Come with me, and I will tell you a story that begins in a sacred place not too far away." His mere mention of another time and space takes us to it, a familiar place deep into our Mother Earth.

I begin another dream.

Bibliography

Alarcon, N. (1981). Chicana's Feminist Literature: A Re-Vision through Malintzin/or Malintzin: Putting Flesh Back on the Object. In Moraga, C. and Anzaldúa, G., Eds. (1981). This Bridge Called My Back: Writings by Radical Women of Color. Watertown, MA: Persephone Press, Inc.

Anaya, R. A. and Lomeli, F., Eds. (1989). Aztlán: Essays on the Chicano Homeland. Albuquerque, NM: University of New Mexico Press.

Anonymous. (1975). A Course in Miracles. Glen Ellen, CA: The Foundation for Inner Peace.

Anzaldúa, G. (1999). Borderlands/La Frontera: The New Mestiza. San Francisco, CA: Aunt Lute Books.

Avila, E. (1999). Woman Who Glows in the Dark. NY: Jeremy F. Tarcher/Putnam.

Barrón Druckrey, E. (2009). Corn Woman Sings: A Medicine Woman's Dream Map. Bloomington, IN: iUniverse.

Braden, G. (2008). Fractal Time: The Secret of 2012 and a New World Age. Carlsbad, CA: Hay House, Inc.

Della-Madre, L. (2003). Midwifing Death: Returning to the Arms of the Ancient Mother. Austin, TX: Plainview Press.

Duran, E. (2000). Buddha in Redface. Lincoln, NE: Writers Club Press.

Castaneda, C (1968). The Teachings of Don Juan: A Yaqui Way of Knowledge. NY: Ballantine Books.

Castillo, A. (1994). Massacre of the Dreamers. New York, NY: Penguin Books, USA.

Facio, E. and Lara, I. Eds. (2014). <u>Fleshing the Spirit</u>. Tucson, AZ: University of Arizona Press.

Federici, S. (2004). <u>Caliban and the Witch</u>. Brooklyn, NY: Autonomedia.

Galland, C. (2007). <u>Longing for Darkness: Tara and the Black Madonna</u>. New York, NY: Penguin.

Gonzales, P. (2012). <u>Red Medicine: Traditional Indigenous Rites of Birthing and Healing</u>. Tucson, AZ: The University of Arizona Press.

Graves, R. (1974). <u>New Larousse Encyclopedia of Mythology</u>. London: The Hamlyn Publishing Group Limited.

Greene, B. (2004). <u>The Elegant Universe</u>. NY: W.W. Norton & Company.

———. (2012). *Why is Our Universe Fine-Tuned for Life?* TED Tanks video.

Gutierrez, R. A. (1991). <u>When Jesus Came, the Corn Mothers Went Away</u>. Stanford, CA: Stanford University Press.

Prabhavananda, S. and Isherwood, C. Trans. (1953). <u>How to Know God: The Yoga Aphorisms of Patanjali</u>. New York, NY: A Signet Book, the New American Library.

León Portilla, M. (1980). <u>Native Mesoamerican Spirituality.</u> Mahwah, NJ: Paulist Press.

Magaña, S. (2011). <u>2012–2021: The Dawn of the Sixth Sun</u>. Torino, Italy: Edizioni Amrita, srl.

Matos Moctezuma, E. (1988). <u>The Great Temple of the Aztecs: Treasures of Tenochtitlan</u>. New York, NY: Thames and Hudson, Inc.

Medina, L. in Facio, E. and Medina, L., Eds. (2014). <u>Fleshing the Spirit</u>. Tucson, AZ: University of Arizona Press.

Moraga, C. and Anzaldúa, G., Eds. (1981). <u>This Bridge Called My Back: Writings by Radical Women of Color</u>. Watertown, MA: Persephone Press, Inc.

Moraga, C. (2011). <u>A Xicana Codex of Changing Consciousness: Writings, 2000–2010</u>. Durham & London: Duke University Press.

Nicholson, I. (1967). <u>Mexican and Central American Mythology</u>. London: Paul Hamlyn Limited.

Pinkola Estés, C. (1992). <u>Women Who Run with the Wolves</u>. New York: Ballantine Books.

Taube, K. (1993). <u>The Legendary Past: Aztec and Maya Myths</u>. TX: University of Texas Press.

Tellez, M. in Facio, E. and Lara, I. Eds. (2014). <u>Fleshing the Spirit, Spirituality, and Activism in Chicana, Latina, and Indigenous Women's Lives</u>. "Pero tu no crees en dios": Negotiating Spirituality, Family and Community. Tucson, AZ: University of Arizona Press.

Townsend, C. (2006). <u>Malintzin's Choices</u>. Albuquerque, NM: University of New Mexico Press.

Villanueva E. F. (2013). <u>Lost Worlds: Palenque</u>. Video.

Waters, F. (1977). <u>The Book of the Hopi</u>. New York, NY: Penguin Books.

Wilcock, D. (2013). <u>The Synchronicity Key</u>. New York, NY: Dutton, Penguin Group.

Index

A

agreement, xxix, 11, 59, 96, 154, 177, 180, 201
AIDS (acquired immune deficiency syndrome), 70, 150
Akau (Chanah's brother), 103
Aki-no-No (Japanese diner), 113
alcoholics, 104, 120
Alcoholics Anonymous, 110
alienation, 95–96, 105
ancestors, xxi, xxxiv, xlvii–xlix, li–liii, 2, 4–6, 48, 51, 57, 59, 109, 121, 136, 149, 154, 166, 169–70, 181, 189, 191–93, 200–201
Anzaldúa, Gloria, xxi, xxvi, xxxii, xxxviii, xlvi–xlvii, xlix
Arizona, 84, 115, 206–7
Atlantic Ocean, xlix
Aurora (dreamer), xxi, liv, 1, 16, 26, 192, 195–97, 199
Avila, Elena, xxiv–xxv, xlvii
awareness, xxvii, xxxi, liii, lv, 11–14, 33, 40, 49, 52, 99, 129, 136, 147, 153, 155, 157, 162, 169, 173, 177, 183, 185, 187–88, 197, 199, 201, 203
Aztec cultures, xii, xxxviii, xli, xlix
Aztecs, xxii, xxiv, xxviii–xxx, xxxii–xxxiii, xxxv–xxxvi, xxxix–xli, li, 3
Aztlán, xxi, xxix
Aztlán: Essays on the Chicano Homeland (Anaya), xxix

B

Baby Beach, 110
Bailey, Mary, 79
balance, xxxii, xxxiv, xxxvii, li, 56, 118, 140, 146, 155, 161
battle, xxxiii–xxxiv, 114, 188, 200
Bay Area, 28, 187
Becker, Ray, 101–4, 107–16
Beth (Kaela's sister), 103
Betsy (therapist), 117–18
blessings, 8, 16, 22, 110, 114, 134, 160–62, 174, 176, 202
Blue Light, 94
Book of the Hopi (Waters), xxviii
Borderlands—La Frontera (Anzaldúa), xxxii
Braden, Gregg, xxxv

C

Caliban and the Witch (Federicci), xliv
California, 23, 51, 69, 72, 76, 109, 114–15, 134, 174
Canyon De Chelly, 115
Carlos (La Curandera's brother), 168
Casas Grandes, 115
Castaneda, Carlos, xlvi–xlvii
Castillo, Ana, xxi, xxxviii, xli–xlii, xlv
Catholic church, xxxviii, xlii–xlv, xlviii, l
Celia (Gracia's best friend), 78
Centzon Huitznahua, xxxiiin27
ceremony, xlviii–xlix, 2, 41, 65, 105, 158, 174–75
Chaco Canyon, 115
Chalice and the Blade, The (Eisler), xliii
Chanah (Akau's sister), 103
Charlotte (La Curandera's friend), 150–51
Chela (Gracia's friend), 65–66
Chicana/o culture, xxi, xxviii–xxxi, xxxiii, xxxvii–xxxviii, xlix, 63
Christopher (La Curandera's nephew), 151–52, 168
Christ the Victor Lutheran Church, 134
City College of San Francisco, 52
Claudia (author's friend), 149
Clavijero, Francisco Xavier, xxviii
Coatlicue (Mother of the Universe), xxvi, xxxiii, xxxv, lv, 180
commitment, xxiii, 86, 96, 126, 130, 132, 148, 153, 159
compassion, 4, 148, 154, 160, 180, 182
consciousness, xxiii–xxiv, xxvi–xxvii, xxix, xxxi, xxxiv–xxxv, xxxvii, xlviii, lii–liii, lvi, 2, 9, 11–14, 16, 35, 37, 40–41, 49, 52, 57, 95, 97–99, 126, 130, 136, 140–41, 144–48, 150–51, 153, 155, 157, 162–63, 166, 171–72, 180–81, 183–89, 191, 193, 197–99, 201

Corea, Chick, 111
Corn Woman Sings: A Medicine Woman's Dream Map (Druckrey), xxii, xlix, lii
Cortez, Hernan, xxxix, xli
courage, 92–93, 96, 120, 123, 163, 177, 199, 201
Course in Miracles, A (Schucman), xxix, 98, 165–66, 188
Coyolxauhqui (Aztec goddess), xxiii–xxvii, xxxiii–xxxiv, l, lii–liii, lvi, 9, 92, 129, 133, 138–39, 155, 179–81, 186–89
Crater Highway, 102
creation, xxiii, xxvi, xxix, xxxi, xxxvii, lii, liv, lvi, 9, 130, 141, 148, 156, 162, 166, 179–81, 185
creativity, xxiii, xxvi–xxvii, xxxii, xxxvii, xliv, xlvii–xlviii, lii, lv, 25, 181, 188
cruelties, 138, 140
Cruz, Gracia de la, 47–48, 51–53, 55, 58
curandera, xxvi, l, 51, 146, 163, 197
curanderismo, xxv, xlviii–l
Cynthia (Holden's ex-wife), 107

D

Dalai Lama, 134–35
Dark Feminine, xxi, xxiii–xxiv, xxvi–xxvii, liii
death, xxx, xxxii, lvi, 27, 51–52, 74, 81, 122, 128, 142, 144, 146, 148, 151, 163, 167
deceit, xxxvi, 63, 138
della-Madre, Leslene, xxviin12
destiny, xxvii, xxxii, xxxvi–xxxvii, xlix, lii–liii, lv, 5, 10, 13, 23, 83–85, 96, 179, 182, 193, 202
destruction, xxxix, xlii, 180–81, 200
De Young Museum, 71

divine, xxxii, xxxiv–xxxvi, xxxvin35, xxxvii, li, 5, 13, 22, 32, 54, 98–99, 127–28, 131–33, 172
divorce, 108, 110, 116
dreamtime, 58, 96, 171
dream yoga, xxxi, 49
Druckrey, Eleanor Barron, xxix
duality, xxv, xxxi–xxxiii, li–lii, lvi, 9, 11–12, 105, 135–36, 138–39, 141, 146, 155–56, 162, 165–66, 168–69, 173, 179–83
Duran, Eduardo, xlviii

E

Eisler, Riane, xliii–xliv
El Norte, xxi, xxvi, xlviii, 49, 84
Elsa (Gracia's roommate), 122–23
emotions, 108, 147, 163, 165, 195, 197–98
emptiness, lvi, 13, 25, 27, 71, 83, 130, 177
encouragement, 37, 40, 42–43
England, xlv, 26, 84
essence, xxxv–xxxvi, 12, 14, 45, 54, 59, 84, 144, 159, 194
eternity, lv, 2, 36, 62, 94, 139, 181, 184, 193, 204
Europe, xxxviii–xxxix, xlii–xliii, xlix
Eva (pastor's wife), 78

F

Fairfax, California, 125, 134
Father William, 58, 170
Federicci, Silvia, xliv–xlv
feminine, xii, xxi, xxiii–xxiv, xxvii, xxxi, xxxiv–xxxv, xxxvii, xxxix, xlii–xliii, xlviii–liii, 129–30, 179
  creative, xlix, li–lii
feminine consciousness, xxiii, xxvi
feminine energy, xxiii, xxv–xxvi, xxxiii

feminine principle, xliii–xlv, xlix
forgiveness, 163, 168–69, 172
Frank (Aurora's friend), 40
freedom, xlvii, 10, 87, 92, 105, 115, 126–27, 155–56, 161, 199

G

Galland, China, xxv–xxvi
Georgina (Aurora's coworker), 29–30
Gimbutas, Marija, xliii
Gnostic Gospels, The (Pagels), xliii
Golden Gate Bridge, 69, 124, 145, 174, 187
Golden Gate Park, 45, 71, 197
Gonzales, Patrisia, xlviii, li
Gracia (dreamer), xxi, liv, 2, 17, 47–48, 51–53, 55, 58, 65–66, 85, 117, 135, 192–95, 197–99, 203–4
Grandfather Sun, 5, 186
Great Star, 9, 155, 181, 186
Gutierrez, Ramon, xliv

H

Hana, 68
Hawaii, 52, 69, 71, 94, 102, 111, 116, 195
Hawes, Hampton, 111
higher power, 109, 120–21
Holden (Gracia's husband), 66–67, 69–71, 83, 97, 100, 106–8, 110–13, 116, 118
Holocaust, 122
Honolulu, 113
"How Music Came to Earth" (Nicholson), xxxvi
Huitzilopochtli (god of war), xxviii, xxxi, xxxiii–xxxiv, 7–10, 13–14, 16, 138, 180–81
Huitznahua, xxxiv

humanity, xxxiv, lv, 9, 12, 126, 146, 148, 155, 182, 185
Hyatt Hotel, 101, 113

I

I-580, 109
illusions, xxxii, lii–liii, 125, 140, 148, 154–56, 165–66, 181, 183, 189, 197–99, 201–3
India, xxxi
innocence, 156

J

Jesus Christ, xliii
Joe (Gracia's uncle), 100–103
José, Don (teacher), 174–76
Juan, Don (Carlos Castaneda's teacher), xlvi
Julie (Aurora's niece), 40

K

Kaela (Gracia's relative), 102–4
Kahului, 107, 113
Kaiser Hospital, 122

L

La Curandera (dreamer), xxi, liv, 2, 17, 142, 197, 199, 203–4
La Llorona, xxvi, xlvii
La Malinche, 88, 200
La Virgen, xxvi, xlv, 19, 31–32, 49, 84, 160, 182. *See also* Virgen de Guadalupe
León Portilla, Miguel, xxxix–xl
Linda (roommate), 122
loneliness, xli, 16, 25, 74–75, 91, 96, 118, 126, 140, 149, 168

Longing for Darkness: Tara and the Black Madonna (Galland), xxv
Looking for Love in all the Wrong Places (Newton), 117
Los Angeles, 18–19, 23, 84, 113–14, 151

M

Macy's, 103
madness, 32, 117
Magaña, Sergio, xxiii, xxvii, xxxi–xxxii, xlvii
Mahalo House, 104–5, 108, 111
Malinalxochitl (Aztec goddess), 1–2, 8, 14, 17, 197
Malintzin (Hernan Cortez's translator), xxxix–xlii, xlv–xlvi
marginalization, xlix, 90, 93, 95
Marin County, xviii, 124–25, 151
Martinez, Hermano, 76
Marto, Diana, 112
masculine, xxiii–xxiv, xxvii, xxxi, xxxiv, xxxix, xlii–xliv, xlix
Massacre of the Dreamers (Castillo), xlv
Matson Lines, 114
Matt (La Curandera's friend), 150
Maui, 94, 97, 101
Mayahuel (goddess), xxxv–xxxvi, 85, 87, 89
Mayan, xv, xxii, xxx
Maysie (Ray's daughter), 115
Medina, Lara, xxxii
meditation, xxxi, 51–52, 134–36, 142, 151, 162, 167–68, 177, 179, 182, 186
Mexico, xxi, xxv, xlii, xlv, 18–20, 48–49, 95, 158, 174
Mexico-US border, 1
Midwifing Death: Returning to the Arms of the Ancient Mother (della-Madre), xxvii

Milky Way, xxiii, xxxiv, lv, 9, 22, 130, 135–36, 139–40, 179–81, 186, 189
Mirror Lake, 94
Modesto, 47, 76
Moraga, Cherrie, xxi, xlvi, li
Mother Earth, xxiii, 2, 42, 62, 146, 180, 202, 204
Mother Ocean, 42–43
music, xxiii, xxvi, xxxii, xxxvi–xxxvii, 10, 13, 19–20, 22–24, 26, 31, 33, 36–37, 42–43, 46, 49, 52, 54, 56–57, 72, 82–83, 101, 103–4, 107, 113, 126, 132, 153, 155, 169, 175, 177, 179–81
musician, xxxvii, 10, 32–35, 40, 42–43, 57, 59, 119, 131, 133, 155
myths, xxviii–xxix, xxxv, 86, 165, 180

N

Nahuatl, xxiv, xxix, xxxi
Native Meso-American Spirituality (Portilla), xxxvin35
nepantla, xxxii
New Mexico, xliv, 115, 205
New York, xvii–xviii, 31, 158, 205–7
Nicholson, Irene, xxiv, xxviii, xxx, xxxiv–xxxvi
Not Always So: Practicing the True Spirit of Zen (Suzuki), 142
Novato, 116
Nyingma Institute, xxxi, 194

O

Oahu, 103
Ocelotl (dream guide), 2, 9, 11–12, 17, 49, 57–59, 95–97, 115, 135–36, 147, 149, 166, 170, 194, 197, 204
Oklahoma, 115
Old Europe, xxxix, xlii–xliii, xlix

P

Pacific Ocean, 65
Padmasambhava, 194
Pagels, Elaine, xliii
Paia, 68, 110, 112
passion, 20, 23, 52, 84
peace, xxxi, 31–32, 52, 56, 94, 110, 125, 136, 146, 150, 163, 166, 188
perfection, 121, 156, 201–2
Pinkola Estes, Clarissa, xxvi–xxvii, xlvii, 145
Pinky (cockatiel), 111–12
power, xxi, xxv, xxxiv–xxxv, xxxviii, xli, xliii–xlv, l, lii–liii, 8, 13, 16, 45, 63, 92, 94, 99, 109, 121, 126–27, 130, 136, 139, 149, 153, 157, 159, 161–64, 168–69, 172–73, 179, 182–83, 188, 191, 194, 198–200, 202–3
prayers, xxxi–xxxii, 22, 78, 82, 99, 109–10, 119, 121, 133, 142, 149, 153, 162, 174–76, 182, 186, 202

Q

Quetzalcoatl (feathered serpent), xxiv, xxxi, xxxiii–xxxv, 62–63

R

Raul (Roberto's elder brother), 86
reality, 34, 163, 181–84, 187, 189, 191, 193, 195, 199, 201–2
Red Medicine (Gonzales), xlviii
rejection, 16, 74, 88, 90–91, 108, 140, 171
Richmond Bridge, 187
Rio Bravo, 84
Robert (support group's member), 125, 128, 131–32
Roman Empire, xliv, xlix

Romano, Elena, 54–55, 132
Roshi, Richard Baker, 142
Roshi, Shunryu Suzuki, 142
Rosy (niece), 158–59

S

Samadhi, 135
San Francisco, 28–29, 52, 69, 76, 109, 116, 124, 127, 142, 146, 150, 165, 178
San Francisco State University, 70, 111
San Mateo, 124
San Rafael, 117, 119, 151
senshin (meditation), 142
separation, xxxv–xxxvi, xlviii, 94, 129, 139, 156, 168, 185, 196
serenity, xxxi, 36, 125, 136
Sixtus IV (pope), xliv
"Somewhere over the Rainbow," 102
Spain, xxvii, 70–71, 84, 118
Stockton, 20, 23, 28–29, 42, 45, 47, 51, 58, 76
Stockton Delta College, 51
Suzuki, Mitsu, 142
Suzuki, Otohiro, 142
Suzuki, Shunryu, 142
Sylvia (minister's daughter), 24

T

Tamalpais, Mount, 91, 145–46, 151, 172
Tara, 116
Tasajara Zen Mountain Center, 142
Taube, Karl, xxxv
Teachings of Don Juan: A Yaqui Way of Knowledge, The (Castaneda), xlvii
Texas, xxiv–xxv, 112, 114–15
This Bridge Called My Back (Anzaldúa), xlvi
Tijuana, Mexico, 76

Tito (Celia's best friend), 78
Toltec, xxii
Toltec Secret, The (Magaña), xxiii
Townsend, Camilla, xxxviii, xl–xlii
tranquility, 31, 94, 146
transformation, xxiii–xxiv, xxxii, xxxiv, 135, 140, 169, 181, 186–87
treachery, xxxvi, xxxix, 138

U

United States, xliv, xlvi, xlviii, 84
universe, xxiv, xxxi, xxxiii, 10, 13, 32, 121, 127, 130, 135, 139–40, 146, 154, 156–57, 162, 173, 179–80, 185, 188
University of California, xxii, 48, 77, 111–12, 177

V

Victoria (Aurora's friend), 38–39
Virgen de Guadalupe, xxvi, xxxix, xlv, 31, 182

W

war, xxiii, xxx–xxxi, xxxiii, xxxix, xli, xliv, 94, 143, 180–81
  holy, xxiv
Waters, Frank, xxviii
wedding, 69, 71, 129–30
wisdom, xxv, xxxviii, xlvii, lii, liv, 4, 8, 10–11, 13–15, 69, 84, 92, 99, 121, 130, 134, 139–40, 148, 157, 169, 173, 186, 198, 200–201
Woman Who Glows in the Dark (Avila), xxiv–xxv

Y

Yosemite National Park, 94